THE FREE PRESS

New York   London   Toronto   Sydney   Singapore

The

EMPTY
CHURCH

*The Suicide of
Liberal Christianity*

THOMAS C. REEVES

THE FREE PRESS
A Division of Simon & Schuster Inc.
1230 Avenue of the Americas
New York, NY 10020

THE FREE PRESS and colophon are trademarks
of Simon & Schuster Inc.

Manufactured in the United States of America

10 9 8 7 6 5 4 3 2 1

Library of Congress Cataloging-in-Publication Data

Reeves, Thomas C., 1936–
    The empty church / the suicide of liberal Christianity / Thomas C. Reeves.
        p.   cm.
    Includes bibliographical references and index.
    ISBN 0-684-82811-1
    1. Liberalism (Religion)—United States—History—20th century.
  2. Liberalism (Religion)—Protestant churches—History—20th century.
  3. Church membership.   4. United States—Church history—
  20th century.   I. Title.
  BR526.R434   1996
  280'.4'09730904—dc20   96-13401
                                                           CIP

To STANLEY AND MAUREEN ATKINS

CONTENTS

PREFACE

In the course of the intense debate between Republicans and Democrats in the mid-1990s over the future of the welfare state, congressional leaders and conservatives in general hoped that churches would play a more active role in providing assistance to the poor. Mainline Protestant leaders, however, were among the first to remind Americans that their churches were in no condition to assume new and potentially awesome responsibilities. Indeed, an abundance of literature revealed that these once prominent and affluent denominations were declining and in disarray—ironically, at a time when religious belief in America seemed to be extraordinarily high.

Some years earlier, I had begun investigating the mainline churches. Long interested in the relationship between religion and politics, I sought to know why these and other religious bodies had lost much of their effectiveness in recent decades, especially since that volatile period from 1965 to 1975, often referred to as the sixties. The sad condition of the nation's churches was reflected in the puzzled and at times disdainful expressions and comments people made when learning of my research topic. In a variety of ways I was asked: Do churches, well, really matter any more?

Scholars, journalists, and religious leaders had been examining the plight of the mainline churches since the 1970s. Sociologists and professors of religion were more active in the field than were historians. Early in my research I became convinced that there was ample room for a fresh examination of the subject, especially one that offered historical perspective and strove to be reasonably succinct, clear, and calm.

This book is designed for a broad, nonspecialized audience—the great majority, who may well know little about history or even the basics of Christianity but who ponder the deepest issues of life and wonder why so many churches in our time seem so consistently unappealing and irrelevant. Many such people are active in churches, and a great many others are not.

The discussion that follows must and will step beyond ecclesiastical concerns. Religion always intersects politics, education, law, the family, cultural standards, and so on. What human beings do is in large part determined by what we are; and what we are rests on what we believe, on the way we perceive reality. "There is hardly any human action," wrote Alexis de Tocqueville in *Democracy in America,* "however particular it may be, that does not originate in some very general idea men have conceived of the Deity, of his relation to mankind, of the nature of their own souls, and of their duties to their fellow creatures. Nor can anything prevent these ideas from being the common spring from which all the rest emanates."

A personal note is appropriate here. Almost all my life I have belonged to a mainline denomination. Confirmed in the Lutheran Church as a boy, I have been a member of the Episcopal Church since 1960. Since 1976, I have been active in organized efforts to move the Episcopal Church in a direction it chooses not to go. Since 1983, I have been a trustee of an Episcopal seminary, Nashotah House, and I am highly familiar with the turmoil mainline theological education is experiencing.

In one sense, then, I am an insider. But in another and deeper sense, I am an outsider, keenly interested in understanding things within an historical framework, aware of the fallibility and evanescence of all human endeavor, certain that no earthly vessel contains all the truth that will free us from ourselves and automatically bring temporal and eternal bliss. A great admirer of C. S. Lewis, I have taken to heart his admonitions, in *Mere Christianity*, against smug denominationalism.

In general I have much affection for the mainline churches. They have appealed in large part to the middle- and upper-middle classes because of their dignity, respectability, and learning as well as their spiritual resources. They deserve much credit for braving the storms of modern knowledge, for their long record of social and political activism (at least from the Social Gospel to the civil rights movement), and for their advocacy of tolerance and ecumenism. That these churches have become unattractive and superfluous to many in recent years should not prompt us to forget their many valuable contributions to untold millions of Christians and others, here and around the world.

This study documents attitudes and actions that are leading toward the serious debilitation, if not extinction, of these historic churches. But there is nothing inevitable about the demise of the mainline; its fate is not beyond its control. Perhaps this book will play a small role in persuading members of the liberal Protestant churches, both lay and clerical, to reconsider some of their assumptions, especially about the faith. For readers not directly involved, there is still much to be learned about the past and present from an examination of the struggles of Christians coming to grips with modern life.

I wish to express my special thanks to James Miller and the Wisconsin Policy Research Institute for financial assistance with this project. I am indebted in various ways to Prof. Louis Geiger, Gary Brazer of the National Association of Scholars, Patrick Kuhlmann, Beverly McCumber, Dawn Greathouse, and Melissa Mattioli. My editor, Susan Arellano, has been splendid in every way. As always, I owe the most to Kathleen.

Advice from one devil to another on how to destroy a Christian's faith: "Talk to him about 'moderation in all things.' If you can get him to the point of thinking that 'religion is all very well up to a point,' you can feel happy about his soul. A moderated religion is as good for us as no religion at all—and more amusing."

—C. S. Lewis, *The Screwtape Letters*

1

CONFUSED AND HELPLESS

This book about religion in America focuses largely upon the mainline or liberal Protestant churches, denominations that claim to be the spiritual homes of almost a quarter of the American people. The mainline consists of the "seven sisters" of American Protestantism: the American Baptist Churches in the USA, the Christian Church (Disciples of Christ), the Episcopal Church, the Evangelical Lutheran Church in America, the Presbyterian Church (USA), the United Church of Christ, and the United Methodist Church.[1]

This study places liberal Protestantism in a historical context, describes its current plight, and makes recommendations for its revitalization.

The mainline churches have played major roles in the shaping of the United States. For centuries, membership was often a sign of respectability, prosperity, and upward mobility. A recent study by the sociologists Barry A. Kosmin and Seymour P. Lachman showed that the Disciples of Christ, the Congregationalists (members of the United Church of Christ), the Episcopalians, and the

Presbyterians still lead other Christians in income, education, and property ownership.[2]

All of our presidents, except Roman Catholic John F. Kennedy and Southern Baptists Jimmy Carter and Bill Clinton, came from mainline churches. Of United States Supreme Court Justices from 1789 to 1992, 55 of 112 have been either Episcopalians or Presbyterians. Both denominations have long been heavily overrepresented in Congress. In the 101st Congress (1989–91), for example, one fifth of the senators were Episcopalians, ten times their proportion in the general population. The 104th Congress (1995–97) contained 68 Baptists (many of whom were mainliners), 63 Methodists, 63 Episcopalians, and 59 Presbyterians.[3]

And yet today, these one-time pillars of the religious establishment are frequently ignored, their power to bestow social prestige has greatly dissipated, and their defining theological doctrines have been largely forgotten. It has often been noted that mainline church membership sharply declined in recent decades. But in fact the strength of mainline churches has been eroding for the better part of this century.[4] Some observers have predicted their eventual demise. Even friends and insiders have acknowledged that the mainline churches have lost their impact, their zeal, even their meaning.

Some critics, especially on the right, have gone beyond this to argue that these liberal churches are in part responsible for the moral and spiritual decline that has shaken the nation during the past three decades. Why are the churches failing to teach right from wrong, they ask. Why are young people abandoning them? Why are church leaders so quiet in the face of growing moral anarchy? And why do they spend much if not most of their time promoting counter-productive social and political causes?

In the story of America's mainline churches, especially since the sixties, we encounter the larger drama of a country and a civilization in intense turmoil over the nature of truth. We may learn much about what has been called the "culture war" by studying the deterioration of the religious bodies that once established our spiritual and moral standards.

But there is more to this than current events. The critical issue, in my judgment, has deep roots in Christian history, so deep that it was addressed by St. Paul.[5] Is there truth, supernaturally revealed in Christianity, that lies beyond our present understanding of things, truth that is unchanging and absolutely vital to our present and future?

This is not about the acceptance or rejection of fundamentalism; for most Christians, certainly in the mainline churches, that struggle ended long ago. The issue involves the line that must be drawn, by all thinking Christians, between certain knowledge and revelation. What, in short, are the essentials of the religion without which it loses its authenticity and power? And what are the implications for personal conduct? At a time when many Christian churches seem to be on the brink of some sort of profound division between those who accept the traditional faith and those who do not, these questions are especially relevant.

A LARGE BODY OF EVIDENCE, from public opinion polls to election returns, shows that the American people are deeply concerned about the quality of life in this country. Faced with dramatic increases in crime, violence, drug use, pornography, divorce, illegitimate births, abortion, child poverty, and teen suicides, along with enormous declines in academic standards, public taste, and basic civility, millions have concluded that there is something seriously wrong. We seem to be dying from within of a malady that has affected our moral sensibility and seems to be rushing us toward anarchy.[6]

Exit polls in the elections of 1994, for example, found 56 percent of voters agreeing that the problems facing the country were "primarily moral and social" and that 65 percent were more likely to support the candidate or political party whose top priority was a reversal of the nation's moral slide. Democratic Party pollster

Celinda Lake said, "Values were below the surface in everything in today's elections and will play even more of a role in '96."[7]

The nation's condition is ironic, of course, for with our great wealth, our enormous commitment to higher education, our dramatic expansion of individual rights, and our status as world leader after the end of the Cold War, something like a golden age might have been expected for the United States. If money, education, democracy, and power are unable to produce peace, goodness, enlightenment, and joy, what else can?

Our goals have proved deceptive and our utopians are few. Hand wringing has long been part of the intellectual's job description, but the dire warnings emanating from the professionally literate have rarely seemed so significant. The social scientist Os Guinness, for example, has written that

> the United States has become afflicted over the last generation with a crisis of cultural authority similar to that which the ancient Greeks spoke of as "the gods switching sides," the traditional Chinese as "the crisis of the Mandate of Heaven," and nineteenth-century Europeans as "the death of God." Metaphors such as fraying, eroding, unraveling, and decomposing have become popular, but the prosaic fact is this: Under the conditions of late twentieth-century modernity, the cultural authority of American beliefs, ideals, and traditions is dissolving.[8]

The Yale classics professor Donald Kagan agrees.

> Jefferson and his colleagues could confidently proclaim their political rights as the gift of a "Creator." By now, however, the power of religion has faded, and for many the basis for a modern political and moral order has been demolished. Nietzsche announced the death of God, and Dostoevsky's Grand Inquisitor asserted that when God is dead all things are permitted.

Kagan sees nihilism looming, and the forecast is far from pleasant.

Nihilism rejects any objective basis for society and its morality, the very concept of objectivity, even the possibility of communication itself, and a vulgar form of nihilism has a remarkable influence in our educational system today.[9]

The New York University psychologist Paul C. Vitz also stresses the significance of the educational establishment, identifying the nation's colleges and universities as the major source of the permissiveness, pluralism, and intellectual and moral chaos threatening to engulf us.

Deconstructionists have powerfully argued that no written text has any fixed meaning, that all interpretation lies in the beholder; and thus we see individual moral relativism being advocated at the highest intellectual levels. Values clarification for the kids; deconstruction for graduate students. Meanwhile, feminists, gay and lesbian advocates, and other minority groups are arguing that all truth (especially morality) is ideological.

Vitz contends that the malady is spreading.

At present, this intellectual and academic anarchy is primarily found on our nation's campuses, but their tribalism has already begun to move out into the whole society. . . . At present there is certainly no answer to this social incoherence, and it looks like we are headed into a period of disintegration and increasing domestic conflict."[10]

Some point to politicians, the courts, big business, feminism, or the media as the principal source of our problems. Much attention has been paid to the media. George Gilder has observed, "Under the sway of television, democratic capitalism enshrines a Gresham's law: bad culture drives out good, and ultimately porn and pruriency, violence and blasphemy, prevail everywhere from the dimwitted 'news' shows to the lugubrious movies." The impact on the citizenry, Gilder contends, has been acute.

Boobissimus has already laid waste a generation of American youth, who have slipped to the very rear ranks of the industrial world in academic and intellectual achievement and leapt into the lead in violence and bastardy. Now, impelled by the still more far-reaching Kultursmog of direct broadcast satellite technology, Boobissimus is preparing to lay waste the rest of civilization as well.[11]

Public opinion polls have shown much dissatisfaction with the media. A 1991 Gallup survey found that 62 percent of Americans did not believe television represented their values.[12] A *Times-Mirror* survey conducted in the summer of 1993 found that 80 percent thought television violence directly harmful to society, while almost 50 percent classified the effect as "very harmful."[13]

When Senate majority leader Bob Dole said in 1995 that there was too much violence and sex in movies, television, and popular music, 71 percent of those polled by the *Los Angeles Times* agreed. Sixty one percent believed that the content of American entertainment was getting worse.[14] That same year, critics noted that the movie *Casper,* a comedy for kids, contained sexual innuendos and dialogue peppered with blasphemies.

William J. Bennett's *Index of Leading Cultural Indicators* attracted considerable public attention in 1993 for documenting concisely much of what troubles Americans. Between 1960 and 1990, when the population increased 41 percent, there was a 560 percent increase in violent crime, a more than 400 percent increase in illegitimate births, a more than 200 percent rise in the teenage suicide rate, and a nearly 200 percent rise in divorce. The percentage of children living in single-parent homes had more than tripled during that period, and the fastest-growing segment of the criminal population was the nation's children.

At the same time, total social spending at all levels of government (measured in constant 1990 dollars) had climbed from $143.73 billion to $787 billion. Inflation-adjusted spending on welfare had gone up 630 percent, and inflation-adjusted spending on education had risen 225 percent. In short, the illness had grown worse as the prescribed medicine increased. Bennett quoted Nobel Prize–winning author Aleksandr Solzhenitsyn as saying that "the West . . . has been undergoing an erosion and obscuring of high moral and ethical ideals. The spiritual axis of life has grown dim."[15]

In 1993, according to a study published in the *Journal of the American Medical Association*, one in four youngsters ages 10 to 16 reported being assaulted or abused within the previous year, and 1 in 10 reported being sexually abused or assaulted.[16] According to the Justice Department, an estimated 1.3 million Americans were victims of gun-related crimes in 1993. Guns were used in 29 percent of the 4.4 million murders, rapes, robberies, and aggravated assaults in the United States in 1993—an 11 percent increase over the previous year.[17]

As of June 30, 1994, there were more than a million people in American prisons for the first time in history. The number was more than double that of 1984, and the rate of prison population to the general public during that period had doubled. One out of every 260 Americans was imprisoned for terms longer than one year, and another approximately 440,000 were in jails awaiting trial or serving short sentences. More than 90 percent of all prisoners were in state prisons, and 93 percent of that number were either violent criminals or repeat offenders. More than a quarter of federal prisoners and more than a third of the state prisoners had an immediate family member who had also been jailed.[18]

The relationship between the breakdown of the family and societal ills was obvious and well documented. The conservative political scientist Charles Murray, in a widely noted essay for the *Wall Street Journal*, pointed out that in 1991, 1.2 million children were born to unmarried mothers—practically 30 percent of all live births. The rate for black women was 68 percent. Murray argued that "illegitimacy is the single most important social problem of our time—more important than crime, drugs, poverty, illiteracy, welfare or homelessness because it drives everything else."[19]

In 1995, the National Center for Health Statistics reported that the birth rate for unmarried women had increased more than 50 percent between 1980 and 1992. The white out-of-wedlock birth rate soared 94 percent, while the black rate rose 7 percent.[20]

Data released by the U.S. Census Bureau in August 1994 showed that only 50.8 percent of American children lived in a traditional nuclear family (defined as one in which both biological parents were present and all children were born after the marriage). One-half of all African American children, nearly one-third of Latino children, and one-fifth of white children lived with a single parent.[21] According to one study, some 60 percent of the nation's rapists, 72 percent of adolescent murderers, and 70 percent of long-term prisoners came from homes where the father was absent.[22]

In 1995, according to the Social Science Research Institute at the University of Southern California, there were some 4,000 gangs in the United States with more than 500,000 known members. More than 800 cities had documented gang problems. Irving Spergel of the University of Chicago has noted the direct relationship between the rise of gangs and the breakdown of the family.[23]

For all their squabbling, leaders of both the left and right today readily acknowledge the moral crisis. Although conservatives may blame the welfare state, permissiveness, and materialism for our troubles, and liberals may point their fingers at racism, sexism, and inadequate educational and social welfare expenditures, both sides agree that forceful actions are necessary to stem the current cultural blight.

In 1992, liberals harshly ridiculed Vice President Dan Quayle for complaining about the television program *Murphy Brown* and its advocacy of single motherhood. Two years later, Health and Human Services Secretary Donna Shalala supported Quayle's position, and President Clinton publicly admitted that the Republican had been right.[24]

The "character issue," dismissed by many liberals in 1988 as irrelevant and worse, has become important in election campaigns at all levels of government. In 1994, liberal *Newsweek* columnist Meg Greenfield wrote of elected officials, "The kind of people they are—their values, their strong points, their weaknesses, their intelligence, their characteristics as people, in short—is what makes them good or bad at public office. It is everything."[25] In California that year, for example, where $100 million was spent on campaign advertising, the personal integrity of candidates was a major issue of both parties. In Virginia, where Oliver North was running for the Senate, the question of character was predominate. After the G.O.P. landslide in November, Democrats expressed intense interest in the character of House Speaker Newt Gingrich.

President Clinton's principal political problem, said public opinion polls, was that people did not trust him or consider him a moral leader. And Congress consistently has a lower admiration level than the president. In 1994, *Parade* magazine asked its readers whether the nation's leaders "were setting good moral examples" for young people. Of the nearly 40,000 people who responded, only 7.9 percent replied yes, while 84.7 percent said no.[26] In 1995, a nationwide poll showed that only 18 percent gave Washington officials a high rating for honesty and integrity.[27]

Given the significance of the crisis and the widespread recognition of it, what role is being played by the nation's most prominent churches in reaching solutions? If our problem is moral, it is also spiritual. William Murchison has rightly observed, "As morality is the heart of culture, so religion is the heart of morality."[28] Therefore, what better place to seek assistance than the venerable, respectable religious institutions led by the nation's most highly educated clergy?

Little would be achieved by such action. As is quite well known, the mainline churches have been shrinking dramatically during the last three decades and appear to be confused and helpless at a time when the nation is crying out for inspiration and guidance.

A 1985 study revealed that laity in the United Church of Christ (formed in 1957 out of a merger between the Congregational Churches and the Evangelical and Reformed Church) had great difficulty in identifying anything distinctive about their denomination. The sociologist William M. Newman concluded that little more than freedom of religious choice and religious tolerance, practiced at the local level, could be found. "Of course, these themes are entirely consistent with broader civic values in the United States."[29]

In 1993, bishops of the United Methodist Church's Executive Committee pushed their official papers aside and for three hours spoke earnestly about such questions as "What does it mean to be a United Methodist?" and "What, if anything, is distinctive about our church?" "Churches without any self-understanding lose members," says The Rev. Jim Andrews, head of the Presbyterian Church (USA).[30]

At the Episcopal Church's General Convention of 1994, the House of Bishops fell into bitter quarrels about homosexuality, concluding that each prelate would deal with the issue as he or she pleased. Two weary observers exclaimed: "The Episcopal Church is an institution in free fall. We have nothing at all to hold on to, no shared belief, no common assumptions, no agreed bottom line, no accepted definition of what an Episcopalian is or believes."[31]

A large number of Americans lack firm commitments to denominations, and many switch denominations several times during their adult years. The mainline churches are especially affected because of their lack of exclusive or often even special features. A survey of 1,100 Presbyterians nationwide showed 73 percent agreeing with the statement: "There are several other denominations where I could serve and be just as satisfied."[32]

Since the cultural revolutions of the 1960s and 1970s, the mainline churches have been in a serious and unprecedented numerical decline, losing between a fifth and a third of their membership. In 1993, Methodists, for example, rejoiced that their losses had slowed from 64,344 in 1991 to 58,866 in 1992.[33] In 1995, a researcher observed that the Methodist Church had lost 1,000 members every week for the last 30 years![34]

Churches use various methods of acquiring membership data and report figures in different ways. The standard source for the official numbers is the *Yearbook of American and Canadian Churches*, published annually by the National Council of Churches. In 1994, and using the "Full, Communicant or Confirmed Members" category, the American Baptist Churches in the USA had 1.5 million members; the Disciples of Christ had 605,996; the Episcopal Church had almost 1.6 million; the Evangelical Lutheran Church in America had 3.8 million; the Presbyterian Church (USA) had 2.7 million; the United Church of Christ had 1.5 million; and the United Methodists had 8.5 million. (Four of the seven churches list higher numbers in an "Inclusive Membership" category, while Baptist, United Church of Christ, and Methodist officials list the same figure in both categories.)[35]

In contrast, there were 4.1 million Mormons in 1994, 15.6 million Southern Baptists, and 60 million Roman Catholics.[36] (As early as 1890, Roman Catholicism was the nation's largest single denomination.)[37]

A major reason for the numerical decline of the mainline churches is their failure to retain their own children once they have reached the age of decision.[38] Presbyterians, Methodists, and Episcopalians lose nearly half their young people for good. Indeed, fully 48 percent of Presbyterian youth drop out of churchgoing altogether.[39] This alienation and indifference is revealed on the college level by the difficulty students today often have even spelling "Presbyterian" and "Episcopalian." Denominational history and theology interest my students about as much as baroque opera or the insects of Paraguay.[40]

The mainline membership is graying rapidly. By 1983, nearly half of all mainliners were 50 years of age or older. In 1994, 61.4 percent of the laity in the United Methodist Church were 50 years or older.[41] (In the general population, 25.5 percent were over 50.) Conservative Protestants are younger than liberal Protestants in part because they are more successful in keeping their children in church.[42]

Few observers anticipate a dramatic resurgence in mainline membership. The Methodist theologian Stanley Hauerwas of Duke Divinity School said in 1993, "God is killing mainline Protestantism in America, and we goddam well deserve it."[43]

Giving as a percentage of annual income decreased in Protestant churches between 1968 and 1993, from 3.35 percent to 2.97 percent in eight denominations affiliated with the National Council of Churches. Indeed, a study of eleven denominations between 1921 and 1993 reported that per member giving as a percentage of income was lower in 1992 than in 1921, and even lower than in 1933, the depth of the Great Depression.[44]

Giving to overseas Protestant ministries based in the United States was $2 billion in 1992—less than what Americans spent on guns ($2.48 billion) in 1994.[45] This figure looks even worse when compared with consumer expenditures for illegal drugs (an estimated $49 billion in 1993); alcohol ($44 billion in 1992), legal gambling (nearly $40 billion annually), leisure travel (an estimated $40 billion in 1992), and cosmetics ($20 billion in 1992).[46] This plus the decline in membership have caused serious financial problems in the mainline denominations.[47]

The Presbyterian Church (USA), faced with a $5 million budget deficit in 1993, sacked more than 200 national staff members.[48] In 1994, a top official at the Presbyterian Center in Louisville said, "We see the need to trim our budget by about 5 percent a year."[49] The Evangelical Lutheran Church in America, created out of a merger of three smaller Lutheran groups in 1988, racked up more than $21 million in deficits in its first three years and cut some twenty positions from its national offices.[50] Between 1991 and 1995, the Episcopal Church cut its national office staff by about one-third, and its budget declined more than $3.6 million between

1994 and 1995. The budget was cut $2.45 million for 1995–96.[51] At the National Council of Churches, created and maintained largely by the mainline churches, contributions from members dropped 50 percent between 1975 and the late 1980s, and the full-time staff was cut to 61, down from 187 two decades earlier.[52]

Morale throughout the mainline ranks is low. One major study concluded that "The liberal Protestant community is mired in a depression, one that is far more serious and deeper than it has suffered at any time in this century."[53] A Gallup poll revealed that only 27 percent of Protestants gave their church an excellent rating. The Methodists, scoring the highest among the mainline bodies, reported 25 percent; the Presbyterians, 18 percent; and the Episcopalians, 9 percent.[54]

Missionary zeal has been almost lost. Gallup reports, "Invitation and evangelism are virtually ignored by the mainline churches."[55] In 1985 a third of the nation's Methodist churches had performed no baptisms; almost two-thirds offered no membership training or confirmation classes; and nearly one-half lacked a list of potential new members.[56] The Episcopal Church in 1996 sponsored just 25 overseas missionaries worldwide (one was in England), down from 59 in 1989.[57]

Colleges and universities founded by mainline churches have in large part become either secular, largely secular, or obscure. In 1990, the presidents of 69 Presbyterian colleges and universities issued a manifesto that discussed "the demise of Protestant hegemony, the decline of mainline churches and the importance of denominationalism" and concluded that "The Presbyterian Church could be close to the point where its involvement in higher education might be lost forever."[58]

Mainline church headquarters, conventions, organizations, and agencies seem almost inevitably to fall under the control of liberals— a generic, albeit at times slippery term for those on the left. Thus official pronouncements and actions often disturb people in the pews, who by and large are more moderate or conservative. (In 1994, more than 40 percent of mainline church members were Republicans, while about 25 percent were Democrats.[59] According to an exit poll taken that fall, only 11 percent of the nation's voters called themselves liberal, while 12 percent said they were "somewhat liberal".[60] In 1992, 43 percent of mainliners voted for Bush and 34 percent for Clinton.)[61] Two Methodist professors of religion have declared, "it seems inconceivable that an agency of any mainline, Protestant denomination should espouse some social position unlike that of the most liberal Democrats. The church is the dull exponent of conventional secular political ideas with a vaguely religious tint."[62]

In 1992, the Presbyterian Church (USA) elected The Rev. John H. Fife to its top post. Fife had been arrested in the 1960s for picketing in front of the suburban homes of central-city landlords, and during the same years counseled draft resisters and marched in Selma and Birmingham, Alabama. In 1986 he was found guilty of federal charges of conspiracy and two counts of aiding the transportation of an illegal alien. While running for office in the Presbyterian's annual convention, he favored a committee report supporting abortion rights. Fife's election made him "symbolic leader of the church for the year."[63]

That same year, the United Church of Christ moved its headquarters from New York City to Cleveland, Ohio, in an attempt to counter charges that East Coast liberals were running the show. Not long after the furniture arrived, denominational leaders began alienating locals by attacking Chief Wahoo, the Cleveland Indians' popular logo, as offensive to Native Americans.[64]

In 1995, the largest church lobby in Washington, D.C., was the United Methodist Board for Church and Society. With a staff of nearly forty, the board was spending $2.5 million a year. On what? Mark Tooley of the Institute for Religion and Democracy observed in a trenchant report on the Board:

Like fossils trapped in amber, directors and staffers embraced yesterday's causes by calling for an unlimited welfare state, praising Fidel

Castro's Cuba, urging global U.S. military withdrawal, bemoaning the revival of free market economics, and affirming, of all things, the sexual revolution.[65]

The obvious question is, Why do liberals dominate? As we have seen, liberals have long been prominent in the mainline. But there is also an important principle of group dynamics involved here: moderate, otherwise busy people are no match for zealous, ideological interest groups eager to attain power. This is as true for churches as it is for any other institution.

Conservatives within the mainline often become emotional when speaking of the tactics liberals use to control denominations. The Rev. David Runnion-Bareford of the United Church of Christ, for example, thinks that liberals are not spiritually motivated. "It's all about power and money." There are, he believes, about 10,000 people in his church who went to the same schools and share the same sixties, left-liberal bias. They support, appoint, and elect one another, he says, and "They control everything."[66]

The Rev. Jim Heidinger of the United Methodist Church shares the same general view. Liberals, he claims, go wrong theologically. They often have difficulties in the parish because of their views, and then they begin searching for power. There is little else for them to do. Conservative evangelicals, on the other hand, he says, tend to stay out of the political side of church life and concentrate on spreading the gospel. The inevitable result is a liberal takeover of church authority.[67]

In the Episcopal Church, I watched organized liberals narrowly win an episcopal election in a historically conservative diocese and quickly take over all operations as though they were the vast majority. Their opponents, who had practiced courtesy and said their prayers before and during the election, were thereafter assumed not to exist.

Leonard R. Klein, a Lutheran, has written of a liberal "bureaucratic inner circle" that tends to dominate. "The dysfunctional politeness of church culture empowers the most aggressive, and virtually no one says so until things have gone too far, especially if someone who claims to have suffered pain is pressing the issue." This sort of takeover is preceded, Klein believes, by a "prior decay of theological coherence."[68]

Dr. David Carlson, a one-time resistance leader in the Evangelical Lutheran Church in America, thinks that widespread ignorance of Scripture, theology, and history contributes greatly to liberal dominance. Appeals to anything beyond current events often get nowhere with church members, he says, for people no longer know what you are talking about. "We've lost the Scriptural and doctrinal underpinnings."[69]

Despite their considerable variety, mainline seminaries and the schools of theological training that supply clergy to the mainline are routinely dominated by the left. Indeed, liberal theologians, as the dean of the University of Chicago Divinity School has pointed out, have played major roles in the very formation of mainline Protestantism.[70]

Seminaries are frequently the scenes of "pathbreaking" statements, publications, courses, and bizarre events designed to reveal the "latest breakthroughs" by their faculty (as though, like scientists, they were constantly bombarded by new information) and win denominational support for an assortment of liberal causes. Graduates often emerge with little faith in the integrity of Scripture, a minimal grasp of church history and orthodox theology, and armloads of politically correct positions on social and political issues.

Seminary president Manfred T. Brauch has written of "the near-stranglehold that the major voices in critical biblical scholarship continue to exercise on theological education," the result being, among other things, that "Jesus's miracles become inventions of the early church. Accounts of God's intervention on behalf of the people of Israel become legends or myths. Expressions of hope in the coming of Christ as a future event in God's redemptive work become the wishful projection of unfulfilled expectations of Jesus' early followers."[71]

The Methodist theologian Thomas C. Oden of Drew University has complained of a seminary education "awash in antisupernatural assumptions," one that is "radically relativized." "There is not only no concept of heresy, but also no way to raise the question of boundaries for legitimate or correct Christian belief where absolute relativism holds sway. The very thought of asking about heresy has itself become the new arch-heresy."[72]

The Duke University Divinity School professors Stanley Hauerwas and William H. Willimon have written that the "roller coaster of clever new theologies has subjected clergy to one fad after another and has misled pastors into thinking that their problem was intellectual rather than ecclesial." They added of their profession, "We have no stake in saying something new. That is a favorite game of academia and is of little use to a church more interested in saying something true than something new."[73]

The emphasis at the Episcopal Divinity School, said its academic dean, Frederica Harris Thompsett, is feminist liberation theology. "Certainly we do attract students who are left of center."[74] Barbara G. Wheeler, president of Auburn Theological Seminary, reported, "Gender studies, race studies and deconstructionism are present to some extent at all the theological schools."[75] A student at the prestigious, interdenominational Harvard University Divinity School declared, "Pluralism is the God at Harvard. The basic presumption is that Western religion is not good, and Christianity is the worst. The new slur, like being 'homophobic,' is being 'Christo-centric.'"[76] Another student at the same institution recalled, "I learned word games. *Capitalism, patriarchy, Christianity, patriotism, America, tradition, Republican, hierarchy*—these were bad words. *Feelings, liberation, oppression, victimization, conversations, dialogue, caucus,* and *empowerment* were good words."[77]

This dogmatism is a product of several factors. For one thing, as we shall see, liberalism has dominated mainline seminaries for decades. Moreover, hiring to achieve "diversity" since the 1960s has brought gays, lesbians, blacks, and feminists in large numbers into faculties and administrations, and very few of them have turned out to be orthodox or conservative. (One Harvard Divinity School graduate has observed: "Diversity may be defined as the gathering together of as large a group as possible of the left-minded.")[78] A sympathetic researcher visiting a class at the Episcopal Divinity School, "Genealogy of Race, Sex, Class Oppression," taught by the popular black feminist Katie Cannon, observed: "Current events were mixed with ideology in class that morning, and the world was found consistently wanting."[79]

Then, too, the intellectual caliber of seminarians as a whole in this country has declined sharply in recent decades. Most North American theological schools are "open admission" institutions that rarely reject anyone with a bachelor's degree.[80] One researcher reported that the energy level of seminary students was "shockingly low."[81] The New Testament professor Katherine Grieb of the Protestant Episcopal Theological Seminary in Virginia said in 1995, "We're all working against increasing illiteracy, however, not only biblical illiteracy but general illiteracy. We're having to teach English as well as teaching our disciplines."[82]

Since the 1960s, seminaries (like virtually all colleges and universities) have designed their curricula to the "felt needs" of their students. The results have included a decline in academic rigor and an emphasis on the therapeutic, the trendy, and the easy assimilation of leftist views. One student at Harvard Divinity School discovered that classmates who had not read an assignment could derail class discussion completely simply by accusing the author of sexism, homophobism, misogyny, or some similar offense.[83]

In 1994, the Yale University Divinity School professor Christopher R. Seitz complained of his students: "Most don't know the names of half of the books of the Bible, whether Calvin lived before or after Augustine, what it means to say that Christ descended to the dead or acted 'in accordance with the Scriptures,' what the wrath of God means or how to understand a final judgment of the quick and the dead." Seminary students, he wrote, are prepared to think critically about their faith while lacking a "substantive base."[84]

Not all the seminary news is bleak; there are still institutions, directly or indirectly connected with the mainline, that offer a balanced and challenging theological education and produce graduates interested primarily in the spiritual dimensions of the faith. Asbury Theological Seminary, for example, a campus with over a thousand students, provides many orthodox clergy for the United Methodist Church. Eastern Seminary and Northern Seminary, serving the American Baptist Churches in the USA, now have orthodox leaders. Princeton Theological Seminary has become more moderate in recent years under the leadership of Thomas Gillespie. Two conservative student groups, the Theological Student Fellowship and the scholarly Charles Hodge Society, reveal a refreshing diversity of opinion on the Presbyterian campus.[85]

Dean Gary Kriss of Nashotah House boasts that his seminary is a place where Episcopalians and others can combine rigorous learning, through a core curriculum, with free discussion of all topics and the pursuit of personal holiness. "In a sophisticated society, the Church needs leaders (both lay and ordained) who are equipped to witness intelligently to the gospel. It has been suggested that the clergy ought to be the most intelligent and best educated people in a community."[86] But Kriss and his ideals are by no means popular in his church. Indeed, most Episcopal bishops will not send students to the "reactionary" seminary.[87]

From support for the welfare state and affirmative action to opposition to prayer in the public schools, mainline positions on domestic issues are extremely predictable. Feminism is wholly endorsed. Abortion rights are backed. (Since 1988, American Baptists have left the morality of the issue up to each individual congregation.) Homosexual activity is often condoned.

The United Church of Christ and certain regional organizations of the Disciples of Christ have ordained practicing homosexuals.[88] (As early as 1977, the UCC was being called the first major post-Christian church in the United States, in part because of its avant-garde position on homosexuality.)[89] In mid-1994, a UCC church in Seattle hired a gay couple to share a job as associate minister, and the church headquarters called the men "outstanding candidates."[90]

In 1991, a resolution in the General Convention of the Episcopal Church to prohibit sexual intercourse by the clergy outside of marriage was defeated. Three years later, seventy-one bishops publicly defied church policy and declared their willingness to ordain practicing homosexuals and bless same-sex unions.[91] The Episcopal Women's Caucus, a semi-official arm of the church with an aggressive lesbian contingent, boasted in 1995 that it existed to free the church from, among other things, "heterosexism."[92] Episcopal Bishop John Spong is one of several gay rights proponents who have claimed that St. Paul was a repressed and frustrated homosexual.[93]

John Boswell's *Christianity, Social Tolerance, and Homosexuality*, published in 1980 and called by one critic "a kind of sacred text for those who want to morally legitimate the homosexual movement," is routinely invoked in studies by Methodists, Lutherans, and Presbyterians. Similarly popular is Boswell's *Same-Sex Unions in Premodern Europe*, published in 1994, which claims that homosexual marriages were well established in the medieval church.[94] (On the other hand, the American Baptist Churches of the West, affiliated with the American Baptist Churches in the USA, expelled four northern California congregations in early 1996 for welcoming homosexuals as members without teaching that homosexual activity was sinful. At about the same time, the ELCA expelled two Lutheran churches in San Francisco for having appointed openly homosexual members as pastors. Kim Byham, a gay rights leader in the Episcopal Church, warned of a backlash: "It's a sad tale, but Christianity has always been washed in the blood of martyrs."[95])

The only disease to attract major mainline attention is AIDS, which largely stems from anal intercourse by homosexuals and the use of contaminated needles for intravenous drug consumption. (A study published in 1995 in the *American Journal of Epidemiology* concluded that one-third of gay men continued to engage in unprotected anal intercourse.[96])

Once a year, special prayers are offered in all Episcopal churches for AIDS victims. A National AIDS Hotline has three telephone numbers: one in English, one in Spanish, and one for the "Hearing Impaired."[97] At the General Convention in 1994, the National Episcopal AIDS Coalition distributed condoms and delegates passed no fewer than three resolutions on AIDS.[98]

At the same conclave, Bishop Jane Dixon wore a large button that read "SEXUALITY, NOT SPIRITUALITY." There seems to be a mainline obsession with sex, a topic of often intense debate at meetings and conventions of all sorts. This again reflects the mainline's absorption of contemporary liberal mores. As William Murchison put it, "a healthy and vigorous sex life is the great modern desideratum—the Holy Grail of a self-regarding society."[99]

In the fall of 1993, the Evangelical Lutheran Church in America released a twenty-two–page first draft of a statement on human sexuality that said there was biblical support for homosexual relationships, that masturbation was healthy, and that teaching teens to use condoms was a moral imperative.[100] The Presbyterian Church (USA) voted in 1993 to begin a human sexuality curriculum for *preschool* children in its churches.[101]

At the same time, comprehensive ethical guidelines from mainline headquarters are frequently opaque. A woman consulting the book *United Methodist Social Principles* on divorce complained, "Our church seems to think that the main thing is to do what you personally think is right. What help is that?" The Methodist minister William H. Willimon commented, "It doesn't require a great amount of courage for a church to say to contemporary American culture: First be sure in your heart that what you are doing is right, then go ahead and do it and to hell with what anybody else says."[102] Wheaton College historian Mark A. Noll believes that modern Protestantism has lapsed "into pallid cultural captivity."[103]

In foreign affairs, mainline principals often assume that America is automatically the villain. Many thought their own country responsible for the Cold War; Stalin and his ideological friends appeared to be mere victims of right-wing hysteria. Many supported the Marxist Sandinistas against the Reagan-backed Contras in Nicaragua. President Bush had to turn to evangelist Billy Graham to bless American involvement in the Persian Gulf War when the Presiding Bishop of the Episcopal Church, the church to which Bush belonged, opposed the conflict.[104] Methodist Bishop Melvin Talbert called Bush "the real aggressor in the Gulf."[105] The General Synod of the United Church of Christ declared that the Gulf struggle "was not a just war" and expressed support for the more than one thousand conscientious objectors in the military.[106] (Eighty percent of the American people backed the war, agreeing that there was a "just, moral cause for taking military action.")[107]

To these protagonists of sackcloth chic, it is a given that "American imperialism" is responsible for much of the misery on the planet, especially in Third World countries. There is much wallowing in guilt—actually, the guilt of other, less enlightened Americans. A national meeting of the Disciples of Christ in 1983 declared, "We confess our guilt as one of the wealthiest countries in a world full of starving people, as citizens intent on order in a country full of desperation." Delegates acknowledged breaking faith with earlier generations, "the dead who lived before us and whose dreams we betrayed, the dreams of 1789 and of 1917." The nostalgic reference to the Bolshevik Revolution must have seemed odd to many Americans.[108]

The formidable religious thinker Richard John Neuhaus has estimated that only a quarter of the mainline leadership would endorse the proposition that America is a force for good in the world.[109]

Conditions are often similar on the local level. Complaints about the political partisanship, character, and competence of clergy are commonplace in many denominations. In 1993, it was reported that about 600 United Methodist clergy were being fired or taking a leave of absence each year. A Southern Baptist survey revealed 116 of its ministers being fired every month.[110]

The character of the clergy is a constant concern of the faithful. The vital elements of character—integrity, prudence, temperance, courage, loyalty, responsibility, humility, perseverance, compassion, generosity—are all too frequently missing in our spiritual leaders. Sexual morality is a case in point.

In a 1990 poll taken in the United Methodist Church, 42 of the clergywomen surveyed said they had been sexually harassed by other clergy, and 17 percent of female laity reported being harassed by their ministers.[111] A study released by the Park Ridge Center for the Study of Health, Faith, and Ethics in Chicago suggested that 10 percent of all ministers have had affairs with members of their congregations, and that 25 percent have had some kind of sexual contact with a parishioner.[112] Between 1984 and 1993, 105 claims were filed against Episcopal priests for alleged sexual misconduct, costing the Church Insurance Corporation $7.9 million to settle.[113] After the bishop of the Episcopal Diocese of Massachusetts committed suicide in 1995, the diocese revealed that he had been "involved in several extramarital relationships" over his career as priest and bishop.[114]

(Roman Catholic churches were rocked the hardest of all by sex scandals in the 1990s, many millions of dollars being paid to victims and spent on legal fees and administrative expenses. In 1994 alone, the Archdiocese of Chicago spent $4.3 million, nearly quadruple the cost just two years earlier.[115])

A Hartford Seminary study released in 1995 found clergy divorce rates in fifteen denominations similar to that found among lay persons generally. About 25 percent of clergywomen and 20 percent of clergymen studied had been divorced. The study found that "The divorce rate is far higher in the liberal denominations than in the more conservatives ones." Over a fourth of the Episcopal clergy, for example, had been divorced, while no more than one-sixth of the Southern Baptist clergy had been.[116]

Wisdom, knowledge, even basic competence seem to be in short supply among the clergy these days. In mainline churches all over America, for example, sermons are too often hastily prepared ("Saturday night specials") and deadly dull. Elizabeth Achtemeier, who teaches Bible and homiletics at Union Seminary, Richmond, Virginia, says that poor preaching is contributing to biblical illiteracy and "the cultural captivity of the church."[117]

Solid teaching is at a premium, and the basics about sin, repentance, judgment, and hell frequently go unexplored. Theological education has been neglected in the mainline churches to the point that one student of the subject contends, "theology no longer plays an important role in the church's life."[118] It is all too often presumed that God is wholly and merely . . . nice.

What does the Episcopal chaplain at Princeton University tell young people who come to him with questions? The Rev. Frank Strasburger declared in 1994 that he is not in the business of dispensing dogmatic answers about anything. "For better or worse, we are a church with broad tolerance both for the anomalies in our own understanding of the truth and for the possibility of its being accessible to those beyond our fold." His job, as he sees it, "is to help students out of their parents' faith and into their own."[119]

Music (frequently with bowdlerized lyrics to meet feminist demands) and liturgy often echo this vapidity. "Stripped of His awesome majesty," the church musician Thomas Day has noted, "God becomes merely a 'soft,' endearing old distributor of love."[120] Little or nothing is expected of parishioners beyond a measure of amiability. The church historian D. Newell Williams has commented, "Many people now see no reason to be Christian. The mainline churches are just plain boring."[121]

Of course, thousands of mainline parishes do not fit this general description, congregations that are happy, knowledgeable, orthodox, and growing—growth usually being a natural sign of a healthy parish. The conservative Methodist minister Jim Heidinger believes that this healthiness is especially true among the thirty-six thousand churches in his denomination. He cites a scientific poll taken in 1988 revealing that 69 percent of Methodists describe themselves as conservatives on moral and theological issues, while more than three-quarters of all surveyed opposed the ordination of homosexuals. "We are a basically conservative church being controlled by liberals."[122]

There is resistance from pulpits and the pews to the predilections of denominational leaders and elected bodies. In the 1960s Presbyterians United for Biblical Concerns, the Presbyterian Lay Committee, and the Good News Movement of the Methodists were formed to attack leftward lurches. Dissidents within the Episcopal Church created, among other groups, the Evangelical and Catholic Mission, Episcopalians United, and, in 1989, the Episcopal Synod of America. In the late 1970s, United Church of Christ members formed the United Church People for Biblical Witness (since 1984, the Biblical Witness Fellowship) to curb their denomination's liberal policies. Lutherans for Religious and Political Freedom, founded in 1985, is known for its sharp criticisms of liberal and secular trends within the ELCA. Disciples Renewal was created in 1987 as a conservative alternative within the Christian Church. American Baptist Evangelicals was created in 1992 to return the American Baptist Church to its biblical and evangelical emphasis.

In 1992 a thousand elected delegates to the General Convention of the United Methodist Church reaffirmed their opposition to homosexual behavior and overwhelmingly rejected a special committee's report to revise church teaching on the issue.[123] When the Evangelical Lutheran Church in America released the first draft of its statement on human sexuality, noted above, some twenty thousand telephone calls clogged the lines at church head-quarters the following day.[124] In 1994, four hundred local United Church of Christ leaders attended a series of conferences attempting to find ways of combatting liberalism in their denomination. Among the complaints was an attempt to remove the word "Lord" from a new church hymnal, on the ground that it was patriarchal, and to delete male language from the classic Trinitarian formula of Father, Son, and Holy Spirit.[125]

A variety of reasons are given for the decline of the mainline churches. On the left, a common explanation is that the churches are too stodgy and traditional. At the most basic level is what I call the "Sister Act" (after the popular movie) school of thought, which states in general that as soon as the clergy start dancing and singing rock music, multitudes will pour through the doors. "Meeting the people where they are" is one way of stating the underlying principle. The less genteel might say simply that pandering pays off.

Episcopal (former Roman Catholic) priest Matthew Fox, for example, has designed a *Planetary Mass* that incorporates loud rave music, gyrating dancers, an altar in the shape of a sun and crescent moon, tai chi exercises, and a profusion of television monitors. When performed at Grace Cathedral in San Francisco in October 1994, a reporter observed: "As the gospel was being read, videos of televangelists were projected over the word 'sorcery.' There were scenes of violent video games and bombs hitting Iraq during the Persian Gulf War. Fr. [Chris] Brain crossed himself with soil, symbolizing the sacredness of the earth. 'Mother God' was referred to and the Holy Spirit was called 'the spirit of life' or 'the passion for living.'" Bishop William Swing said of the mass, "I was very carried away by it."[126]

Feminists devised a Summer Solstice Party that featured an all-night picnic and camp-out, a totem pole, individual totems (each "representing an important aspect of her identity"), songs, stories, dances, chanting, and the Hatha Yoga Sun Salutation in thirteen body postures.[127]

Sometimes one may see the direct impact of "Sister Act." At a Faith of Women service in 1994, held in the Princeton University chapel, the twenty-two–member choir, accompanied by piano and drums, broke into a swinging version of the hymn "Salve Regina"—as arranged for the movie. Perhaps with Hollywood also in mind, the offering was designated for the state network for women with AIDS.[128]

At the University of Delaware, Episcopal, Lutheran, Presbyterian, United Methodist, Baptist, and Roman Catholic chaplains sponsor Christian rock 'n' roll concerts. A leader of the ecumenical group, an Episcopal priest, summarized his strategy by saying: "I did the Anglican thing. I said, 'Let's have a party!' "[129]

During a weeklong Episcopal Youth Event, Bishop Edmond Browning, presiding bishop of the Episcopal Church, balanced a spoon on his nose, wore his purple "PB" baseball cap backwards, wore a latex "conehead," and sprayed the crowd with water from an oversized squirt gun. One youth said, "I always thought of bishops as really old and stuffy, but he's not. He's fun." Another concluded, "Definitely a pretty cool guy."[130]

It would help, too, many liberals believe, if the churches would abandon their "old-fashioned" moral positions, especially concerning sex. In 1993, a woman priest at the Episcopal cathedral in Chicago displayed a condom during an Easter season service and said that if Jesus were to return he would want everyone to be free to enjoy sex, in whatever form that might be.[131]

In 1995, Episcopal priest Alexander Seabrook wrote of his church, "every time that we ordain someone who is not a heterosexual white male, we gain hundreds of new members."[132]

Some would like to see bolder church involvement in issues of race, the environment, health care, poverty, and so on. Some would like to jettison the very basics of the Christian faith, like the Incarnation and the Resurrection, thereby appealing to those who think Christianity intellectually indefensible. The liberal Episcopalian and sociologist Donald E. Miller refers to the great mysteries of the faith as "social fictions" and argues: "I see no reason why Christians cannot recite the creeds, participate in the sacrament of the Eucharist, and enjoy the rich symbolic structure of the church without feeling that they are somehow being hypocritical if they do not *literally* believe what they are affirming. Not to do so is to be imprisoned within a pre-Enlightenment world view."[133]

To many liberals, in short, the mainline denominations are declining because they have been insufficiently attentive to the "progressive" forces of our time. Churches stuck in the past, they argue, must pay the price for their ignorance and insensitivity.

Some mainliners take a certain pride in what they view as their martyrdom, arguing that the millions who have departed lacked the necessary intellectual and moral training to enjoy the fellowship of enlightened, modern Christians. The Rev. Paul Sherry, the liberal leader of the United Church of Christ, declared, "We've tried to say that we're trying to be responsive to what we believe God is saying to the church these days. And we've said to ourselves that if this means we will lose some members, we are sorry that that has to be the case, but that may be the cost of discipleship."[134]

And there are other ways of putting a positive spin on the negative numbers. One sociologist concluded a statistical study with, "In effect, while there may be fewer participants in the Presbyterian churches, they may be more committed and more involved."[135]

Conservatives, of course, see things quite differently. Many argue that the mainline churches are hemorrhaging because they concentrate on politics. As one critic put it, "To politicize the church by focusing its attention and energies on pronouncements dealing with social issues about which Christians are bitterly divided is to lead the church away from its destiny and toward eventual paralysis."[136]

This "political neutrality" explanation fails, however, to acknowledge the inevitable and intimate relationship between religious belief and social action. Christians, everywhere and at all times, have been active in political affairs. Richard John Neuhaus argues that "Christian truth, if it is truth, is public truth. It is accessible to public reason. It impinges upon public space. At some critical points of morality and ethics it speaks to public policy." Only religion, he adds, "must, by definition, insist upon moral truth that is transcendent, intersubjective, and therefore normative."[137]

In modern times, for example, men and women from the mainline churches have labored for a wide variety of political and social reforms through the Social Gospel movement, Progressivism, and the New Deal. From the 1890s on, many mainline leaders considered themselves liberal and avant-garde. Mark Noll has commented, "Like the early leaders of Calvinism on the Continent and the English Puritans, Americans have moved in a straight line from personal belief to social reform, from private experience to political activity."[138] And yet as late as the 1950s the mainline churches seemed robust by any measurement. Political activity alone did not prompt the recent deterioration.

Then, too, of course, many thriving evangelical churches today are themselves deeply engaged in political efforts. The Religious Right (18 percent of the nation's adult public in 1994) has become a major factor in the Republican Party, favoring an end to abortion on demand, opposing homosexual practices and pornography, and promoting prayer in public schools.[139] Pat Robertson ran for the presidency in 1988, mounting a campaign organized in part by the Assemblies of God, the largest of the Pentecostal churches.

By late 1994, the Christian Coalition, founded six years earlier, claimed to have 1.5 million dues-paying members and the support of between 18 and 20 percent of Americans. Since Clinton's inauguration, the organization reported adding 8,000 members a week.[140] The coalition, run by Pat Robertson, claimed success in a New York school board election in 1993 and in the nationwide Republican sweep of the following year. Its executive director, Ralph Reed, said, "We're hot because we believe in something."[141]

The success of the Christian Coalition prompted the mainline churches in 1994 to form a liberal educational and lobbying organization called the Interfaith Alliance, which had a first-year budget of $4 million. Board member Joan Brown Campbell, general secretary of the National Council of Churches, said: "Our concern is that the radical right lays claim to the fact that they uniquely speak for people of faith in this country, in essence that 'God is on our side.' We feel we must come together as an interfaith group and say to this country there is an alternate religious voice."[142]

In 1995, the alliance publicly blasted the GOP majority and the Christian Coalition and condemned laws passed during the first hundred days of the 104th Congress. The Rev. Hubert Valentine, the alliance chairman, said "there was very little of the Jewish and Christian values of brotherly love" in evidence. Rabbi Arthur Hertzberg, an alliance member, said if congressional conservatives "made the rich richer and the poor poorer, they have not made a contract with America, but a contract with the devil."[143]

Today, Christians of all persuasions regularly take stands on major policy issues and support their convictions with money and effort. On the volatile issue of abortion, for example, serious Christians find silence a highly unsatisfactory option. At stake are the rights of women and the lives of millions of unborn children.

But the "political neutrality" argument usually goes on to assert that mainline churches water down and even discard the gospel in the course of their liberal boosterism. Many conservatives contend that great numbers of people have left in direct protest. A study of baby boomers (the 76 million born between 1946 and 1964) who grew up in mainline churches showed that more than a third switched, 17 percent going to conservative Protestantism. These people seemed to leave in search of stronger moral guidelines and deeper faith. "I got fed a lot of twinkies," said one man.[144]

Some on the right view the plight of the mainline churches as a byproduct of a massive and deliberate assault by left-wing secularists, often called secular humanists, upon the whole of the

Christian faith and the American way of life. Concerned Women for America, the nation's largest women's organization (much larger than the heralded National Organization for Women), has claimed that "the secular humanists, who deny God and traditional moral values, have almost gained total control of our public policies, our schools, even our law-making institutions and courts—in just one or two generations."[145] The historian James Hitchcock contends that secular humanism "has a keen sense of being locked into a continuous philosophical and social struggle with religious belief, in which the ultimate stakes are nothing less than the moral foundations of society."[146] Many conservatives like Hitchcock fail to be distressed by the deterioration of liberal churches, seeing them as collaborators with forces determined to de-Christianize our civilization.

Other observers see the mainline churches as mere victims, casualties of such modern phenomena as urbanism, industrialism, rising educational levels, prosperity, social mobility, the changing nature of the family, and so on. It is true, for example, that liberal Protestants, being higher in the social structure, have lower fertility rates than conservative Protestants, and this has had an impact on the decrease in young members.[147]

One interpretation of the mainline malaise, posited in 1972 by Dean M. Kelley, an official of the National Council of Churches, has warranted frequent commentary. In *Why Conservative Churches Are Growing*, Kelley argued that successful churches make strict demands, both of faith and practice, on their members. The "business" of religion, he contended, was "to explain the ultimate meaning of life" and "the quality which makes one system of ultimate meaning more convincing than another is not its content but its seriousness/strictness/costliness/bindingness."[148] By this standard, then, the mainline churches, light on questions of eternal importance, lacking a distinctive identity, and permissive to the bone, seem doomed.

Two liberal professors of religion, Wade Clark Roof and

William McKinney, concluded in 1987 that Kelley's thesis had in general proved sound. "Careful analysis of membership trends shows that the churches hardest hit were those highest in socioeconomic status, those stressing individualism and pluralism in belief, and those most affirming of American culture."[149] The sociologists Roger Finke and Rodney Stark agreed, concluding in 1992, "to the degree that denominations rejected traditional doctrines and ceased to make serious demands on their followers, they ceased to prosper. The churching of America was accomplished by aggressive churches committed to vivid otherworldliness."[150]

In 1994, a major study conducted by the Catholic University sociologist Dean R. Hoge and three others concluded that members of theologically conservative churches that stress financial sacrifice, personal piety, and personal salvation are the most generous givers.[151]

In contrast to the mainline denominations, many conservative evangelical churches have been prospering. (Evangelicals stress personal conversion and such classical Protestant beliefs as the all-sufficient authority of Scripture. Fundamentalists, who in general defend biblical inerrancy and reject modern ideas and values, are the right wing of the movement and represent about a third of all evangelicals. A recent study showed evangelical Protestants making up more than 20 percent of the nation's population.)[152] An official of the Southern Baptist Convention, for example, could boast in 1994, "We're still growing at the rate of 750 members and five churches a week."[153] Between 1965 and 1989 the Assemblies of God grew 121 percent, the Seventh Day Adventists grew 92 percent, the Church of God (Cleveland, Tennessee) grew 183 percent, and the Church of the Nazarene grew 63 percent. The major metropolitan areas abound in large and affluent nondenominational churches that seem especially successful in appealing to youth.[154]

The success of these bodies, as suggested above, may be due to their rejection of the secular spirit of the age. The sociologist Daniel

V. A. Olson argues that conservative churches prosper because their members are united in basic, orthodox Christian beliefs and values that are distinctive from mainstream American culture.[155]

And yet the burgeoning of conservative churches may well be tapering off. According to figures collected by the National Council of Churches, the Lutheran Church–Missouri Synod grew less than 0.1 percent from 1991 to 1992, while the Southern Baptists increased a mere 0.83 percent. An Associated Press analyst concluded that "the church growth figures indicate a spiritual malaise."[156] Giving as a percentage of income per member in eight denominations associated with the National Association of Evangelicals dropped from 6.19 percent in 1968 to 4.27 percent in 1993.[157]

Perhaps these churches are now feeling the effects of at least a measure of the secularism and relativism plaguing their spiritual cousins in the mainline churches. The theologian David F. Wells of Gordon-Conwell Theological Seminary thinks so, believing he hears the "death rattle" of evangelical Christianity. "We now have less biblical fidelity, less interest in truth, less seriousness, less depth, and less capacity to speak the Word of God to our own generation in a way that offers an alternative to what it already thinks." Evangelicals, he believes, have "come to terms psychologically with our society's structural pluralism and its lack of interest in matters of truth."[158]

What, exactly, is eating away at churches, the mainline in particular, rendering them uncertain guides in a civilization starving for lack of purpose and solid moral and ethical guidelines? There are clearly many pieces to the puzzle, and once they are sorted out, recommendations will be in order for reinvigorating the once proud and vital mainline denominations.

Why bother at all? In part because many mainline members revere their church's traditions and accept their historic theological doctrines. In 1995, on the fiftieth anniversary of his ordination, the Episcopal priest Jack Bunday expressed his joy at being an Anglican and said he would no more leave the church because of its objectionable leadership than he would abandon his country, which he also thought was in bad hands.[159]

Then, too, many are deeply attached to their local church and its people. Millions of mainline Christians have spent all or much of their lives worshipping in the same congregation, and in many cases their ancestors also belonged. For better or worse, their faith is intimately linked with a specific denomination and a particular building within that tradition. To be cast from it could be personally devastating.

This points to yet another important reason for rejuvenating the mainline churches: If they fail, millions of their members may not embrace the available alternatives. This book has already presented data showing that large numbers of people who leave the mainline drop out of church completely. The Rev. Robert Miller, the associate editor of *The Presbyterian Layman*, says that without question a great many who exit his denomination choose to stay home on Sundays.[160]

True, if their denominations collapsed or became intolerable, some conservative Presbyterians would join the small Evangelical Presbyterian Church or the Presbyterian Church in America; a few Lutherans would head for the fundamentalist Missouri or Wisconsin synods; Episcopalians have their choice of several tiny splinter groups. Some mainliners, especially the American Baptists, would find the fundamentalist and charismatic interdenominational churches appealing. Still, one suspects that a great many mainline members would have difficulties elsewhere.

Socioeconomic levels must be taken into account. According to one study, 34 percent of Episcopalians, 25 percent of Presbyterians, and 21 percent of United Church of Christ members are college graduates. In contrast, only 6 percent of Southern Baptists and 2 percent of Assembly of God members have college degrees.[161] When Jeffrey Wallen, an expert on higher education, was asked why he and many of his fellow Presbyterians would not be comfortable in one of the evangelical or fundamentalist churches, he replied with a single word: "class."[162]

But there is more to be considered here. There is a sensibility, a temperament that can transcend the traditional definitions of class. For many mainliners, of varying levels of education and income, there is a profound need for dignity, reverence, beauty, learning, tradition, and a sense of the numinous. In my parish, an Episcopal church in urban Milwaukee, many of the most faithful and deeply Anglican members have virtually no status at all in the eyes of the world.

Few evangelical and fundamentalist churches are designed to satisfy the needs of such people. Warehouselike buildings, sobbing pop gospel soloists, garish theatrics, shouting preachers, and boisterous worshippers cannot appeal to many of us. There is no sense in attempting to gloss over what often amounts to a basic incompatibility among equally devout Christians.

Not all evangelical and fundamentalist churches fit this stereotype. David Carlson of Minneapolis, the lay founder of Lutherans for Religious and Political Freedom, left the ELCA for a large interdenominational church that contains many professionals and features scholarly, sophisticated sermons. Carlson admits, however, that such churches are rare. And he further acknowledges that the popular music and lack of liturgy leave him yearning for more.[163]

There are the Roman Catholic and Orthodox churches, of course—spiritual homes of the great majority of Christians in the world. But for a variety of theological, moral, aesthetic, and ethnic reasons, few mainliners could be expected to embrace those very different systems. The issue of authority alone would be a huge stumbling block.

If the mainline churches become unbearable or fail entirely, many members will no doubt drift away from organized religion altogether, leaving them increasingly vulnerable to the many secular temptations. (This has happened throughout western Europe.) Staying home on Sundays is almost always a destructive option for Christians, who need the spiritual strength available not only in Scripture, sermons, sacraments, and song but in the joys and difficulties of being with people of all sorts and conditions who share the common goal of a life and death in Jesus Christ.

Moreover, such a movement by millions would have national as well as personal implications, for we should have learned by now that the religion of the golf course, the shopping mall, and the television set is no match for the moral poisons that have infected us.

Let us begin sorting out the pieces of the mainline puzzle by examining briefly the role of Christianity in the history of this country. Perspective is always important, and we need to reexamine assumptions now prevalent about the secular nature of the American experience.

2

CONSUMER CHRISTIANITY

Today, few dogmas are as securely held and passionately defended on the left as the idea that America was always meant to be, is, and should always be a secular, pluralistic society. Acceptance of this concept, to liberals, is a litmus test for separating those who are "knowledgeable" from those who are trying to "turn back the clock." The "Christian nation" concept is widely dismissed in the media and in the classroom. Numerous national figures, including Supreme Court justices, have taken the position that the First Amendment commanded not only the separation of church and state but the separation of religion from public life.

An abundance of evidence suggests, however, that this interpretation of the relationship between Christianity and the United States is relatively new and is shared by only a minority of Americans. Placing our churches in a proper historical setting will help us understand how they got where they are and can help us formulate solutions to the many complex problems facing contemporary religious bodies.

The idea of a Christian society is almost as old as the religion itself. The Roman Emperor Constantine in the early fourth century embraced the faith and tried to tie it closely to the state. Later in the same century, Theodosius I established the orthodox Christian state.

The Reformation, while it championed religious freedom, still bound the faith to the state. And as rulers identified themselves and their peoples as either Catholic or Protestant, wars broke out to expand both political and religious authority. The union of church and state, then, for many centuries was thought to be divinely ordained.

This concept was a major force in American history from the beginning. The English settlers—Anglican, Puritan, and Quaker—were convinced that God was on their side and that He was calling them to create a holy society. The Puritans, Calvinists who attempted to establish a "new Jerusalem" in Boston, were especially influential in planting this idea. Cotton Mather's imposing *Magnalia Christi Americana*, for example, taught generations to view New England's past as sacred history.

Very few early Americans of any nationality doubted that their own colony enjoyed a special relationship with the Creator. As the historian Robert Kelley put it, "The colonials were a provincial people, and they regarded their style of living as not only good but of God."[1] Only three colonies failed to unite church and state, and strict laws concerning worship and personal conduct were plentiful.

The men who led the Revolution, tried to make the Articles of Confederation work, and wrote the Constitution held a variety of religious views. While almost all of them were officially Christians, many had been deeply influenced by the Enlightenment of the eighteenth century, with its faith in human reason, goodness, and progress. Some, like Thomas Jefferson, were deists who denied biblical miracles, disliked organized religion in general, and wanted the churches to be kept separate from the state.[2] James Madison was of a similar mind. (However, Madison spoke highly of Christianity at times, once referring to it as "this precious gift" and its propagation as "the victorious progress of truth."[3]) But both men were idiosyncratic among their peers. The great majority of American political leaders and thinkers of the time had no intention of completely separating the cross and the flag.

The Continental Congress employed a chaplain. Article III of the Northwest Ordinance of 1787 declared that "Religion, morality, and knowledge" were "necessary to good government and the happiness of mankind." State constitutions were filled with kindly references to God and religion.

M. E. Bradford wrote of the fifty-five framers of the Constitution, "with no more than five exceptions, they were orthodox members of one of the established Christian communions. An internal transformation of American society in the direction of a secularized egalitarian state was the furthest thing from the minds of these men." They were not French ideologues, said Bradford, their biographer. "They were closer to Hobbes than to Rousseau. Man, they recognized, was made to live in society and under government, out of providential necessity."[4]

The "no establishment" and "free exercise" clauses of the First Amendment to the Constitution were written in response to a prolonged and intense clamor, by Christians and non-Christians alike, against the idea of a national church. (Ironically, some voted for the First Amendment to protect established state churches from the federal government.) Freedom of worship, virtually nonexistent anywhere, was thought to be the best answer to the religious warfare and persecution that had gone on for centuries.

The separation of church and state, then, was created to protect the state from religion and to protect religion from the state. (Denominations quickly flourished and multiplied under this freedom). The policy was not intended to rid the nation of God and Christianity or to completely segregate churches from public life. Robert H. Bork has observed, "The history of the formulation of the clause by Congress demonstrates that it was not intended to ban government recognition of and assistance to religion; nor was it understood to require government neutrality between religion and irreligion."[5] The legal scholar Terry Eastland has written that "Nothing in Madison's original draft of the religion clause, or in the clause itself as ratified as part of the First Amendment, refers to any comprehensive forbidding of every form of public aid or support for religion."[6] As Linda Chavez put it, "America was founded on the freedom of, not from, religion."[7]

President Bill Clinton acknowledged this truth in 1995 while pleading for more religion in American life. "This country, after all, was founded by people of profound faith who mentioned Divine Providence and the guidance of God twice in the Declaration of Independence." The First Amendment, he said, prohibited the establishment of religion by the state but protected the free exercise of religion. "It does not, as some people have implied, make us a religion-free country."[8]

The day after the First Amendment passed in the House, that same body called for a day of national prayer and thanksgiving, and President Washington acceded, expressing official gratitude to "the providence of Almighty God." (One scholar has observed that Washington at the time was often compared to Jesus, noting that "he symbolized the bond between his society's political and religious sentiments."[9]) The very men who proposed the establishment clause employed chaplains for both houses of Congress and provided paid chaplains for the Army and Navy.

The Supreme Court justice William O. Douglas later wrote, "The First Amendment . . . does not say that in every and all respects there shall be a separation of Church and State. Rather, it studiously defines the manner, the specific ways, in which there shall be no concert or union or dependency one on the other. That is the common sense of the matter. Otherwise the state and religion would be aliens to each other—hostile, suspicious, and even unfriendly."[10]

Religion played a major role in all areas of American life in the first half of the nineteenth century. Francis Scott Key's poem "The

Star-Spangled Banner" said of the nation, "And this be our motto: 'In God is our trust!'" Alexis de Tocqueville discovered in the early 1830s that religion and "the spirit of freedom" were "intimately united and that they reigned in common over the same country."[11] Newspapers routinely published sermons on their front pages. Periodic revivals attracted huge audiences all across the country (prompting some mainline clergy to try to have them outlawed as disturbances of the peace). Roman Catholics had their revival meetings as well. Indeed, Finke and Stark report that they occurred about as frequently and regularly in Catholic churches as in Baptist and Methodist churches. "By the middle of the nineteenth century, evangelism had come to the fore of parish life."[12]

Clergymen, educators, businessmen, and Americans from all walks of life attributed their freedom, their prosperity, and their happiness to the God they worshiped in their churches. This was reflected in the nation's public schools, where Protestant morality and nationalism were blended and propagated. The pioneering educator Horace Mann warned, "If we do not prepare children to become good citizens—if we do not develop their capacities, if we do not enrich their minds with knowledge, imbue their hearts with the love of truth and duty, and a reverence for all things sacred and holy, then our republic must go down to destruction, as others have gone before it."[13] Popular textbooks by Noah Webster and William Holmes McGuffey were saturated with references to Christian ethics and virtues. Prayer and Bible reading were common in the public schools.

Churches took official positions on many public issues. Fourth of July orations and political speeches in general were filled with biblical quotations. Congress continued its policy of hiring a chaplain and engaging in official, tax-supported prayer. Churches enjoyed exemption from property taxes. The nation's expansionism was justified with the concept of "manifest destiny," the belief that America had a unique, God-given right to occupy the whole of the continent. What is today routinely described in the class-

The Empty Church

room as the rape, pillage, and exploitation of innocent peoples was then seen, at least officially, as a mission to spread democracy, prosperity, and the promise of salvation.

Both sides in the Civil War cited Scripture to justify their actions. President Lincoln, although not a church member, held powerful views on the relationship between God and the United States. In a proclamation calling for a National Fast Day in 1863, he declared: "[I]t is the duty of nations as well as of men, to own their dependence upon the overruling power of God, to confess their sins and transgressions, in humble sorrow, yet with assured hope that genuine repentance will lead to mercy and pardon; and to recognize the sublime truth, announced in the Holy Scriptures and proven by all history, that those nations only are blessed whose God is the Lord."[14]

Despite the shattering experience of the Civil War and the rise of industrialism, urbanism, massive immigration, and a large number of scientific advances that jolted traditional views in the Gilded Age, the synthesis of religion and culture remained strong. Lew Wallace's *Ben Hur: A Tale of the Christ*, published in 1880, was purchased by millions, and a stage version ran for thirty-five years. Wallace felt compelled to write the novel after a shocking conversation with Robert Ingersoll, the era's most prominent agnostic. "To Wallace's generation," wrote the historian Russell Nye, "the book's affirmation of Christianity and its evangelical tone held great appeal."[15]

Christianity was deeply a part of American higher education at this time. The majority of colleges had clergy as presidents, most faculty were church members, and courses in the faith were routine. In 1890, the president of the University of Michigan reported that twenty-two of twenty-four *state* universities conducted chapel services, that twelve of them required attendance, and that four mandated church attendance as well.[16]

Most Americans continued to assume that they lived in a Christian country. In 1892, following a lengthy review of historical evidence, Justice David Brewer wrote in a majority opinion of the United States Supreme Court (*Church of the Holy Trinity v. United States):* "[T]his is a religious people. This is historically true. From the discovery of this continent to the present hour there is a single voice making this affirmation. . . . this is a Christian nation."[17] That segregationists and imperialists also grounded their views on the Bible illustrates the seriousness with which religion was taken.

Christianity played an important role in the reforms of the Progressive Era. Teddy Roosevelt, for example, was not shy about touting the nation's close relationship to God and wrapping his legislative proposals in righteousness. Woodrow Wilson saw himself as a religious prophet and his nation as the light of the world. Settlement house workers like Frances Perkins believed that their efforts with the poor were intimately connected with their Christian faith.

In 1907, Walter Rauschenbusch's *Christianity and the Social Crisis* caused a national stir by expounding on the "social aims of Jesus." The following year, representatives of thirty-three Protestant denominations created the Federal Council of Churches, which immediately began a policy of militant liberal advocacy. The church historian Sydney Ahlstrom has referred to the council as the "praying wing of Progressivism."[18]

America's churches were highly active during World War I, linking their faith directly with the national interest. Ministers used government propaganda from pulpits, publicly displayed service-star flags, and conducted Liberty Loan drives in their churches. The historian William Warren Sweet declared, "At least for the period of World War I the separation of church and state was suspended."[19]

Even in the Roaring Twenties, when it became fashionable in some circles to belittle piety and altruism, few Americans doubted that their national values were higher than everyone else's. Indeed, this smugness was a major source of the country's isolationist policy. Bruce Barton's best-selling book *The Man Nobody Knows,* which portrayed the Savior as a successful businessman, was only an especially silly example of a huge literature that linked America with Jesus Christ. In 1931, a majority opinion of the United States Supreme Court declared in *U.S. v. Macintosh*, "We are a Christian people. . ., according to one another the equal right of religious freedom, and acknowledging with reverence the duty of obedience to the will of God."[20]

Throughout the Depression years, Christianity retained its vigor. Movie censorship, for example, illustrated the authority of churches to shape public opinion. Stores closed on Sundays, colleges supervised the morals of their students, politicians continued to assure people that they belonged to a God-fearing nation.

During World War II, the government built over six hundred interfaith chapels for the armed forces, and eleven thousand uniformed military chaplains distributed Bibles containing a foreword by the chief executive commending the reading of Scripture. President Franklin Roosevelt often referred publicly to the nation's religious origins, proclaimed days of prayer, and appealed to the public's faith in God. One of the "four essential human freedoms," he declared, was freedom of worship.

At the same time, religious novels were best-sellers. The film *Going My Way*, a sympathetic story revolving around a Catholic priest, was a box office smash, and Bing Crosby, who portrayed the priest, won the Academy Award for best actor that year. A popular song of the day exclaimed: "Praise the Lord and pass the ammunition."

The strong religious sense of the war years increased during the rest of the decade. And government lent its support. In 1946, for example, Brooklyn was the site of the 117th annual Sunday School Union parade, in which some ninety thousand Protestant youngsters participated. On hand were Brooklyn's mayor, the governor of New York, and a justice of the United States Supreme Court. All local schools were closed for the day. The march, observed the sociologist Robert Wuthnow, "betokened an easy, taken-for-granted alliance between church and state."[21]

The 1950s have been called a "golden age" of American Christianity. Church membership, attendance, and financial donations reached new heights. When asked by the Gallup poll whether religion was "very important" in their lives, 75 percent of Protestants and 83 percent of Catholics responded positively.[22]

In 1950, the National Council of Churches (NCC) was created, composed of 29 denominations, with a combined membership of 33 million church members and 143,000 congregations. Before his election as the first NCC Council president, Bishop Henry Knox Sherrill of the Episcopal Church declared that "the Council marks a new and great determination that the American way will be increasingly the Christian way, for such is our heritage. . . . Together the Churches can move forward to the goal— a Christian America in a Christian world." President Truman greeted the formation of the council with the hope that the body would "exert a greater influence in the strengthening of the spiritual foundation of our national life at a time when a materialistic philosophy is rampant."[23]

In 1952, Congress asked the president to proclaim a National Day of Prayer annually. The first National Prayer Breakfast was held in 1953, attended by President Eisenhower. The words "under God" were soon added to the pledge of allegiance, and "In God We Trust" became the nation's official motto.

When Billy Graham held one of his highly successful revival meetings in Washington, D.C., 125 representatives turned out to meet him for breakfast one day, and 56 senators came to a luncheon given by Lyndon Johnson, Everett Dirksen, and others. Vice President Richard Nixon and his wife attended one of the evangelist's regular meetings.[24]

The illustrations by Norman Rockwell on the covers of the *Saturday Evening Post* reflected the widespread view that Americans were a healthy, happy, and devout people. Birthrates were high, and the Christian family was glorified; "The family that prays together, stays together," said the popular slogan.

Both Presidents Truman and Eisenhower expressed their personal commitment to Christian doctrine and values. But it was Eisenhower who stood at the forefront of the religious revival of his day. The mainline historian Martin Marty has observed, "Eisenhower used the White House, Teddy Roosevelt's 'bully pulpit,' to promote a generalized and nationalistic religion. Ike was friendly enough to the churches, but as a priest of this national faith, he found it more important to see the nation itself as a kind of shrine or instrument of God."[25]

This theme was prominent in rhetoric, politically inspired and otherwise, about the Cold War. To Eisenhower, Secretary of State John Foster Dulles, Billy Graham, Senators Joe McCarthy, Henry M. Jackson, and John F. Kennedy, and practically everyone else in the country, the worldwide struggle was between Christian America and the atheistic Soviet Union—a conflict between good and evil.

In 1952, Supreme Court Justice Douglas (himself a most worldly man) declared in *Zorach v. Clauson*, "We are a religious people whose institutions presuppose a Supreme Being."[26] By mid-1963, at least thirty states either required or authorized Bible reading in public schools. For about half of America's schoolchildren, the day began with religious exercises that included Bible verses or the Lord's Prayer or both.[27]

In 1965, writing for Billy Graham's magazine *Decision*, Richard Nixon (ever the adroit politician) declared that "More preaching from the Bible rather than just about the Bible is what America needs." He described religion as "the true fountainhead of America's strength," and expressed his belief "that the whole national experience of our people, the extent to which the American idea has worked, is evidence of the interdependence of a widely shared religious faith and the vigorous health of a free American society."[28]

Today, of course, this sort of thought does not sit well in many areas of American life, especially in the nation's schools and colleges.

Thomas Sowell and others have richly documented efforts in the public schools to indoctrinate students in the dogmas of secularism and "non-judgmental" thinking.[29] An extremely partisan interdisciplinary conference on advocacy in the classroom, held in 1995 and sponsored by sixteen highly prestigious academic organizations, illustrated the stranglehold the left enjoys over liberal arts education in academia.[30] Dinesh D'Souza, in a study of leftist control on campus, concluded that "instead of liberal education, what American students are getting is its diametrical opposite, an education in closed-mindedness and intolerance, which is to say, illiberal education."[31] Richard Bernstein, in a similar book, noted that multiculturalism, the current rage, "is a code word for an expanded concept of moral and cultural relativism."[32]

The courts have played a major role in promulgating this overall point of view. Since 1982, the Supreme Court has followed "the endorsement test" on church-state questions. In the words of the legal scholar Gerard V. Bradley, the principle "holds that public authority may do nothing that might be construed as a sign that religion is a good thing, that religion is a component of human flourishing in a way that something else (assertedly comparable, which the justices call 'nonreligion' or 'irreligion') is not." This is an extremely serious matter, writes Bradley, that results from a misreading of the Constitution and of American history. "The broad neutrality brought us abortion-on-demand and will, in all likelihood, soon christen assisted suicide and homosexual marriage as constitutional rights."[33] Liberals on the Supreme Court, writes the University of Chicago law professor Michael W. McConnell, want to make government "a relentless engine of secularization."[34]

The American Civil Liberties Union, People for the American Way, and several similar groups on the left have prodded the courts relentlessly to promote their secular agenda. In 1995, the ACLU tried to stop recordings of "Silent Night" and other Christian hymns from being piped into a government building in Chicago. The claim was that since the government owned the loudspeaker system, this was an "establishment of religion."[35]

There is, of course, much evidence to show that we are indeed now living in a secular—some call it pagan—society. In the media, for example, religion is denigrated when discussed at all. The Media Research Center found that only 212 of 18,000 network news stories in 1993 dealt specifically with religion. L. Brent Bozell III, founder of the center, observed, "When it is a story, what kind of story is it? There were two big stories in 1993, abortion and gay rights." He added, "There's a sports division on every network, yet only one network has a religion reporter. It's just not on their radar screen. They don't understand the religious experience. When they think of religion, they think of scandal. They see it as a private thing, not as part of culture."[36]

Jeff Sagansky, president of CBS Entertainment, told an interviewer in 1994, "The first thing you learn as a program executive is never program anything whose content has to do with religion and God. It isn't hip."[37] Richard John Neuhaus has described a public discourse on religion that has been "increasingly debased by major media that are as morally ignorant as they are religiously indifferent."[38]

By early 1995, Beavis and Butt-head merchandise had generated more than $100 million in gross revenue, prompting one observer to exclaim that this was an example of how "MTV and others in the entertainment industry turn a financial profit by contaminating civil discourse, ridiculing common decency, debasing morality and corrupting us all."[39] (More about the media later.)

Scholars and journalists increasingly use "BCE" (Before the Common Era) and "B.P." (before the present) in dates to replace the traditional references to the birth of Christ. The Christmas season has been renamed the "winter holiday" and seems to be about shopping. Easter, to millions, is about bunnies and eggs and

"Spring Break." The Madonna we know is hardly a religious figure. The interests of the general public appear to center upon sports, television programs, movies, cars, houses, calories, clothes, celebrities, computers, crime, gambling, and so on.

Do people in bars and beauty parlors talk about holiness, miracles, or justification by faith? How many could, or would even want to, name the president of the Harvard Divinity School? Do more college students major in business than in religious studies? Do more young people know lyrics by 2 Live Crew and Snoop Doggy Dog than the verses of Charles Wesley? What role has religion played in what Michael Rothschild has called America's "epochal transformation from a Machine Age to an Information Age economy"?[40]

And where do we turn for help when faced with life's most difficult decisions? In a *U.S. News and World Report* poll, 81 percent agreed that going to a therapist would be helpful "sometimes" or "all of the time." Arianna Huffington commented, "Our culture increasingly celebrates therapy as an all-purpose panacea—from the public confessionals of daytime talk shows, through presidential retreats featuring group encounters and hug-fests, to the diffusion of 'therapy-speak,' as in 'getting in touch with one's feelings' and 'needing one's space.' Personal salvation is no longer expected to be found exclusively in a pew or on one's knees. The therapist's office is the new sacred place."[41]

It should be obvious that we are a secular, materialistic people. Banks and entertainment complexes appear to be our cathedrals, and journalists and talk show hosts our prophets.

Evangelists as well as professors speak routinely about "post–Christian America." Edward Farley, professor of theology at Vanderbilt Divinity School, has observed, "As a way of thinking and experiencing, religiosity is marginal to most of the institutions in which our culture is now embodied: government, corporations, leisure activities, science, aesthetics, the military, and education."[42] In 1995, Gallup reported, 57 percent thought religion was losing its influence on American life, up from 40 percent in 1985 and 48 percent in 1990.[43]

And then there are the data about crime, pornography, the breakdown of the family, illegitimacy rates, and so on. How could such a dangerous and corrupt country conceivably be called Christian?

But is this evidence the whole story? Is it true, as we are told, that the nation lacks a common faith and that it is held together merely by politics, sports, or just by "diversity" itself? (Vice President Al Gore once mistranslated *e pluribus unum* to read "out of one, many.") There is a large body of evidence, gathered mainly by pollsters, that strongly suggests otherwise.

In *The People's Religion: American Faith in the 90's*, for example, George Gallup Jr. and Jim Castelli contended that "Basic religious beliefs, and even religious practice, today, differ relatively little from the levels recorded fifty years ago." Indeed, "the baseline of religious belief is remarkably high—certainly, the highest of any developed nation in the world."[44]

In 1988, the highly respected Gallup Organization reported that nine Americans in ten said they never doubted the existence of God, eight in ten said they believed they will be called before God on Judgment Day to answer for their sins, eight in ten believed that God still works miracles, and seven in ten believed in life after death. Moreover, 90 percent prayed, 88 percent believed that God loved them, and 78 percent said they had given "a lot" or "a fair amount" of thought to their relationship with God during the past two years. Eighty-six percent said they wanted religious training for their children.

Natural law? Seventy-nine percent believed that "there are clear guidelines about what's good and evil that apply to everyone regardless of the situation." Traditional moral standards? Gallup found that 36 percent of Americans were conservative on the subject, 52 percent were moderate, and only 11 percent were liberal.

A whopping 84 percent said that Jesus was God or the Son of God, about three-quarters had at some time or other sensed Jesus' presence in their lives, and 66 percent reported having made a personal commitment to Jesus Christ. Even 72 percent of the unchurched said they believed that Jesus was God or the Son of God, up from 64 percent in 1978. Almost half of all Protestants described themselves as born-again Christians.

How can that much faith exist in a secular society? If 84 percent of its people believe that Jesus Christ was what he said he was, doesn't that by definition qualify the United States as a Christian country? Gallup concluded that "the degree of religious orthodoxy found among Americans is simply amazing. . . . such a nation cannot by any stretch of the imagination be described as secular in its core beliefs."[45]

Comparative poll data for western European nations strengthens this view. Belief in a personal God was at 31 percent in Great Britain, 26 percent in Italy and France, 25 percent in Finland, 24 percent in West Germany, and 19 percent in Denmark and Sweden. Only 27 percent of western Europeans said that religion was "very important" to them, while the figure in the United States was 56 percent.[46] (When Gallup asked the question in a different way in 1994, 66 percent of Americans said that religion was "extremely" or "very" important in their lives.)[47]

A mere 8 percent of Americans were without a religious preference, and even they, in the words of Gallup, "express a surprising degree of interest in religion and religious belief."[48] (The 8 percent figure was reconfirmed in a 1994 Gallup poll.[49]) In one survey, 69 percent of blacks and 61 percent of all Americans expressed a "great deal" or "quite a lot" of confidence in the church or organized religion. Baby boomers, while less involved in religion than other Americans, were more likely than others to report that they were more interested in religion than they were five years earlier.[50]

In 1990, a poll of 113,000 people around the nation commissioned by the Graduate School of the City University of New York determined that 86.5 percent of Americans were Christians. Jews, with 1.8 percent, were the largest non-Christian faith. (Gallup polls described Jews as highly secular. Only 30 percent called religion "very important" and only one in five attended synagogue in the week before being interviewed.[51]) Only 7.5 percent of those surveyed said they had no religion.[52]

Gallup polls taken in 1991 showed a modest rise in religiousness in America over the past three years. Christians were 82 percent of the adult population. (This figure held steady three years later, with 58 percent of the population being Protestant and 25 percent being Catholic.[53]) About seven out of ten adults reported membership in a church or synagogue (a level reached in the 1970s that remained the same in 1994.[54]) Eighty-six percent of teens said they believed that Jesus Christ is God or the Son of God, and 73 percent considered regular church attendance an important aspect of American citizenship. Fifty-nine percent of interviewees said they agreed completely that a personal faith in Jesus Christ was the *only* assurance of eternal life, and another 17 percent agreed "somewhat." Eighty-one percent believed the Bible to be the literal (32 percent) or inspired (49 percent) word of God.[55]

In 1992, the sociologists Finke and Stark, following a careful analysis of data collected by the Bureau of Census and others, concluded that on the eve of the American Revolution only about 17 percent of Americans belonged to churches. By the start of the Civil War the figure was 37 percent, by 1906 it was slightly more than half, and in 1926 this had increased to 56 percent. The numbers continued to rise until by 1980 church adherence was about 62 percent. In short, America appeared to be more religious in the year Ronald Reagan was elected president than in the days of the Founding Fathers.[56]

In a 1992 poll by the Barna Research Group, 79 percent of those aged 46 to 64 said that religion was "very important to me," a statement concurred in by 65 percent of those 27 to 45, and 54 percent of those 18 to 26. When asked whether they agreed that the Bible is the "totally accurate" word of God, 80 percent of those 46 to 64 years old said yes, and so did 73 percent of those 27 to 45, and 65 percent who were 18 to 26.[57]

The Catholic sociologist Andrew Greeley, after announcing similar data in 1993 from an international study, declared, "In some countries, most notably Ireland and the United States, religious devotion may be higher than it has ever been in human history."[58]

A 1994 USA Today/CNN/Gallup poll found that 70 percent belonged to a church or synagogue and that 66 percent attended services at least once a month. David Roozen of the Center for Social and Religious Research, Hartford Seminary, said that overall membership and attendance statistics "have remained stable over the last 10 or 15 years." The same poll showed that nine adults in ten believed in a heaven and that 79 percent believed in miracles.[59]

Gallup reported that same year that 51 percent of the public said grace before meals either always or frequently, and that only 14 percent never did.[60] Seventy-three percent of adults favored a constitutional amendment to allow voluntary prayer in the public schools.[61] Sixty-two percent believed that religion could solve all or most of the day's problems, a figure that had remained steady for twenty years.[62]

A Harris poll taken in July 1994 revealed that 95 percent of those surveyed believed in God and 90 percent believed in heaven. Of the four in five Americans who described themselves as Christians, 89 percent believed in life after death, 87 percent in miracles, and 85 percent in the virgin birth of Jesus Christ. Even 52 percent of the non-Christians surveyed expressed belief in the Resurrection![63]

A survey of 4,809 Americans released in September 1994 by the Times-Mirror Center for the People and the Press found that nine out of ten did not doubt the existence of God, almost eight out of ten said that prayer was an important part of their daily life, and almost nine of ten said they had "old fashioned values about family and marriage."[64]

A *New York Times*/CBS News poll in December 1994 found that 64 percent of adults believed that "organized prayer" should be permitted in the public schools. Six in ten public school students agreed.[65]

Gallup reported that American confidence in and support of organized religion reached a ten-year high mark in 1995. The index number had risen fifteen points since 1988.[66]

Beyond the polls, there is the large and growing demand for religious literature. About half of the fifty-five thousand new trade books published each year are religious books. Sales in 1993 were at about $2.7 billion, up from about $1 billion in 1980.[67] By 1994, the Christian book industry was growing at a rate of 12 to 15 percent a year.[68] The Roman Catholic catechism, William J. Bennett's *The Book of Virtues*, Pope John Paul II's *Crossing The Threshold of Hope*, and Dan Quayle's *Standing Firm* (which promoted traditional family values as well as the author), were best-sellers in 1994, as were volumes on near-death experiences, spiritual guidance, and angels. Bible sales amount to more than $400 million a year. (There are 450 different versions of the Bible available in English.)[69]

In 1992, Americans donated $56.71 billion to religious groups, or some 47 percent of total gifts.[70]

Richard John Neuhaus has declared, "Statistically at least, America is as much a Christian nation as it ever was, and perhaps more so." He contends that "one of the most elementary facts about America is that its people are overwhelmingly Christian in their own understanding, and that they and many who are not Christian assume that the moral baseline of the society is the Judeo-Christian ethic."[71]

A great many politicians certainly campaign as though they lived in a Christian country. In 1992, there were constant allusions to America as a religious nation with a special, divinely ordained "mission." All the major presidential candidates declared their personal commitment to the faith. George Bush told a convention of the National Religious Broadcasters, "I want to thank you for helping America, as Christ ordained, to be a light upon the world. . . . One cannot be America's president without a belief in God, without a belief in prayer." Bill Clinton, interviewed on an interdenominational religious cable network, professed, "If I didn't believe in God, if I weren't in my view . . . a Christian, if I didn't believe ultimately in the perfection of life after death, my life would have been that much more different." Ross Perot was a Presbyterian who backed traditional family values. Pat Buchanan, a Roman Catholic, advocated an America based on traditional Christian moral standards. Dan Quayle was the darling of the Religious Right. And so on.[72]

And yet Billy Graham could declare that America was no longer a Christian or Protestant nation. It is, he said, "a secular country in which thousands of Christians live and have substantial influence."[73] The Roman Catholic theologian The Rev. Avery Dulles was of the same mind, arguing that the country's moral breakdown was threatening democracy.[74] In 1994, the Jewish medical educator David C. Stolinsky lamented the loss of the Christian values that dominated America in the 1950s. "The reason we fear to go out after dark is not that we may be set upon by bands of evangelicals and forced to read the New Testament, but that we may be set upon by gangs of feral young people who have been taught that nothing is superior to their own needs or feelings."[75]

Is modern America secular or Christian? We seem to be the most religious nation in the advanced industrialized West but at the same time appear to be blatantly, even aggressively secular. Scholars, clergy, judges, journalists, and others have pondered the paradox for years.

In the first place, the polling data declare emphatically and unanimously that the United States continues to be a Christian nation—at least of a sort. The level of faith in the Christian gospel expressed by Americans is indeed, in Gallup's words, "simply amazing."

A truly secular society would have numbers approximating those found in, say, Great Britain, France, or Scandinavia, where interest in God is minimal and church attendance is extremely low (about 2.2 percent in the Church of England on an average Sunday).[76] The historian Alan D. Gilbert has defined a thoroughly secular culture as "one in which norms, values, and modes of interpreting reality, together with the symbols and rituals which express and reinforce them, have been emancipated entirely from assumptions of human dependence on supernatural agencies or influences."[77] That is not a description of American culture—at any time.

Second, Richard John Neuhaus is clearly correct in saying that most Americans ground their sense of right and wrong on what has been called since the 1930s the Judeo-Christian tradition. The polls show that the vast majority believe, at least in general, in a code of conduct that has deep roots in the past, principles that the left often dismisses as "conventional" and "bourgeois."

When nine out of ten Americans tell pollsters they believe in "old fashioned values about family and marriage," there is widespread agreement about what that means. Most people do not condone burglary, rape, or Nazism. Charles Manson, Charles Keating, and Aldrich Ames are not heroes. Not many condemn honesty, courage, or fidelity. Indeed, people yearn for presidents, bosses, and spouses who have such qualities.

Still, the public tells pollsters (64 percent in 1991) that there are few moral absolutes. More people (43 percent) say they rely upon their personal experience instead of outside authorities when weighing right from wrong. Only three persons in ten view Scripture as the ultimate authority in matters of truth. That this seems to contradict other polling data about faith and morals has not escaped the attention of the pollsters themselves, who talk about public ambiguity in determining good from evil.[78]

This ambiguity is in part a reflection of the individualism inherent in Protestantism and the Enlightenment. Americans, among many others, have long claimed the right to define truth as they see it. The uncertainty also reveals the genuine difficulty facing all of us in knowing exactly how to respond to complex issues in the modern world. The great principles by which we live do not always provide us with clear-cut commandments. The historian Jacques Barzun once exclaimed, "The great difficulty of the moral life is that our knowledge of right conduct, as embodied in the Decalogue, the Sermon on the Mount, or the Analects of Confucius, is abstract—like the articles of a constitution."[79] George Weigel has written, "the suggestion that Christian orthodoxy yields a single answer to virtually every contested issue of public policy is an offense, not simply against political common sense, but against Christian orthodoxy."[80]

Abortion is the classic case. A CBS News poll taken in January 1995 showed that while 46 percent of the respondents said that abortion was the same thing as murder, half of those said it still was sometimes necessary.[81] Two presidential families, the Reagans and the Bushes, were divided over the issue. Quarrels over economic redistribution, immigration, welfare, the legalization of drugs, gun control, capital punishment, human embryo research, and other issues are commonplace and inevitable.

And yet for all our disagreements, we are far from being moral idiots—without a past, bereft of authority, and compelled to reinvent basic truths as we go. Pre-Christian peoples, of course, had a strong sense of right and wrong. As the Lutheran theologian Carl E. Braaten has observed, "The idea of a law rooted in the nature of humanity and the world and discoverable by reason has been traced back to the 'dawn of conscience.'"[82] Aristotle and the Stoics, for example, believed in natural morality. Cicero declared,

"For there is a true law: right reason. It is in conformity with nature, is diffused among all men, and is immutable and eternal; its orders summon to duty; its prohibitions turn away from offense. . . . To replace it with a contrary law is a sacrilege; failure to apply even one of its provisions is forbidden; no one can abrogate it entirely."[83]

No civilization has been completely at bay about right and wrong. There have been differences about morality, to be sure, but they have not been total. For all of the rich diversity of detail, there is, and has always been, a vital framework written on human hearts and minds by the Creator. C. S. Lewis has written, "Think of a country where people were admired for running away from battle, or where a man felt proud of double-crossing all the people who had been kindest to him. You might just as well try to imagine a country where two and two made five. . . . Men have differed as to whether you should have one wife or four. But they have always agreed that you must not simply have any woman you liked."[84]

The philosopher Allan Bloom has observed,

> History and the study of cultures do not teach or prove that values or cultures are relative. All to the contrary, that is a philosophical premise that we now bring to our study of them. This premise is unproven and dogmatically asserted for what are largely political reasons . . . the fact that there have been different opinions about good and bad in different times and places in no way proves that none is true or superior to others. To say that it does so prove is as absurd as to say that the diversity of points of view expressed in a college bull session proves there is no truth.[85]

The Princeton political scientist Robert P. George declares: "Moral disagreements among reasonable people warrant the conclusion that not all moral truths are obvious, not all moral questions are easy. They do not warrant the conclusion that moral truth is inaccessible to reason."[86]

The English sociologist David Martin has cited the International Values Survey to conclude that "we are mostly agreed about good and bad." He observed, "People are, it seems, adamantly opposed to lying, stealing, cheating, coveting, killing, and dishonouring their parents." Imagine responses to the following questions, says Martin: "Grinding the faces of the poor, the widowed, and the fatherless is reprehensible/admirable? Drinking and driving is irresponsible/responsible? Causing a little child to stumble is perverse/life-enhancing? Taking your share of the chores is wicked/virtuous? Poking a sharp shard in another person's eye is revolting/entertaining?"[87]

Martin notes that consistent moral relativism, in practice, is hard to find. In contemporary liberal circles, where tolerance and moral relativism are said to reign supreme, "you are continually confronted by a noble rage about the delinquent condition of the world. Here is little else but moral passion for purity: pure jokes, pure speech, pure earth, sky, and sea, pure food and pure bodies, even undiluted equality."[88]

Christian thinkers have long believed that the Law of Moses reinforced and clarified natural law, and that the Saviour fulfilled it. As the *Catechism of the Catholic Church* puts it, "The moral law finds its fullness and its unity in Christ. Jesus Christ is in person the way of perfection. He is the end of the law, for only he teaches and bestows the justice of God."[89]

The existence of natural law is scriptural (although there is but a single reference to it in the New Testament and none in the Old Testament, which even lacks a term for "nature"), and it has been official Roman Catholic teaching for many centuries.[90] The Protestant reformers, with the possible exception of Zwingli, also endorsed natural law and its consummation in the gospel. Calvin wrote in his *Institutes*, "It is a fact that the law of God which we call the moral law is nothing else than a testimony of natural law and of that conscience which God has engraved upon the minds of men."[91]

All major American reform movements have appealed to eternal truth to buttress their crusades. The civil rights movement is an obvious example. Martin Luther King Jr., in his famous letter from Birmingham jail, wrote of "the most sacred values in our Judaeo-Christian heritage" and contended "that there are two types of laws: just and unjust. . . . I would agree with St. Augustine that 'an unjust law is no law at all.'"[92] The anti-abortion movement claims unequivocally that it is rooted in the Judeo-Christian tradition, arguing, as reformers do, that what may be legal can still be immoral.

When 79 percent of the American people declare faith in clear guidelines about what is right and wrong, they are expressing a commitment to what Neuhaus calls a "moral baseline" long accepted in our culture and elsewhere. A majority of Americans understand, at least in general, what is expected of them by a power beyond their own wills. They know, for example, that personal integrity, being generous to the poor, and honoring marriage vows are virtues that do not go out of style. (The University of Chicago's National Opinion Research Center found in 1992 that 91 percent of the American people think extramarital affairs are bad and that the overwhelming percentage of married people remain faithful.)[93] In 1994, the social scientist Robert Wuthnow published a study in which he asked two thousand working Americans what was "absolutely essential" or "very important" to their very basic sense of worth as a person. "Your family" ranked first, followed immediately by "Your moral standards." Ninety-seven percent of weekly churchgoers and 93 percent of the total labor force endorsed this choice.[94]

This strong consensus and the best of the conduct that flows from it are often overlooked by the major media, at times deliberately, but also by oversight. "The News" is dominated by the sordid and the sensational. Beneath this surface lie millions of unheralded, everyday stories involving decency, courage, kindness, generosity, selflessness, and the other virtues that make life bearable, enjoyable, and meaningful.[95] The great majority of Americans, the polls tell us, link these actions with their Christian faith.

Simply labeling America Christian, however, is inadequate. We must ask what sort of Christianity lives in the hearts and minds of most Americans in the late 1990s. It is clearly something unlike the faith practiced by third-century hermits, St. Francis of Assisi, or Martin Luther. Christianity has always absorbed elements of the culture of its adherents, and it is important to consider how extensively the classic faith has been altered by a modern, literate, prosperous, technologically driven society undeniably absorbed with obtaining prosperity, security, and pleasure. In short, what is the content of our Christianity?

First, our faith is not inextricably tied to our churches. Polls show that a majority of Americans have confidence in organized religion. But in 1988, according to Gallup, 44 percent of Americans were unchurched (people who said they were not members of any church or had not attended services in the previous six months other than for special religious holidays, weddings, funerals, or the like.) That figure amounted to about 78 million adults. Gallup found that overwhelming majorities, churched and unchurched, agreed that people "should arrive at their religious beliefs independent of any church or synagogue" and that one can be a good Christian or Jew without attending a church or synagogue.[96] Gallup discovered in polls taken in 1992 and 1995 that confidence in the clergy was at 54 percent of the populace, down from 67 percent in 1985.[97]

When asked why they attended church less often, very few of those interviewed gave reasons that reflected a deep animosity toward organized religion. Only 8 percent said they disagreed with policies and teachings. A mere 5 percent said they were atheists or agnostics. For many, going to church just did not seem that important (a point to which we shall return). Leading the list were 34 percent who said they were too busy.[98]

Religious individualism, to repeat, is at the core of American

Christianity. This is a characteristic in harmony with our historic sense of personal independence as well as the considerable socio-economic mobility we have long enjoyed. Roof and McKinney concluded, "Typically Americans view religious congregations as gatherings of individuals who have chosen to be together, in institutions of their own making and over which they hold control—fostering what sometimes, in the eyes of observers from other countries, appears as 'churchless Christianity.'" For Americans, "religious authority lies in the believer—not in the church, not in the Bible, despite occasional claims of infallibility and inerrancy on the part of some."[99]

This is true of modern American Roman Catholics as well. The massive changes made since Vatican II, consistently celebrated by liberal Catholics, have had unintended results. Gallup reported that 77 percent said they relied on their consciences rather than papal teaching in making difficult moral decisions. Polls show Catholics lending strong support for legal abortion, artificial birth control (they are more likely than Protestants to be childless), "safe sex" education in schools, and the ordination of women, all positions officially opposed by their church.[100]

According to Gallup, Catholic church attendance (people saying they had gone to church in the past seven days) fell from 74 percent in 1958 to an all-time low of 48 percent in 1988.[101] A study published in 1994 by the University of Notre Dame sociologists Mark Chaves and James C. Cavendish found that the national average was a mere 26.7 percent.[102]

Some, including Humphrey Taylor, president of the Louis Harris poll, now think that all church attendance figures reported by pollsters have been exaggerated. In 1993, Gallup found that 41 percent of Americans went to church within the last week. That figure had remained consistent for over a decade. But to some there just did not seem to be that many people in church on Sunday.[103]

In 1993, a much publicized and controversial study conducted by the sociologists Mark Chaves and Kirk Hadaway and the religion professor Penny Long Marler concluded that only 19.6 percent of Protestants and 28 percent of Catholics were in church on any given week. Only approximately 16 percent of self-defined Episcopalians attended worship during a typical week. The researchers challenged the many telephone surveys conducted by Gallup and other pollsters, and suggested that Americans felt a need to appear more religious, and more respectable, than they really were. (Other studies show, for example, that more people say they voted than actually voted.)[104]

The widely noted Catholic sociologist Andrew Greeley called the study "a sloppy piece of work," and others were also critical.[105] The research was conducted among Protestants in a single rural Ohio county and among Catholics in only 18 dioceses. But in any case the study again pointed to the chasm between the professed faith of the American people and their ambivalence about churches. Ironically, it also bolstered the belief that America remained a Christian society, for if the nation were truly secular, why would millions feel compelled to lie in this way to pollsters about church attendance?

Second, Christianity in modern America tends to be superficial. For one thing, its adherents are poorly educated in the faith. Gallup refers to "a nation of biblical illiterates" and presents solid evidence: only four in ten Americans know that Jesus delivered the Sermon on the Mount; fewer than half of all adults can name the four Gospels of the New Testament; only three in ten teenagers know why Easter is celebrated. "More than half of all Americans read the Bible less than once a month," Gallup reports, "including 24 percent who say they never read it and 6 percent who can't recall the last time they read the Bible."[106]

Of course, given the fervently secular nature of the media and education at all levels, this illiteracy should not be surprising. It will no doubt increase. The young people who leave the mainline churches in droves are surely no exceptions. If Sunday schools are teaching about condoms and poverty in Rwanda, there is little time for things like Scripture and church history. And if the clergy present the faith merely as a branch of anthropology or social work, there is little need for anyone to be informed.

A study by the Search Institute of Minneapolis in 1990 revealed that large majorities of mainliners did not read the Bible when alone. The Presbyterians headed the list (77 percent), followed by the Lutherans (75 percent), the United Church of Christ (68 percent), the United Methodists (65 percent), and the Disciples of Christ (62 percent).[107]

According to Gallup, only slightly more than half of the Lutherans, Methodists, and Presbyterians believe in the devil (a being prominent in both the Old and New Testaments), while roughly the same numbers accept ESP. Fifty-six percent of the Lutherans and 49 percent of the Methodists believe in UFOs. A third of the Methodists and 31 percent of the Presbyterians believe in astrology. While 73 percent of the American people believe in hell, 77 percent believe their own prospects for going to heaven are excellent or good.[108]

An in-depth random survey of 4,001 Americans, conducted by a team of political scientists and published in 1993, concluded that 30 percent of Americans are totally secular in outlook, 29 percent are barely or nominally religious, 22 percent are modestly religious, and only 19 percent—about 36 million people—regularly practice their religion. In measuring mainline Protestants (16.7 percent of those studied), for example, the researchers considered church attendance, membership, personal prayer, belief in life after death, and how "important" respondents said religion was in their lives. Those who registered some activity in all five categories were considered "committed" and qualified as part of the 19 percent. "We're not talking about Mother Teresas," said the political scientist John C. Green. "We're looking at people who meet a religious minimum according to their own traditions."[109] In short, if this study is accurate, the vibrant faith pollsters hear about during their telephone interviews is exaggerated and not vitally linked with much of the public's attitudes and actions.

The superficiality of the Christianity expressed by a large majority of Americans can also be seen, of course, in the destructive behavior that increasingly mars our daily lives. Faith without works is dead, orthodox Christianity proclaims. Pious rhetoric is not necessarily the reflection of a deep-seated, life-changing commitment.

Consider the violence, the insensitivity, and the staggering vulgarity we encounter—and enjoy—in the media. In 1990, 2.9 million couples lived together without marriage—up 80 percent from 1980 and 454 percent from 1970.[110] There are 1.5 million abortions a year, and abortion is a $450 million a year business.[111] Venereal diseases are rampant. African Americans are killing each other, going to prison, and succumbing to an assortment of addictions in record numbers.[112] ("American blacks are, by some measures," Gallup reports, "the most religious people in the world."[113]) Drug abuse among teenagers was reported in 1995 to be still on the rise. Between 1992 and 1995, the proportion of eighth graders using illicit drugs almost doubled; among tenth graders it jumped by nearly two-thirds; among seniors it escalated by nearly half. Health and Human Services Secretary Donna E. Shalala warned, "We have a generation at risk."[114]

Corporations blackmail entire states for tax dollars, ruthlessly "downsize" employees, and refuse to pay a living wage. Advertising agencies lie and corrupt. Bureaucrats stifle initiative and waste billions. Radicals work feverishly to undermine the West's moral and rational foundations. (Science, we are now told, is a fabrication of white, heterosexual males bent on suppressing minorities.[115]) Politicians seem to do their best to earn our distrust and scorn. "We have become," said William Bennett, "the kind of society that civilized countries used to send missionaries to."[116]

Then, too, there are our priorities. It is one thing to tell a pollster, perhaps in complete sincerity, that family and personal moral values are our chief concerns. But most of us, it seems clear, expend the great bulk of our time and energies fulfilling the American dream. We are consumed by our jobs, as psychiatrists, divorce lawyers, and millions of latchkey children know all too well, and are locked into an endless pursuit of the power, cash, status, and pleasure that promise "personal fulfillment" and happiness. Probably few clergy address this issue (there is the budget to meet and the new parish hall to be built), and, as Robert Wuthnow puts it, "we therefore go about our lives pretty much the same as those who have no faith at all."[117]

At the same time we are slaving away to obtain the "finer" things in life, we publicly profess a strong distaste for materialism. We are able, following a long tradition in Western civilization, to divide the spiritual from the material realms of existence. The dichotomy makes us somewhat uneasy, but we persist nonetheless. Wuthnow observes,

> The American public voices concern about the reign of materialism in our society while wandering the corridors of the mall. Somehow we have been able to convince ourselves that materialism is bad for our collective health, but we proceed in our individual lives as if nothing mattered more than a fat wallet, especially one made of expensive leather.[118]

People who do not know who gave the Sermon on the Mount may not have read about the rich man and the eye of a needle. More than likely they do know about the warning and have chosen either to ignore it or explain it away—an endeavor long perfected by the wealthy and their minions. (The Judeo-Christian economic ideal, as Dale Vree has put it, "seems to be neither affluence nor poverty; it is more like sufficiency.")[119] In any case, earthly comfort and security, Scripture tells us, are perilous goals for Christians.

Equally dangerous is the passion for power. Overcoming self is one of classical Christianity's highest virtues. C. S. Lewis has observed, "A rejection, or in Scripture's strong language, a crucifixion of the natural self is the passport to everlasting life. Nothing that has not died will be resurrected."[120]

Christianity in modern America is, in large part, innocuous. It tends to be easy, upbeat, convenient, and compatible. It does not require self-sacrifice, discipline, humility, an otherworldly outlook, a zeal for souls, a fear as well as love of God. There is little guilt and no punishment, and the payoff in heaven is virtually certain.

The faith has been overwhelmed by the culture, producing what may be called cultural Christianity. This is not a question of mere influence; acculturation takes place at all times and in all places. Christianity becomes cultural Christianity when the faith is dominated by a culture to the point that it loses much or most of its authenticity.

What we now have might best be labeled Consumer Christianity. The psychologist Paul C. Vitz has observed, "The 'divine right' of the consumer to choose as he or she pleases has become so common an idea that it operates in millions of Americans like an unconscious tropism."[121] Millions of Americans today feel free to buy as much of the full Christian faith as seems desirable. The cost is low and customer satisfaction seems guaranteed.

America is not—not yet, anyway—a thoroughly secular society. But its Christianity, in large part, has been watered down and is at ease with basic secular premises about personal conduct and the meaning of life. Such a religion has an uncertain future for it has absorbed ideas and attitudes that may well lead to its demise. Authentic Christianity and the world are by definition at odds. That was decreed repeatedly and unequivocally by the Founder. The "disciple whom Jesus loved" made the truth crystal clear when he wrote: "If anyone loves the world, the love of the Father is not in him. . . . We know that we are children of God, and that the whole world is under the control of the evil one."[122]

There are still millions of Christians in this country, of course, in many denominations, who cling to the scriptural and traditional faith and the morality that comes with it. They may ingest more than a bit of the worst parts of their culture; it is virtually impossible not to. But their primary allegiance is to the supernatural and living faith enjoyed by orthodox Christians for almost two thousand years.

In our time, a great many such people are worried and angry about the secularism, violence, cynicism, and despair they see welling up about them. One Wisconsin evangelical exclaimed in 1994, "The once-unthinkable is now almost commonplace, and we feel as though we are riding on a wagon out of control, careening down a hill. It is no progress to continue on the wrong path which our culture has already traveled so far."[123]

The evidence strongly suggests that the simile is on target. How we got into that wagon and began our wild ride downhill requires much attention. We are in need of more perspective. Let us begin with a look at the secular religions that largely molded the modern world, faiths that helped enfeeble contemporary mainline Christianity.

3

SECULAR RELIGIONS

To account for the plight of the mainline denominations, one must first understand the impact that three great secular religions have had on them. These religions, developed in the West over the past three centuries, are human-centered and utopian. Their influence on Christian churches would seem puzzling without historical perspective. The story can be told only in outline form here, but its importance should not be underestimated. The roots of the decline of the mainline are deep.

HISTORIANS HAVE FREQUENTLY GRAPPLED with the complex story of the rise of the modern Western world view out of the ashes of the medieval Age of Faith. They have described the rebelliousness, curiosity, and genius of the Renaissance humanists; Protestant contributions to individualism, nationalism, capitalism, and democracy; and the development of scientific rationalism and empiricism in the seventeenth century. The culmination of much of this cascade of change was the Enlightenment of the eighteenth century, which interpreted human existence in a way that would transform the Western world.

The basic idea of the Enlightenment, according to the historian Crane Brinton, was "the belief that all human beings can attain here on this earth a state of perfection hitherto in the West thought to be possible only for Christians in a state of grace, and for them only after death."[1] Because human reason could understand the workings of nature (the writings of Galileo, Descartes, and Newton inspired the Enlightenment prophets, and the research of Linnaeus, Buffon, Hutton, Lavoisier, van Leeuwenhoek, Priestly, Boerhaave, and others surrounded them), the objective mind was capable of great things. And if society conformed to the plans designed by educated, rational people, harmony and happiness were inevitable. Centuries of superstition, ignorance, and faith had kept humans in chains, but no longer. (The Protestant reformer Martin Luther called reason "the devil's whore.")

A second generation of Enlightenment thinkers tended to follow Rousseau and stressed intuition and feeling, rather than reason, as the pathway to truth. But the rationalists and romantics had much in common, and they covered over their discord.

The prophets of the Enlightenment distrusted authority and tradition. They condemned historic Christianity and rejected the idea of an all-knowing, intimately concerned God who is active in history. (At best, the Creator did his work and left. To most deists, God was inscrutable and indifferent.) They believed that each person was basically good, or at least neutral, by nature and formed by the environment. Truth, they said, could be gleaned through the natural law, and in it they found the "rights of man." They championed equality, liberty, tolerance, justice, and mass education. Progress, through reason and science, was certain. "The perfectibility of man," wrote Condorcet, "is indefinite."[2]

Although lip service was paid to the worship of God, the Enlightenment was itself a religion. As the historian Carl Becker said of the *philosophes* (best translated as "intellectuals"), "They denounced Christian philosophy, but rather too much after the manner of those who are but half emancipated from the 'superstitions' they scorn."

> They ridiculed the idea that the universe had been created in six days, but still believed it to be a beautifully articulated machine designed by the Supreme Being according to a rational plan as an abiding place for mankind. . . . They renounced the authority of church and Bible, but exhibited a naive faith in the authority of nature and reason. . . . They denied that miracles ever happened, but believed in the perfectibility of the human race.[3]

The Enlightenment was a secular religion and, following in the footsteps of many Renaissance thinkers, its focus was on the exaltation of the human species. In this religion, pride, rather than being the first of the seven deadly sins, was the cornerstone. A certain measure of self-respect is, of course, a healthy thing, but the emphasis here was on the glorification of the self—one's intellect, self-sufficiency, and all-importance.

For the Christian, the self is the problem; pride must be combated with repentance, humility, and trust in God. Centuries earlier, Thomas a Kempis had written in *The Imitation of Christ*, "Be assured of this, that you must live a dying life. And the more completely a man dies to self, the more he begins to live to God."[4] The modern Christian mystic Evelyn Underhill once quoted Meister Eckhart, "Where I left myself I found God; where I found myself, I lost God," and added, "Our eyes are not in focus for His Reality, until they are out of focus for our own petty concerns."[5] That was exactly the faith the Enlightenment prophets came to destroy.

Thomas Paine declared boldly, "I do not believe in the creed professed by the Jewish Church, by the Roman Church, by the Greek Church, by the Turkish Church, by the Protestant Church, nor by any Church I know of. My mind is my own church."[6] C. S. Lewis has written, "Which of the religions of the world gives to its followers the greatest happiness? While it lasts, the religion of worshipping oneself is the best."[7]

The French Revolution, grounded on Enlightenment thought, was, especially in its later stages, a religious crusade, complete with dogmas, liturgies, festivals, and saints. The historian R. R. Palmer said that the revolution itself was a religion, and wrote of the Jacobins, "It was their burning faith in things human, their absolute certainty of being right, their passionate and absorbing devotion to the indivisible Republic that was their church, their willingness to die for a cause without whose triumph life would be empty."[8] A hymn chanted in the dechristianized Cathedral of Notre Dame went:

> Come, conqueror of kings, Europe's example;
> Come, over false Gods complete thy success!
>
> Thou, Saint Liberty, inhabit this temple,
> Be of our nation the Goddess![9]

The pillaging of Catholic churches and the busy work of the guillotine illustrated the underside of this faith, which for all its laudable contributions to human liberty did not turn out to be as merciful and humane as advertised. Jean-Jacques Rousseau, one of the most influential of Enlightenment prophets, had helped set the stage for the violence by espousing, in *The Social Contract*, an assortment of totalitarian views draped with gushy generalities about the wisdom and goodness of "the people." At one point, he advocated the banishment or execution of those defying a patriotic civil religion imposed by the state, a faith in which intolerance was the only sin.[10]

Maximilien Robespierre, said Lord Acton, maintained order and authority "by regulated terror."[11] The English conservative Edmund Burke referred to the revolutionary leaders as "savages" and "madmen."[12] During the course of the single year of the Reign of Terror, at least twenty thousand French were executed and hundreds of thousands were imprisoned. The butchery in the Vendée by Jacobins was such that the historian Leo Gershoy exclaimed: "the record of man's inhumanity to man is unparalleled."[13]

The slaughter was committed to establish a future kingdom of virtue on earth. It was benevolent murder; those who would not listen to Reason had to be eliminated for the common good. As the terrorist St. Just put it, "What constitutes the Republic is the complete destruction of everything that is opposed to it."[14] Much more bloodshed and violence would accompany the lofty ideals of the Enlightenment as they rolled through the eighteenth and nineteenth centuries.

The political scientist Bruce Frohnen has written, "Speculative reason is more dangerous than passion because it respects no limits save to its own internal logic. Immoderate by nature, this reason may blind men to the good in their society and so destroy it and themselves. . . . The fruit of Jacobin rationalism was mass murder."[15]

David F. Wells has observed, "The capacity for ultimate knowledge that we are given by creation is a fearful thing when it is unhitched from the knowledge of sin. This uncoupling gives rise to individuals who are unsuspicious about themselves, who infuse their own ideas with divine authority, who are oblivious to the inherent darkness of human nature."[16]

(This is a side of the Enlightenment that modern liberals would rather not discuss. As James Hitchcock has observed, "When they want to invoke the specter of murderous intolerance they talk about either the Catholic Inquisition or the 'witch-burnings' carried out by both Catholics and Protestants. Rarely is there reference to the 'Committees of Public Safety,' which implemented the Reign of Terror in the name of humanity."[17])

Despite a considerable amount of moral theorizing, the faith of the Enlightenment lacked the high sense of personal morality taught by Christians. For individuals, the goals included happiness, pleasure, self-love, fellowship—all in moderation and in accord with what was loosely defined as nature and reason.[18]

F. L. Lucas has written of "the civilized decency of the Enlightenment."[19] But there was often more rhetoric about the nobility of man than noble conduct toward others.[20]

It is not, of course, that the Enlightenment faithful had a corner on hypocrisy. Christians, among others, have always had an ample supply. The point is, to repeat, that this secular religion tended to focus on the self and its desires. As a leading woman of the Enlightenment put it bluntly, "The chief thing is to look after number one, is it not?"[21] This often leads to the mistreatment of others, for the self is a demanding tyrant.

The truth of a religion, at least to Christians, may be judged in large part by the love, compassion, and respect it demands of the faithful toward others. And not just in general; individual men and women matter the most. It is easy to love humanity, because humanity is an abstraction. Loving specific people, especially the unfortunate and the disagreeable, can often be another matter entirely. Malcolm Muggeridge has written of "the great moral fallacy of our time—that collective virtue may be pursued without reference to personal behaviour."[22]

Note the life of Rousseau, an idol of the Enlightenment frequently given to exhortations on morality. One scholar has described him as a "masochist, exhibitionist, neurasthenic, hypochondriac, onanist, latent homosexual afflicted by the typical urge for repeated displacements, incapable of normal or parental affection, incipient paranoiac, narcissistic introvert rendered unsocial by his illness, filled with guilt feelings, pathologically timid, a kleptomaniac, infantilist, irritable and miserly." His character was such that he made a long-time sex slave of one poor woman and calmly sent five of their illegitimate children to virtually certain death in an institution. (His influential novel, *Emile*, contained instructions about the moral education of young people.) Such men in history have often had the sheer gall to tell others how to live.[23]

The life of Voltaire, another major prophet, contains similar stories. Observe him in his old age, a time in life when what we truly are often becomes luminous: self-obsessed, filled with rage, devoting much of his energy to cursing Christianity and the Bible, coming to be known even to embarrassed friends as the "genius of hate." His colleague Denis Diderot thought him the Antichrist. The historian Paul Hazard has written, "That the eighteenth century witnessed the birth of a race of men, thereafter perpetuated, whose sole spiritual nourishment was anti-clericalism, who made anti-clericalism the sole item on their programme, and who deemed that that would suffice to remodel governments, to perfect societies, and lead the way to happiness—for this, many men are responsible . . . but none of them to same degree as Voltaire."[24]

And then there was Karl Marx, a child of the Enlightenment. He was violent, tyrannical, intolerant, self-absorbed, power-hungry, untruthful (utterly reckless with facts and quotations), anti-Semitic (although born a Jew), and hypocritical (he detested working-class socialists and probably never set foot in any sort of industrial workplace). Much of his life he was drunken and dirty, and he was unwilling to provide for his family. His wife once had to beg money from a neighbor to buy a coffin for one of their children. At the lowest point in his family's financial misery, Marx sired an illegitimate son, thereafter ignoring him. Michael Bakunin said of him, "Marx does not believe in God but he believes much in himself and makes everyone serve himself. His heart is not full of love but of bitterness and he has very little sympathy for the human race."[25]

And yet Marx was the founder of another great secular religion, one of the most attractive, powerful, and destructive the world has ever seen. The historian Isaiah Berlin has said that Marx was "among the great authoritarian founders of new faiths, ruthless subverters and innovators who interpret the world in terms of a single, clear, passionately held principle, denouncing and destroying all that conflicts with it."[26] The church historian Ralph Lord Roy notes, "Certainly, Communism has a faith, a sacred literature, a concept of a 'Kingdom of God,' of a devil and saints, of a chosen people."[27] The economist Robert L. Heilbroner has written, "If we are to judge by a count of worshiping noses, Marx must be considered a religious leader to rank with Christ or Mohammed, and Engels thus becomes a sort of Saint Paul or a John."[28]

Marx knew his Enlightenment authors well, and it is no coincidence that Communism and the earlier faith, despite profound differences, had more than a little in common. They both lauded reason, human rights, peace, and brotherhood, and looked forward to a millennial state of perfect happiness and harmony on earth. They claimed to be the bearers of total truth and were the sworn enemies of the Christian faith. More specifically, the philosopher Allan Bloom reminds us that "The *bourgeois* is Rousseau's great invention," and his "critique of modern economics and his questions about the legitimacy of private property are at the root of socialism, particularly Marxism."[29]

Communism, of course, was also eager to persecute unbelievers. In his lifetime, Marx was popularly known as "The Red Terrorist Doctor."[30] The horrors inflicted upon millions of Christians and others by Communists in eastern Europe, China, and elsewhere during the following century are well documented.

It is difficult for some to understand the appeal of these two great secular religions. Rousseau's *Social Contract* and Marx's *Das Kapital*, for example, are murky and tedious polemics filled with much that is highly questionable and blatantly wrong. It should be obvious that human nature is far from benign, that living "reasonably" and being "educated" are not (as Jefferson believed) objective and automatic prescriptions for happiness, that progress is neither inevitable nor uniform. And how could any sensible adult believe that people would willingly live in a classless society? Borrow a neighbor's car or lawn mower more than twice to sample humanity's natural inclination toward sharing. Simply observe toddlers with their toys!

But millions have been swayed by the worldly faiths, including, even especially, those glowing with the consciousness of superior academic credentials. The English professor and historian Herbert J. Muller spoke for a great many of his peers when he wrote of the Enlightenment faith, "It let into Europe a clear, steady daylight, and focused this light on many time-honored prejudices and barbarities, in particular the unreason of political and religious tyranny."[31] Marxism in the West made deep inroads among the intelligentsia. In recent decades, it is to be found in this country almost exclusively on campus.

There were many reasons and combinations of reasons for the popularity of the secular religions. Certainly, we must not discount the appeal of the genuine idealism inherent in them. Not many in this country today would tolerate the tyranny, injustice, misery, ignorance, and cruelty that haunted reformers. Liberty, equality, fraternity—watchwords taken from *The Social Contract*—are concepts people will die for. The French revolutionaries of 1789 first introduced universal male suffrage on a national scale, planned a national system of public schools, and proclaimed the abolition of slavery.

In the Great Depression, many American intellectuals became Communists or fellow travelers because of their devotion to what were essentially Christian principles concerning injustice. In the revealing volume *The God That Failed*, Richard Crossman wrote, "You can call the response masochistic, or describe it as a sincere desire to serve mankind. But, whatever name you use, the idea of an active comradeship of struggle—involving personal sacrifice and abolishing differences of class and race—has had a compulsive power in every Western democracy."[32]

On the less lofty side of the question, we encounter the person whom Eric Hoffer called the True Believer, a familiar figure in history on the left and right. He is a totalitarian, filling an emotional as well as an intellectual need by attaching himself totally to an ideology. The historian Leo Gershoy wrote of Robespierre, "He was sincere, fanatically sincere, with the type of narrow dogmatic sincerity which marks single-minded reformers and religious crusaders."[33] The historian J. M. Thompson called Robespierre "a moral fanatic," a "Cromwell, but without his soldiery directness; a Calvin, but without his cramping theology."[34] Jean Bethke Elshtain had this sort of zealot in mind when she referred to those who "go on automatic pilot as the corpses mount."[35]

Many intellectuals became Marxists because they hungered for just such an all-encompassing faith, seeking release from what Crossman has called "the privilege of freedom."[36] The political scientist Guenter Lewy has written about this appeal in the 1930s: "Politically and morally disoriented by their alienation from American society, a considerable number of American intellectuals became ensnared by a closed system in which the whole of history as well as their own person could find their place and meaning."[37]

The complete surrender of the will and mind required of Marxists has often been described. Ignazio Silone, calling socialist policy "a faith," noted, "For me to join the Party of Proletarian Revolution was not just a simple matter of signing up with a political organization; it meant a conversion, a complete dedication."[38] Arthur Koestler has written, "To one who himself for seven years found excuses for every stupidity and crime committed under the Marxist banner, the spectacle of these dialectical tight-rope acts of self-deception, performed by men of good will and intelligence, is more disheartening than the barbarities committed by the simple in spirit."[39]

Envy, hatred, and the lust for power also played a role in wooing people into the secular religions. Both the Enlightenment and Communism promised revenge on the wealthy and well born (many of whom scorn intellectuals as well as exploit the poor). Some joined the secular religions for the sheer love of violence. And there was the possibility of gaining authority in the eventual paradise. More than one professor has dreamed of having the power to "rule by reason"; many a failed bookseller has been eager to nudge the "iron laws" of history along while drawing a handsome state salary. The French philosopher August Comte (whose character was similar to Rousseau's) proposed a "religion of humanity" in which the priesthood, given enormous governmental authority, was to be composed of sociologists!

Lewy has observed, "Intellectuals, it appears, are especially vulnerable to the totalitarian temptation. They see themselves as the moral conscience of society and therefore find it easy to justify the use of the coercive power of the state in order to free ordinary folks from 'false consciousness.' Intellectuals are fond of social engineering and, to use Rousseau's classic phrase, they have little difficulty countenancing schemes that 'force people to be free.' "[40]

The secular religions were also fueled by what I call the Lemming Impulse: the willingness of people to conform out of the fear of being different. The line between conviction and fashion is often hard to draw, of course, but the historian must not discount the great power of the latter to woo those unwilling or unable to think for themselves. One observes this routinely, especially among adolescents and politicians.

And let us not overlook the appeal offered by the rejection of the Christian religion, with all its talk about sin and forgiveness, faith and selflessness, and, perhaps above all, its "bourgeois" morality. Freedom from the demand for personal holiness undoubtedly increased the attractiveness of these two great secular religions.

Essays on sexual liberty, for example, were popular in the salons of the Age of Reason. Paul Hazard wrote of the Enlightenment:

> Now, when all the old disturbing hypotheses were, as far as possible, put aside, things like predestination and original sin; when it was satisfactorily established that whatever was natural was good, that pleasure was natural, and that the greatest of all pleasures was sensual pleasure, not, indeed, all women, but all who were in the fashion, conformed to the new Art of Love.[41]

The great *philosophe* Denis Diderot—a brilliant moralist who was also an adulterer, petty swindler, pornographer, narcissist, shameless liar, plagiarist, and hater of God and Christianity—gave this practical advice, at age 62, to a friend: "In the midst of the public excitement, keep well; be gay; drink good wine; and when you get a fancy for love, look for women who won't make you sigh too long. They amuse as much as the others; they take less time; you possess them without worries and leave them without regrets."[42]

Lenin defined morality merely as that which "serves to destroy the old exploiting society and to unite all the toilers around the proletariat." He said in 1920, "We repudiate all morality taken apart from human society and classes. . . . We say that our morality is entirely subordinated to the interests of the class struggle of the proletariat."[43] Anything can be, and has been, justified by such a moral standard. The discovery of the secret Lenin archive in 1991 has documented the stunning magnitude of Lenin's brutality toward the Soviet people.[44]

Of course, immorality was neither a requirement nor an inevitable result of membership in a secular religion. Disciples could display the most noble features of personal character. But the temptations to be otherwise were, and are, extremely powerful in these faiths, and the historical record is filled with the pain, misery, and heartlessness of those who focused their lives on the glories of humanity and the earthly paradise to come. (Many of the sins recorded in the history of Christianity have had the same cause.)

Both the *philosophes* and the Marxists wholly admired science, and it is important to observe at this point that modern science is itself another great secular religion. It offers a world view, dogmas, sacred texts, high priests, temples, professional (if not personal) ethics, and so on. People give their lives to it and trust its methodology as the exclusive arbiter of truth. In universities and elsewhere today, "scientific" is a magical word, virtually a synonym for objective, thorough, quantifiable, modern, hard, real.

Science is indeed one of the glories of civilization. Despite its destructive side, which the great wars of our century have revealed clearly, it is the crowning achievement of modernity. It has broadened our minds, healed our bodies, and provided us with wealth and comforts that not even the utopian novelists of the last century could imagine. And yet it bears the essential characteristics of the secular religions and should be celebrated with caution, at least by Christians.

Science tends to stress the all-sufficiency of the human intellect, to be scornful of the past, and to dismiss or at least distrust the value of anything beyond its rigorous examination, including the supernatural. Its modern practitioners, never particularly known for their lowliness and compassion, often dream aloud, as did their forebears in the Enlightenment, of a world ruled by those who are allegedly superior, rational, and objective, beginning with themselves.

Moreover, there is a crucial limitation to this faith: it has little meaningful to say about the deepest moral and spiritual issues of our lives. The psychologist Paul Vitz reminds us, "At present there is no satisfactory evidence that science can verify any value."[45] Science cannot, for example, shed light upon or inspire fidelity, courage, prudence, temperance, and the other classical virtues. It cannot tell us how to become good. Milton Mayer has written that "the lifelong crisis of man is moral. . . . We know that goodness—and not law at all—is the bond of men in community and that even a band of thieves is held together by goodness and by goodness alone. Good men will make good laws, and if they make bad laws they will correct them; but bad men will subvert good law and good societies." Natural science, he continues, "fortifies certain moral virtues such as patience, persistence, initiative, and open-mindedness; but so do burglary and philosophy."[46]

Science, even assuming that psychiatry qualifies as a component, is a most fickle guide to the moral decisions we must all make. It offers little comfort to those experiencing the great sorrows of life and yields no source of thanksgiving beyond itself or blind fate. It cannot deal effectively with sin and forgiveness. It stands mute when confronted with the greatest question of all: What about eternity?

(In a classic confession of faith in science, the historian Ray Ginger admits that his god cannot—yet—answer certain questions. "It deals only with probabilities. . . . Science knows nothing of Absolute Truth. . . . For those who need the amniotic warmth of certainty, dogma is the proper womb." As for those who want to know even if life is worth living, Ginger declares, "Science teaches us also that anybody who asks this question is a desperately sick man.")[47]

In general, the same may be said about science's cousins, the social sciences. For all of their extremely important intellectual contributions, social scientists have grounded their work on materialist and positivist assumptions to support their claim to be scientific. It is a claim that has often fallen short. Moreover, these disciplines have given us answers to critical questions that have sometimes proved ineffective and destructive. Paul Vitz's *Psychology as Religion: The Cult of Self-Worship*, for example, has shown convincingly how the major "helping profession," owing to its commitment to narcissism, egoism, and the worship of self, "has become more a sentiment than a science and is now part of the problem of modern life rather than part of its resolution." The "selfist philosophy" taught by psychologists, Vitz contends, has had a devastating impact on the lives of untold millions of modern men and women. "With monotonous regularity, the selfist literature sides with those values that encourage divorce, breaking up, dissolution of marital or family ties. All of this is done in the name of growth, autonomy, and 'continuing the flux.'"[48]

All too often, the formulas used by social scientists to deal with life's most profound issues are based upon the question asked by Pontius Pilate: What is truth? And moral relativism (more about this later) does little to help a business executive be compassionate, teach a teenager to be chaste, enable a criminal or a drug addict to turn his life around, or help any of us to love one another.

All three of the great secular religions—the Enlightenment, Marxism, and science—profited from the revolutionary research of Charles Darwin. (Marx wanted to dedicate *Das Kapital* to the British scientist.) In Darwin's view, crude chance and senseless struggle, not a Creator, decided what would and would not appear and survive on this planet. Thus there was no longer any reason for the Supreme Being of the Enlightenment to exist. One could explain things by reference to natural developments over vast distances of time. Nature was not static, as the *philosophes* had believed. Studies in astronomy, geology, and paleontology, as well as biology, were pointing to a world in constant flux.

And what was the human species in this scheme of things? Darwin, as the historian John C. Greene put it, "converted the scientific community to the belief that early man was simply an anthropoid animal equipped with a better brain than his cousin anthropoids."[49] If he was correct, beauty, love, integrity, and their opposites were fleeting human inventions. Ideas were as meaningless as ideals. Men and women were of no more ultimate significance than the bacteria exciting scientists in the 1860s and 1870s. As the biologist Julian Huxley put it, "Man could no longer be regarded as the Lord of Creation, a being apart from the rest of nature. He was merely the representative of one among many Families of the order Primates in the class Mammalia."[50]

To some "advanced" intellectuals of the late nineteenth century, the human species was, to use Carl Becker's memorable words, "little more than a chance deposit on the surface of the world, carelessly thrown up between two ice ages by the same forces that rust iron and ripen corn, a sentient organism endowed by some happy or unhappy accident with intelligence indeed, but with an intelligence that is conditioned by the very forces that it seeks to understand and to control."[51]

In recent times, the physicist Paul Davies has written of the possibility that humanity is "an accident of mind-numbing improbability and irrelevance."[52] The writer Molly Finn has described "the bleak emptiness into which the scientific view of the world has led contemporary man, stranding him befuddled on the stage of life, barely able to remember the name of the drama he is acting in, much less its meaning or its purpose, and unable to consult the dead playwright as to his original intention."[53]

Only a relatively few have ever been able to bear such a grim outlook. When Social Darwinism began to attract widespread attention, for example, many interpreted evolution as yet another force leading to progress. Some wealthy people linked their success with nature's preference for the "fit." It was useless, even counterproductive, they argued, to help the "unfit," for things were taking their regular course. Herbert Spencer said that nature was "a little cruel that it may be very kind."[54]

If religion is defined very broadly as a system of beliefs held to with ardor and faith, there were other secular religions in evidence at this time. Nationalism is an obvious example. Business, which consumed the lives of millions and played a major role in shaping the modern character, is another. Politics, nature, any academic, aesthetic, or leisure pursuit could be made into a secular religion. (Gender and sexual orientation would later be transformed into all-consuming faiths. One writer, after her "conversion" to radical feminism, changed her name to Elana Dykewomon.)[55] Humans were made to worship, if not one thing then another.

In the late nineteenth century, then, there were several secular alternatives to Christianity. Many were especially seductive because they offered, among other things, an assortment of personal rewards, intellectual stimulation, a sense of personal freedom, and a feeling, terribly important to many, of being on the cutting edge of developments. In this era of movement, rapid change, opportunity, and an explosion of knowledge, it was inevitable that the Christian faith would seem to some to be badly out of date.

But, of course, the dividing lines between the secular religions and Christianity were often blurred. The Christian businessman, patriot, and politician were commonplace. There were Christian socialists and scientists. (A Christian anthropologist is at least a theoretical possibility.) Most thoughtful citizens of Great Britain and western Europe scrambled to find ways, however unwieldy and unsystematic, to blend their Christianity with the secular religions. In doing so, they faced many awkward questions about Scripture.

Attacks on the Bible were an integral part of the three great secular religions. Such Enlightenment polemicists as Voltaire, Diderot, Baron d'Holbach, Ethan Allen, and Thomas Paine mocked Scripture as a preposterous product of the ignorant. Paine's *Age of Reason* was a powerful tirade against mystery and miracle, based upon an examination of both Old and New Testament stories. The Bible, to this ardent deist and rationalist, was "a book of lies, wickedness and blasphemy" and "an ocean of improbable, irrational, indecent and contradictory tales." The "fable of Jesus Christ" was "blasphemously obscene." And the Christian Church was a "system of falsehood, idolatry and pretended revelation."[56]

Bible scholars, many of whom were German Protestants, were also at work in the eighteenth century. Johann Gottfried Eichhorn, Johann Jakob Wettstein, Johann August Ernesti, Hermann Samuel Reimarus, Benjamin Kennicott, and Johann Salomo Semler, among others, were pioneers in the field.

In the first half of the nineteenth century, Ferdinand Christian Baur and the Tübingen School of scholars propounded historical theories about the origins of the New Testament and assigned later dates than had previously been assumed to documents. (Baur thought the Gospel of John could not have been written before A.D. 150). H. E. G. Paulus at Jena tried to explain away gospel miracles. (Perhaps Jesus only swooned from the cross, and the apparent resurrection was made possible by an earthquake that revived him and opened the tomb.) David Friedrich Strauss's *Life of Jesus Critically Examined* went further, casting doubt on almost all the New Testament accounts of the Christ. Joseph Ernest Renan's widely discussed *Life of Jesus*, published in 1863, dismissed the supernatural elements in the gospel, portraying Jesus as merely a charming preacher.

By the 1870s and 1880s, intellectuals were paying increasing attention to biblical criticism. Textual, or lower, criticism attempted to reconstruct the history of the Old and New Testament writings. Johann Jacob Griesbach and Constantin Tischendorf in Germany were major New Testament scholars. Brooke Foss Westcott and Fenton John Anthony Hort in England produced a celebrated critical edition of the Greek New Testament in 1881. Higher criticism sought to trace the literary methods and sources used by biblical authors. Old Testament studies by William Robertson Smith in Scotland and Julius Wellhausen in Germany inspired further research and stirred major controversies.

The underlying assumption of the scholars was that the Bible was another piece of ancient literature, the product of many different people over many centuries, reflecting myths and folklores current at the time of authorship. Modern scientific research, it was thought, could clarify and explain biblical accounts much the way other scholars had scrutinized, say, the documents of the Roman Empire. Archaeologists, philologists, and students of comparative religions were also at work.

The miraculous in Scripture was, of course, minimized or eliminated altogether in this process. Adam and Eve, Jonah and the whale, the virgin birth, the coin in the fish's mouth, people being raised from the dead—these were stories that modern, enlightened individuals did not have to swallow. If Jesus believed in Noah's Ark, well, he was a man of his time. Reason and experience decreed that miracles did not happen and thus had never happened.

Eighteen centuries of faith in the inerrancy of Scripture was shaken. What were the faithful to think when they read, for example, that Mark 16:9–20 and John 7:53–8:11 were added to the Bible at a later date, that Paul was not the author of the Book of Hebrews (Baur denied the Pauline authorship of everything but Galatians, First and Second Corinthians, and Romans, and rejected the apostolic origin of Acts), that the Psalms had been col-

lected over different centuries, and that the Pentateuch had been
written by many hands after the death of Moses?

Christians were also faced with the hostility of major philosophers. The highly educated were reading Spinoza, Hobbes, Leib-
niz, Hume, Kant, Hegel, Schopenhauer, Feuerbach (whose fiery
condemnation of Christianity had a direct impact on Marx and
Engels), Comte, John Stuart Mill, and the young Nietzsche (who
proudly declared the "death of God"). These thinkers were not
alone in their emphasis on reason, science, materialism, progress,
and individualism. In biology there were Haeckel and Thomas
Henry Huxley. In history there were Gibbon, Carlyle, Buckle,
and Lecky. Indeed, as the academic disciplines were formally created and the modern universities emerged, it seemed to some
that, on the highest levels at least, learning and Christianity had
parted company.

The impact of the advanced intellectual outlook of the nineteenth century in England and western Europe was intensified by
the rising prosperity stemming from capitalism and the industrial
revolution, the growth of democracy, increased secular education,
the emergence of modern medicine, and technological innovations beyond number. Church and state began separating, and in
some western European nations, notably France, governments
were hostile to Christianity. Massive population shifts often resulted in separation from traditional church affiliations and practices. The urban proletariat frequently seemed indifferent or hostile, seeing the church as part of the class exploiting them.
(Marxists told the proletariat that Christianity used humility and
submission to enslave the masses.) There was a trend toward civil
marriage. Anticlericalism was fashionable in many places.

For many, it was increasingly difficult to think of this planet as a
temporary testing ground for eternity. The scriptural command to
be not of this world seemed dated and unreasonably severe. The
historian Kenneth Scott Latourette observed that this was a perilous period in the history of the Christian faith: "in some respects

the danger was now greater than at any time since the great recession between the close of the fifth and the middle of the tenth century."[57]

The response of the Roman Catholic hierarchy to modernity was determined. In 1864, Pope Leo IX issued the Syllabus of Errors, which attacked, among other things, socialism, communism, clerico-liberal societies, and the idea of the separation of church and state. The document concluded by declaring it erroneous to think that the "Roman Pontiff can and ought to reconcile and adjust himself with progress, liberalism and modern civilization." The First Vatican Council of 1869–70 and papal decrees of 1899, 1907, and 1910 further condemned liberalism and biblical criticism. (The Catholic Church would remain officially opposed to the latter until 1943). This rigid stance was by no means debilitating. Throughout the nineteenth century, the church increased its missionary zeal, grew in numbers, and realized a deeper spirituality.[58]

The Protestant response was, quite naturally, more varied and complex. Some churches in England and on the Continent found ways to accommodate modern thought, while others rejected it flatly.

In the eighteenth century, the Church of England, for example, drank deeply of the Enlightenment and suffered from apathy and irreligion as a result. The historian A. D. Gilbert called the period 1740–1830 "an era of disaster," with numbers falling off so rapidly that the church was in danger of becoming a minority religious establishment. The rise of Methodism within the church in the 1740s was a cry of religious yearning from tens of thousands of men and women.[59]

In the early nineteenth century, a steadily growing evangelical movement and the Oxford Movement brought new spiritual life into the state church. Keble, Newman, and Pusey were antiliberal, romantic, completely dependent upon the supernatural, totally devoted to personal holiness. Pusey condemned Bible critics and thought that all good Christians should do the same. Still, both the evangelicals and Anglo-Catholics were minorities within the church. Mainstream Anglicans were less enthusiastic about otherworldly influences and more inclined to welcome current thought.[60]

Biblical criticism, in one degree or another, was widely accepted in the Church of England by the 1890s. Certain accounts in Scripture, many thought, could be considered as legend or myth. Charles Gore, in the controversial and influential book *Lux Mundi*, pointed out that Clement of Alexandria in the third century and Anselm of Canterbury in the eleventh had both treated the seven-day account of creation in Genesis as allegory, not history.[61] The extent to which this revisionist thinking was shared from the pulpit was left up to the conscience of the individual parish priest. To some, "The Word of God is in the Bible" became preferable to the traditional "The Word of God is the Bible." Liberal clergymen, who had no desire to defend the infallibility of Scripture and had the fewest problems with modernity, grew increasingly influential.[62]

Between 1860 and 1885, most educated men and women in England concluded that evolution and Christian doctrine were compatible. When Darwin died in 1882, he was buried in Westminster Abbey with full Christian rites (although he had lost his faith years earlier), and the general committee on his memorial fund included the archbishops of Canterbury and York and the bishop of London. By 1900, there no longer seemed to be a conflict between religion and science. As the historian Owen Chadwick put it, "peace was established because religion had abandoned, or was abandoning, an ancient claim to give truths about the physical world."[63]

Most thoughtful members of the Church of England were no doubt pleased by the compromises with modernity. The historian Albert Marrin wrote of Anglicans, "Neither the Protestant sects nor the Roman Catholic church could, in their estimation, hold a candle to [the Church of England's] comprehensiveness, intellectual freedom, and ability to adapt to external forces and enlist these in training national character."[64] Some Anglican Church evangelicals and members of smaller Protestant bodies in England wondered aloud, however, about the consequences of giving reason and science an authority that was equal, if not superior, to Scripture. The very forces that could dismiss Genesis could also toss out the creeds of the early church, for both rested on supernatural revelation.

On the continent, Protestantism showed extraordinary vigor in the nineteenth century. In Germany, a powerful wave of antirationalist orthodoxy (albeit it blended with Prussian nationalism) swept the country after the revolutionary year of 1848. Frederich Julius Stahl, a leader of the "New Lutherans," denounced revolution and rationalism, emphasized the sacraments and episcopacy, and argued that the state should be governed by Christian principles. A revival of Pietism (which, in general, stressed personal religious experience) in the country also denounced rationalism, revolution, and the radical interpretations of Scripture.[65]

Lutheranism in Scandinavia prospered after 1815. There were orthodox revivals in Switzerland and the Netherlands at the same time. Protestant missionaries from many countries were vigorous throughout the century, covering the globe with the gospel for the first time. Those most active, at home and abroad, were Christians who rejected Enlightenment rationalism and theological liberalism.[66]

THE ENLIGHTENMENT MADE a deep and lasting impression on Americans, of course. But largely because of the abundance and opportunity offered in this land, the power of evangelical Protestantism, and the strong sense of reasonableness inherent in British culture (illustrated by the great popularity of the philosopher John Locke and an intellectual tradition called Common Sense Realism, employed by many Christians for a century to immunize the faith from the claims of *philosophes* and scientists), the ideas of this great secular religion did not become as volatile as they did in France and elsewhere. Sydney E. Ahlstrom noted that "the wines of the Enlightenment were sipped with cautious moderation."[67]

The faith in reason, progress, and democracy was blended with the Calvinist emphasis on work and prosperity and tempered with a strong sense of transcendent values.

As we have seen, Americans saw their nation as firmly Christian and Protestant, chosen of God, and uniquely qualified to bring the light of the gospel to the rest of the world. They held that science and common sense led inevitably to the highest truths, as revealed in a literal interpretation of Scripture. They endorsed stern public and private morality, free enterprise capitalism, individualism, and a generally optimistic view of human nature. "The old order of American Protestantism," the historian George M. Marsden observed, "was based on the interrelationship of faith, science, the Bible, morality, and civilization."[68] By 1870, however, this self-confident climate of opinion began to fall under attack.

In the decades after the Civil War, many intellectuals here as elsewhere began seriously reexamining Scripture in light of modern science, scholarship, and philosophy. At the same time, thoughtful people were confronted with the confusion and turmoil prompted by soaring urbanization, industrialization, immigration, and secularism. The stories and eternal verities long accepted by Christians seemed to some to be products of a much simpler and less enlightened time.

Some Christian thinkers wrestled mightily with modern scholarship, producing what has been called liberal theology, a synthesis of the faith with the contemporary culture. Liberals found ways to accept science and the theory of evolution. They endorsed biblical criticism, contending that the Bible was historically limited and only a part of God's continuing self-revelation. They also stressed the goodness of human nature over original sin, emphasized the love of God rather than his wrath, gave more weight to religious experience than doctrinal purity, disparaged the sacramental nature of the faith, and argued that "progressive" ethics were the test for religious truth. By the 1880s, the movement known as the New Theology, or Progressive Orthodoxy, was especially popular among leaders of the mainline denominations, with the exception of the Lutherans.

Such liberal scholars as the Baptist William Newton Clarke, the Congregationalist Theodore Munger, the Methodist Borden Parker Bowne, and the Presbyterian William Adams Brown contributed important publications to the movement. Liberal seminaries and theological schools included those at Andover, Yale, Union, Boston University, and the University of Chicago. Union Theological Seminary, which broke away from the Northern Presbyterian Church in 1892 over the issue of biblical criticism, had a highly respected liberal faculty. Thoughtful and articulate ministers such as Henry Ward Beecher of Plymouth Congregational Church in Brooklyn and Phillips Brooks of Trinity Episcopal Church in Boston eased the anxieties of their more learned and wealthy parishioners by assuring them that Christianity was entirely compatible with the world around them.

The historian Sydney Ahlstrom wrote of the liberals, "they led the Protestant churches into the world of modern science, scholarship, philosophy, and global knowledge." In doing this, "They forced a confrontation between traditional orthodoxies and the new grounds for religious skepticism exposed during the nineteenth century, and thus carried forward what the Enlightenment had begun. As a result, they precipitated the most fundamental controversy to wrack the churches since the age of the Reformation."[69]

Shortly after the turn of the century, with the Progressive movement in full force, some liberal Christians put their ideas to work in a practical way. The Social Gospel was a powerful reform movement within American Christianity that emphasized the social demands of the faith, particularly in the nation's cities. While conservative evangelicals were part of the effort, the prime movers were mainline Protestants, strongly influenced by liberal theology and social thought. The historian C. Howard Hopkins has called the Social Gospel "American Protestantism's response to the challenge of modern industrial society."[70]

Social Gospel activists welcomed the economic and sociological data then becoming prominent and used it to call for government intervention to create a more humane and Christ-like society. The belief that Christians had a moral obligation to reshape society can be traced to the Puritans and had a rich history in the nineteenth century. But Social Gospelers, influenced by advanced movements in Britain, Germany, and Switzerland, went further to the left than most Americans, prompting a great many church members to find their ideas objectionable.

Much of what the liberals proclaimed contained a strong critique of laissez-faire capitalism. As Hopkins put it, "Competition was declared to be the opposite of Christian love and cooperation, freedom to buy labor as a commodity in the cheapest market was condemned on religious grounds, and the practical materialism of the profit motive was branded as ethically subversive." The solutions that social Christianity proposed were sometimes specific, but more often than not they were general and sentimental prescriptions for "the application of the law of love to society."[71]

The movement's leadership included the Congregationalist minister Washington Gladden, a prolific author and popular speaker who sought to apply the gospel to such issues as labor, politics, and race. The Baptist minister, author, and seminary professor Walter Rauschenbusch was also eager to build the Kingdom of God on earth, and his book *Christianity and the Social Crisis*, published in 1907, brought him national fame. Richard T. Ely, who like so many reformers was trained by German scholars, was the nation's most widely read economist and an activist in the Episcopal Church. The Congregationalist minister Josiah Strong was an important organizer and writer. The Congregationalist minister Charles Monroe Sheldon wrote the most successful novel of the late Gilded Age, *In His Steps*, the story of a town transformed by a minister who asked his congregation to first ask "What would Jesus do?" and then act accordingly.

The participation of Episcopalians and Congregationalists, primarily, and to a lesser degree Methodists, Baptists, and Presbyterians in this movement laid the groundwork for the creation in 1908 of the Federal Council of the Churches of Christ in America.[72] Four years later, the council, representing thirty denominations, formally endorsed a list of reforms that included child labor laws, uniform divorce laws, occupational safety laws, the six-day week, care for the unemployed and elderly, and "a new emphasis upon the application of Christian principles to the acquisition and use of property, and for the most equitable division of the product of industry that can ultimately be devised."[73] This declaration was not overly controversial, for in 1912 three of the major presidential candidates were Progressives and the fourth was a socialist.

Some Christian reformers were socialists and Marxists. The list includes the Episcopal priest William Dwight Porter Bliss, the Methodist minister Edward Ellis Carr, the Methodist activist and temperance leader Frances Willard, and Ely and Rauschenbusch. Three bishops of the Episcopal Church, the most reform-minded of the mainline denominations, were also socialists.[74]

But socialism did not capture the churches and was not a major factor in the Progressive Era. The Church Socialist League, created by Episcopalians in 1911, had fewer than one hundred members five years later. Still, socialism unquestionably had an impact on liberal church leaders. The numerous injustices it documented in untold numbers of publications during the Gilded Age and the early decades of the twentieth century would not be forgotten. The dreams of an earthly paradise where everything would be held in common and all would live in peace and love were to reappear in succeeding decades.[75]

With the New Theology and the Social Gospel, then, mainline leaders and thinkers made crucial compromises with the great secular religions. Many Christians now thought differently than they had a few decades earlier about God, Scripture, human nature, progress, science, evolution, dogma, worship, and the responsibility of the faithful to society.

Still, orthodox Christianity remained very much in evidence at this time. Most Christians continued in their evangelical faith, and most liberals were not prepared to abandon the supernatural essentials of their religion, such as the Incarnation and Resurrection. The conclusion of the Federal Council of Churches statement of 1912 called attention to the importance of the words *God, sin, judgment,* and *redemption*—"they are gigantic and capacious words, belonging to a vocabulary that can interpret the whole universe of right and wrong, both individual and social."[76]

Many factors accounted for the move of mainline leaders and theologians in the direction of modernity. To begin with, they accepted scientific research because there seemed to be no rational alternative. One did not care to quarrel with the findings of, say, modern chemistry, microbiology, or medicine. They were demonstrably true.

Moreover, on the whole, the mainline membership was of a higher socioeconomic level and thus tended to respect the judgments of the most educated. When science and religion clashed, such as in accounts of creation, liberals felt inclined, often uneasily, to be sure, to side with the geologists, paleontologists, and biologists. While the theory of evolution and the observations on the origins of humanity in *Descent of Man*, published in 1871, were controversial, Darwin was endorsed by the most widely respected scientists in the world.

Liberal Christian thinkers explored several avenues for aligning the historic faith with the new evidence. Some, for example, defended Genesis by claiming it was designed exclusively to present moral and spiritual truths (such as, for example, that humanity's knowledge of good and evil came from God and is not our own invention). Some argued that the six "days" of creation did not necessarily mean six twenty-four–hour days; in both the Old (Psalm 90:4) and New Testaments (2 Peter 3:8), we are told that God does not view time as we do, and that a thousand years are like a single day to Him. Others chose to abandon so-called natural proofs for the existence of the Creator and emphasized personal faith and the presence of God in the human conscience.

Such efforts were successful. By the late 1890s, the theory of evolution was largely absorbed into the mainstream of American intellectual life, and the leading mainline figures were in accord. The historian Cynthia Eagle Russett has concluded, "Darwinism reigned over Victorian culture as supremely as Newtonian mechanics had over the previous century."[77] Later, in the 1920s, when evolution would again become an issue among Christians, mainline Protestant college presidents would be in the frontline against efforts to impede scientific teaching. As the Baptist historian Glenn Miller put it, "In simple terms, Protestant educators consistently stood for the best available scholarship."[78]

Liberal Christians approached biblical criticism in much the same way that they looked at science; indeed, Bible scholars were widely thought to be themselves scientists of a sort. And the same respect was paid for the burst of new and often exciting literature and data coming from scholars in the social sciences. In short, it seemed only sensible to accept what appeared to be undeniable.

It is important to note a dramatic change taking place in American higher education at this time. The secularization of colleges and universities began in the 1870s and was well underway twenty years later. There was a burgeoning demand for practical, money-making programs and fading interest in religious and classical studies. The rise of specialized academic disciplines and advanced research degrees encouraged an empirical approach to learning. Pragmatism (the belief, in short, that truth is what "works" or "pays") would soon become popular with the writings of John Dewey and William James.

The liberal Christians who succeeded their evangelical brethren in the leadership of higher education interpreted the growing ideological secularism on campus in a positive way, arguing that faith and objective scholarship were allies. Daniel Coit Gilman, the founder of Johns Hopkins, the nation's first research university, said in 1887 that churches had to recognize "that Science is the handmaid of Religion, that every effort made to extend the domain of human thought, and to interpret the plan of creation, is an effort to extend the reign of righteousness and truth."[79]

Richard T. Ely was not alone among Christian scholars in thinking that independent scientific inquiry could work hand in hand with the Social Gospel, both fulfilling the will of God. In the first report of the American Economics Association, Ely declared that "our work looks in the direction of practical Christianity."[80]

Protestant seminaries and divinity schools were also increasingly committed to scholarship and beginning to embrace a more secular outlook. Harvard Divinity School was a bastion of Unitarianism by 1879. In 1880, the Methodists had 11 theological seminaries, 44 colleges and universities, and 130 women's schools, and critics were complaining that the religious doctrines that helped win the western frontier to the faith were being watered down and secularized. The same was said of the Northern Baptists. One modern scholar has concluded that "all the Northern Baptist seminaries were firmly in the liberal camp by the end of the century."[81] A historian noted in 1915 that "all of the older theological seminaries of the North have on their faculties scholars of the modern type who are outspoken in their acceptance of modernistic views of the Bible and of the evolutionistic philosophy, and no one of them . . . [has] a stalwart and aggressive advocate of the older conservatism."[82]

The Social Gospel grew in large part out of liberals' genuine compassion for the victims of the industrial revolution. Most church leaders lived in urban environments and could witness the social and political tragedies firsthand. Of course, Christianity requires its followers to do good works as an expression of their faith. Christianity is a religion of love based upon God, who Himself *is* love. Reformers saw their activities on behalf of the poor and the exploited as wholly in keeping with biblical commandments. "Instead of a society resting on coercion, exploitation, and inequality," wrote Walter Rauschenbusch, "Jesus desired to found a society resting on love, service, and equality."[83]

That liberal Christians at the time espoused a generous view of human nature and a faith in progress indicated an attachment to the Enlightenment, of course, but it also had much to do with the fact that they were Americans, an incurably optimistic and cheery people, buoyed by economic abundance, political democracy, and freedom from external aggression. Before World War I, many in this country and elsewhere believed that humans were on the verge of unprecedented and unlimited joy.

There were no doubt many other reasons as well for bowing to the "advanced" spirit of the age. Some mainline leaders, for example, were surely eager to make themselves and their faith relevant at a time when, at least at the highest intellectual levels, people were growing skeptical of the ancient and the supernatural. It was also true, as the church scholars Roger Finke and Rodney Stark have pointed out, that mainline clergy received better pay and were more widely respected in polite society than their more evangelical, rigidly moral, and otherworldly brethren in the sects.[84]

Others signed on, no doubt, out of the simple desire, even need, to be trendy. Edmund A. Opitz, a Congregational minister, has wisely observed:

> Churchmen in every age are tempted to adopt the protective coloration of their time; like all intellectuals, churchmen are verbalists and wordsmiths; they are powerfully swayed by the printed page, by catch-words, slick phrases, slogans. . . . In consequence, they are pulled first this way then that by whatever currents of public opinion happen at the moment to exert the greatest power over their emotions and imagination.[85]

The Lemming Impulse would become more obvious later in the century. Liberal clergy, like liberals at all levels in colleges and universities, are especially vulnerable to causes and standards of personal conduct that seem modern and "progressive."

A great many Christian leaders and laity, however, refused to compromise with the great secular religions. To them, Scripture came from the Creator and was to be interpreted either literally or with the utmost gravity. The Bible, in their judgment, was truth, providing all that we needed to know about our origins, proper conduct, and our ultimate destination.

One such leader was the evangelist Dwight L. Moody, thought by many to be the greatest figure in American Christianity from the mid–1870s until his death in 1899. Moody had left school at age thirteen and supported himself for a time as a shoe salesman. He was without seminary training and was never ordained. But Moody had a good mind, a winning personality, a solid command of Scripture, and a zealous faith. He also had the ingenuity to devise techniques of revivalism that won vast numbers of city dwellers to the Christian faith.

Moody preached a simple and often sentimental message of personal conversion to Jesus Christ. He emphasized a loving God and the importance of motherhood and the family. He urged Christians to follow a strict moral code that condemned, among other things, drunkenness, Sabbath breaking, theater attendance, and "telling vile stories." "A line should be drawn," he said, "between the church and the world, and every Christian should get both feet out of the world."[86]

Moody flatly rejected formal education and liberalism. "I have one rule about books," he said. "I do not read any book, unless it will help me to understand *the* book." He laid no claim to a theology, liberal or otherwise. The theory of evolution, in his mind, was absurd. "It is a great deal easier to believe that man was made after the image of God than to believe, as some young men and women are being taught now, that he is the offspring of a monkey."[87]

Moody was uninterested in the labors of liberal reformers. His nondenominational ministry was devoted to the conversion of individuals. True reform, he believed, would spring from souls wholly in love with God. This dictum was of value for the family, community, and nation. "Revival," he said in 1899, "is the only hope for our republic, for I don't believe that a republican form of government can last without righteousness."[88]

This view of the primacy of personal salvation was no doubt accepted by a majority of Methodists, Baptists, and Presbyterians at the time. The historian Henry F. May has written of the Methodists, "Filled more than any other denomination with revivalist traditions, Methodism long insisted on sin as the sufficient explanation of all social evil, and individual redemption as the only remedy."[89] Moody's general rejection of modernism was especially welcome in the South, an area of the country long dominated by evangelicalism and conservatism, and largely outside the range of the more advanced scholarship.

During the Gilded Age, Christians were dividing into two camps: those who had come to terms, at least in part, with the great secular religions and those who mostly or completely refused. The most critical issue was the authority of Scripture. Not all conservatives held to the inerrancy of the Bible, but most probably did.

Clashes broke out within denominations and in seminaries all across the country. In the Presbyterian Church, where the fighting was especially intense, the theologian and scientist James Woodrow (Woodrow Wilson's uncle) was dismissed from his position at the seminary in Columbia, South Carolina, for finding the theory of evolution compatible with Scripture. The General Assembly declared in 1886 that "Adam's body was directly fashioned by Almighty God, without any natural animal parentage." A few years later, the liberal Bible scholar Charles A. Briggs of Union Theological Seminary was tried for heresy and convicted, and the General Assembly officially endorsed the doctrine of biblical inerrancy.[90]

Some of those who rejected modernism were respected scholars. The Presbyterian Benjamin Breckinridge Warfield of Princeton Theological Seminary, for example, thoughtfully defended the inerrancy of Scripture and argued that preconceptions against the supernatural blinded liberals to the truths of the faith. The Baptist theologian Augustus H. Strong, president of the Rochester Theological Seminary, though not subscribing to the inerrancy of Scripture, was an influential conservative.

Evangelicals began organizing during the Gilded Age, both within the major churches and in a spate of often contentious independent denominations. One of their activities was the creation of Bible institutes and colleges designed to train people for active Christian service at home and abroad and to resist liberal theology. A. B. Simpson's New York Missionary Training College (now Nyack College and Alliance Theological Seminary) and the Moody Bible Institute in Chicago were early and effective models. The movement was led by a number of highly energetic and effective ministers, including Moody's Reuben A. Torrey and James M. Gray.

Torrey and Gray both defended scriptural inerrancy, and Gray was one of the seven editors of the *Scofield Bible*, published in 1909. This popular volume, published by Oxford University Press (and revised as recently as 1967), proclaimed a divine plan for the world based upon a literal interpretation of Scripture. It began in the Garden of Eden and concluded with Christ's return to earth to establish the millennial kingdom.

In 1910, the first of twelve paperback pamphlets appeared called "The Fundamentals." This series, sent free of charge by the hundreds of thousands to church leaders, contained ninety articles written by conservative scholars and Bible teachers. The tracts covered a wide variety of topics but became famous for defending biblical inerrancy (one article referred to "a Book dropped out of heaven") and the "fundamental" doctrines of the faith, including the Incarnation, miracles, and the Resurrection. The authors tended to be neither anti-intellectual nor antiscientific. Indeed, they argued that biblical truths were compatible with reason and "true" science—by which they meant a Baconian, inductive science that, they thought, did not threaten the faith. At the heart of liberal thought, they argued, was an irrational bias against the supernatural and the miraculous.

These volumes marked the beginning of the organized fundamentalist (a term coined in 1920) movement, described by George M. Marsden as a "self-consciously conservative coalition against modernism."[91]

The trenches were being dug for a full-scale battle with liberal Christianity. But there was still room for dialogue. The single article in "The Fundamentals" covering socialism was sympathetic, and some form of evolution was acknowledged possible. This moderate spirit was not to last long, however, for conservatives and liberal leaders would soon conclude that compromise between Christians over the assumptions, the methodologies, and the conclusions taught by the great secular religions was virtually impossible.

4

UP TO THE PRECIPICE

A merica's churches, liberal and conservative, energetically supported United States involvement in World War I. From the pulpits of virtually every denomination came the message that the country was involved in a holy crusade to end German militarism and bring peace, democracy, and international brotherhood to the world. The Rev. Randolph H. McKim, rector of an Episcopal church in Washington, D.C., described the war in sermons as "a Crusade. The greatest in History—the holiest. . . . a Holy War."[1] The mainline-dominated Federal Council of Churches declared: "The war for righteousness will be won! Let the Church do her part."[2] Some fundamentalists saw the Kaiser as the Antichrist of Scripture and linked the Great War with the end of the world. Wartime efforts and support of the League of Nations created a strong spirit of teamwork among denominations.

This cooperation was also an important ingredient in the successful crusade to pass national prohibition legislation. The campaign, which met its goal in January 1920, enjoyed remarkable support from all ideological positions within Protestantism. (German Lutherans and northern Episcopalians were exceptions.[3]) Methodists and Baptists were particularly active. In general, conservatives backed prohibition as part of their emphasis on personal holiness, while liberals saw the effort as a means of transforming society for the better. Protestants of all persuasions were eager to curb the power of the liquor industry (especially the German brewers and distillers) and crack down on the saloon, widely thought to be a major source of moral corruption.

On the other hand, Protestant churches were unsuccessful in sustaining the Interchurch World Movement, designed after the armistice by Presbyterians and dedicated to world evangelism and reform. An attempt to raise $336 million collapsed in the summer of 1920. Eldon G. Ernst, the movement's historian, concluded that the failure of this interdenominational drive revealed a decrease in church authority and influence. "The long-developing pattern of a rising urban, secularized, religiously and culturally and racially pluralistic, American population, which had caused increasing alarm to Protestant leaders since the Civil War, had begun to come of age after World War I."[4]

There were many sides to the complex and fascinating decade of the 1920s. The entire nation seemed disillusioned with the Social Gospel, Progressivism, and Wilsonian idealism overseas. Millions were moving into urban areas, intent on getting good jobs, cars, homes, and diplomas. Business was king, skillfully orchestrating the vast machinery of mass production and consumption along with the best politicians money could buy. The opportunity to acquire personal wealth seemed unlimited, and people from all walks of life, from cabbies to bankers, were intensely interested in the latest stock market reports. Newspaper headlines focused on gangsters, athletes, and movie stars. Writers were often cynical and shocking. Many women, now eligible to vote, bobbed their hair, smoked cigarettes, wore short skirts, and danced the Charleston.

In intellectual circles, science and Freudianism were the rage. The latter not only provided intellectual excitement but gave "modern" people an excuse to denigrate self-control, "whole-someness," and anything "Victorian" or "Puritan." Within a single page of one book, Freud called religion a "neurosis," an "illusion," a "poison," and an "intoxicant," and declared: "But surely infantilism is destined to be surmounted. Men cannot remain children for ever; they must in the end go out into 'hostile life'. We may call this *'education to reality.'*"[5]

Not a few thoughtful observers, then and later, dismissed the roaring twenties as an era of vast wickedness and silliness. While that is debatable, one can say with certainty that modern America was born.

Popular religious books of the 1920s often echoed the era's fads and fancies, stressing positive thinking and successful living, and linking business and wealth with Christian virtue. Bruce Barton's best-seller called the parables of Jesus "the most powerful advertisements of all time." Reading the Bible, another writer exclaimed, put money in your pocket. Even the dean of the University of Chicago Divinity School told a reporter that you could make more money by praying about your business.[6]

Liberal theologians likewise absorbed much that was fashionable, especially in academic circles. They continued to move to the left, choosing increasingly to shun the supernatural and flirt with pragmatism, empiricism, and science. Social reform remained high on the liberal agenda.[7] The Federal Council of Churches, for example, played a major role in ending the twelve-hour steel mill shift, campaigned for a child labor amendment to the Constitution, conducted social and labor research, and disseminated the Social Gospel point of view in numerous publications.[8]

The number of mainline churches decreased during the 1920s, while the Southern Baptists and other evangelical and fundamentalist denominations flourished. Between 1916 and 1926, the Disciples of Christ lost 2.7 percent of their membership, the Methodists 5.3 percent, the Congregationalists 6.1 percent, the Northern Baptists 11.5 percent, and the Methodists 12.3 percent.

Small gains were shown by the Presbyterians (USA) (1.4 percent) and Episcopalians (3.8 percent).[9]

Salaries of Protestant clergy fell behind those of other professionals and even some merchants and craftsmen. In 1923, according to the *Literary Digest*, weekly salaries of ministers (for example, Congregationalist, $28.86 and Northern Methodists, $29.44) were considerably lower than those of plumbers ($47.17) and bricklayers ($55.92). This pattern was not to change, prompting many bright and ambitious people to seek other fields of employment. The historian Edwin S. Gaustad observed, "In the struggle over image, the clergyman unsure of his role as prophet or moral leader as citizen or therapist, found little reassurance in observing the swift deterioration of his economic and professional standing."[10]

It was no secret during the 1920s that something vital was leaking out of most of the liberal denominations. Missionary enthusiasm, for example, was drying up, Sunday school enrollments declined, and the number of converts dropped. Many clergy reportedly suffered from a debilitating inertia.[11]

Harry Emerson Fosdick, the famed pulpit minister at First Presbyterian Church in New York City, stirred controversy by declaring in a widely distributed sermon of 1922 that the Virgin Birth, the inerrancy of Scripture, and the Second Coming of Christ were outmoded and unessential concepts. The brilliant journalist Walter Lippmann, in *A Preface to Morals*, noted that liberal churchmen were highly ambivalent about their faith. Missing was "that ineffable certainty which once made God and His Plan seem as real as the lamp-post."[12]

Frederick Lewis Allen, a cogent observer of the 1920s, said that "the Modernists threw overboard so many doctrines in which the bulk of American Protestants had grown up believing (such as the Virgin birth, the resurrection of the body, and the Atonement) that they seemed to many to have no religious cargo left except a nebulous faith, a general benevolence, and a disposition to assure everyone that [the modernist] was really just as religious as they."[13]

Nowhere was religious skepticism more obvious than on campus. By 1910 the leading American colleges and universities had severed their denominational ties, and what religion remained on these campuses in the twenties tended to be liberal.[14] Many faculty by this time were outspoken about their faith in reason, science, and progress. In the 1920s, the social sciences, like the natural sciences before them, began to dismiss religion as at best an anachronism, at worst a social pathology.[15] Liberal Protestants, ever eager to be intellectually respectable, often directly or indirectly endorsed this secular world view.[16] Allen recalled, "It is doubtful if any college undergraduate of the 'nineties or of any other previous period in the United States could have said 'No intelligent person believes in God any more' as blandly as undergraduates said it during the discussions of compulsory college chapel which raged during the 'twenties.'"[17]

Fundamentalists were outraged by the actions of their liberal brethren, convinced that in their efforts to accommodate the world, liberals were destroying the integrity of the Christian faith. Some went so far as to blame World War I on biblical criticism and the acceptance of evolution.[18]

There was a growing inclination by evangelicals and fundamentalists in this era toward anti-intellectualism and a retreat into the past. Many revealed a frustrated and at times angry rejection of a culture that celebrated the likes of John Dewey, Al Capone, Clara Bow, and F. Scott Fitzgerald. The popular evangelist Billy Sunday (a high school dropout and former professional baseball player) expressed this mood when he said: "Thousands of college graduates are going as fast as they can straight to hell. If I had a million dollars I'd give $999,999 to the church and $1 to education." And again, "When the word of God says one thing and scholarship says another, scholarship can go to hell!"[19]

A great many Americans, especially in small towns, rural areas, and in the South, were hostile to the sophisticated, secular world they saw looming in the 1920s. They feared for their faith and their families, and for the future of their nation. As the historian Richard Hofstadter put it, "the city was the home of liquor and bootleggers, jazz and Sunday golf, wild parties and divorce. The magazines and newspapers, the movies and radio, brought tidings of all this to the countryside, and even lured children of the old American stock away from the old ways." Often the blame fell on immigrants, Catholics, and Jews in such Babylons as New York and Chicago. "The Anglo-Saxon Americans now felt themselves more than ever to be the representatives of a threatened purity of race and ideals, a threatened Protestantism, even a threatened integrity of national allegiance."[20]

H. L. Mencken, whom the historian William E. Leuchtenburg has aptly described as "less a true satirist than a sophomoric nihilist," called fundamentalists, among other things, "anthropoid rabble," "morons," "one-horse Popes," and "amateur Messiahs."[21] Some liberal Protestants were equally harsh, referring to fundamentalists as "barbarians" and "extremists," and finding them guilty of "militant ignorance." One modernist minister declared, "Religious zealots barricade the road of progress, put out the eyes of intelligence, mutilate learning and nail reason to the cross."[22] The close, albeit informal, link between fundamentalism and the Ku Klux Klan in the 1920s contributed to this stereotype.[23]

Still, there were intelligent, prosperous, and educated Christians who also believed that God had given them in the Bible an infallible and definitive account of His truth.[24] Among them was the brilliant New Testament scholar J. Gresham Machen of Princeton Theological Seminary. In *Christianity and Liberalism*, published in 1923, Machen made a highly articulate and learned case for fundamentalism and contended that liberal Christianity and the historic faith were different religions: "at every point the two movements are in direct opposition." The "liberal attempt at reconciling Christianity with modern science has really relinquished everything distinctive of Christianity, so that what remains is in essentials only that same indefinite type of religious aspiration which was in the world before Christianity came upon the scene."25

Take the question of biblical miracles. Liberals tended to find some if not all of them unbelievable. Machen, however, argued that they were essential to the faith. "The New Testament without the miracles would be far easier to believe. But the trouble is, it would not be worth believing. Without the miracles the New Testament would contain an account of a holy man. . . . But of what benefit would such a man, and the death which marked His failure, be to us? The loftier be the example which Jesus set, the greater becomes our sorrow at our failure to attain to it; and the greater our hopelessness under the burden of sin." Far more is needed in a sinful world, Machen wrote, than a model man. "Without the miracles we should have a teacher; with the miracles we have a Saviour."26

Machen contributed to the friction between left and right by calling for the removal of liberals from orthodox Christian churches. "In the intellectual battle of the present day there can be no 'peace without victory'; one side or the other must win."27

Few liberals shared Walter Lippmann's enthusiasm about this book. Still, many of them, including the editor of the mainline magazine *Christian Century*, could agree with the "two religions" thesis. "Two worlds have crashed," an editorial exclaimed, "the world of tradition and the world of modernism. One is scholastic, static, authoritarian, individualistic; the other is vital, dynamic, free and social." The clash was "as profound and as grim as that between Christianity and Confucianism." And separation was inevitable. "'Blest be the tie' may be sung until doomsday but it cannot bind these two worlds together."28

Shailer Mathews, the liberal dean of the Divinity School of the University of Chicago, took the same approach in his popular book *The Faith of Modernism*, published in 1924 as a reply to Machen. Mathews condemned church history, traditional theology, and biblical literalism while pleading the case that Christianity had to be squared with modern science and biblical criticism and put to work meeting the needs, especially the social needs, of modern man.

At the heart of much of the struggle between modernists and fundamentalists, Mathews acknowledged, were two irreconcilable views of Scripture. Modern men and women could draw inspiration from the pages of the Bible, the dean wrote, but were freed by objective scholarship from having to swallow it whole, miracles and all. He dismissed the Virgin Birth, for example, and rejected the whole concept of the Atonement. "Belief in the providence of God can be expressed in poetry, folk-tale and legend just as truly as in literal statement." This was a position, Mathews acknowledged, that was unacceptable to the "dogmatic mind."[29]

In the early 1920s, battles between fundamentalists and liberals broke out among Episcopalians, Methodists, the Disciples of Christ, Northern Baptists, and both Southern and Northern Presbyterians. The fiercest struggles occurred within the Baptists and Presbyterians of the North.

While liberals were a minority in all the mainline denominations, they were able to fend off efforts in the early 1920s to curb their influence. At church conventions where policies were hammered out, fundamentalists invariably came away empty-handed. Sometimes they were divided among themselves over theological matters. Moderates and conservatives often supported liberals when they appealed to their denomination for tolerance and unity.

In some cases, the frustrations of fundamentalists led to schism. Presbyterian fundamentalists, for example, created their own seminary in 1929 and laid plans for their own denomination when Princeton Theological Seminary opted for a broader theological program by reorganizing the seminary board. The Princeton Seminary, old (1812), distinguished, and influential (six thousand graduates by 1912), had long been the home of a most rigid Calvinist orthodoxy. The conservative professor Charles Hodge, who trained more than two thousand students at Princeton between 1822 and 1878, had once boasted that "a new idea never originated in this Seminary."[30]

Schism often seemed sensible, for the intellectual and spiritual chasm between liberals and fundamentalists was enormous. (There were often important socioeconomic differences as well.) Both sides searched for truth in different ways and often arrived at sharply contrasting conclusions. Moreover, both liberals and fundamentalists were convinced that their opposition was ignorant, arrogant, and un-Christian, making constructive dialogue virtually impossible.

William Jennings Bryan was the best-known and most widely admired fundamentalist of his time. In many ways, he represented the best and the worst of that movement, and he unintentionally played a major role in minimizing its public credibility.

Bryan was a graduate of Illinois College who had gone into law and journalism before being catapulted into the national spotlight in 1896 with his famous "Cross of Gold" speech at the Democratic national convention. By 1925, when he was sixty-five, Bryan had run for the presidency three times and had served as Wilson's secretary of state. A Populist and Progressive, keenly interested in the Social Gospel, he had championed women's suffrage and had been, in historian Lawrence W. Levine's words, "as militant and extreme a prohibitionist as was to be found in this country."[31]

Bryan was intensely sincere, honest, and outspoken. (By his own estimate, he delivered five thousand lectures between 1894 and 1924, and annually traveled the equivalent of once around the world). He was also a shallow, anti–intellectual, and dogmatic man who gave himself virtually no time for reflection or reading. A catalogue of his convictions consisted largely of a firm faith in the innate goodness and wisdom of the average person, the sanctity of the Bible ("the only Book that is good always and everywhere"), and the primacy of the rural way of life.[32]

Bryan despised the theory of evolution, arguing that it undermined Christianity and public morality and, moreover, was bad science. "All the ills from which America suffers," he said in 1924, "can be traced back to the teaching of evolution." In the early 1920s, wrote his biographer LeRoy Ashby, he "resembled a one-man army against Darwinism," traveling across the country arguing for laws prohibiting its teaching."[33]

The clash between liberalism and fundamentalism reached its zenith in the famous Scopes Trial of 1925. The immediate issue involved the violation of a Tennessee law prohibiting the teaching of evolution in public schools. The liberal American Civil Liberties Union was searching for a test case, and the young high school science teacher John T. Scopes of Dayton obliged.

Bryan was chosen to defend the law by the executive committee of the World's Christian Fundamentals Association. This was an interdenominational body of fundamentalist churches founded in 1919 to combat liberal Christianity. In conjunction with the Anti-evolution League, the Association had succeeded in getting legislation passed in a number of states outlawing the teaching of evolution in public schools. In 1923, at an annual meeting hosted in Fort Worth by the flamboyant Southern Baptist preacher J. Frank Norris, the organization had held a full-scale trial of Texas colleges, charging them with teaching rationalism, evolution, and biblical criticism. (That same year, Norris, in an editorial in *Moody Monthly*, expressed the view of many fundamentalists by declaring that "evolution is Bolshevism in the long run," and with it goes "all authority and government, all law and order."[34])

The opposition stood in sharp contrast. Scopes was defended by a formidable group of learned, liberal, urbane defense lawyers, including the famed Clarence Darrow, an agnostic and champion of free speech. The defense was prepared to offer expert testimony on evolution by a number of distinguished scientists and social scientists. Four liberal clergymen—a Rabbi, an Episcopalian, a Methodist, and Dean Shailer Mathews—were also ready to testify that Christianity and evolution could live together in peace.[35]

From the beginning, Darrow and his allies made Bryan and the fundamentalists the issue in the case. The ACLU lawyer Arthur Garfield Hays wrote that the trial "was a battle between two types of mind—the rigid, orthodox, accepting, unyielding, narrow, conventional mind, and the broad liberal, critical, cynical, skeptical and tolerant mind."[36]

Bryan saw the struggle in a different light: "The contest between evolution and Christianity is a duel to the death . . . If evolution wins in Dayton Christianity goes—not suddenly of course, but gradually—for the two cannot stand together. . . . The atheists, agnostics and all other opponents of Christianity understand the character of the struggle, hence this interest in this case."[37]

There was indeed great media interest in the trial. Reporters and telegraph operators poured into tiny Dayton. Mencken was on the scene early for the *Baltimore Sun*, writing about "morons" and "hillbillies" and "peasants," and the "degraded nonsense which country preachers are ramming and hammering into yokel skulls." Each day the case was in court, reporters sent about 165,000 words from Dayton. A radio hookup made this the first national broadcast of an American trial. Tens of millions of Americans followed the case.[38]

The most memorable moments of the eight-day trial occurred during an hour and a half confrontation between Bryan and Darrow, the former having taken the stand. Darrow, raised on Darwin, Buckle, Spencer, and others, mercilessly revealed Bryan's ignorance about ancient history, science, and comparative religion, and got him to admit, to the scandal of some fundamentalists, that a few portions of the Old Testament need not be taken literally. (The six "days" of creation might have been "millions of years.") Bryan admitted having placed his whole trust in his religion and the literal truth of Scripture, saying at one point, "I have all the information I want to live by and to die by." His self-assuredness rankled Darrow, who sneered, "You insult every man of science and learning in the world because he does not believe in your fool religion." And again, "I am examining you on your fool ideas that no intelligent Christian on earth believes."[39]

Bryan displayed considerable wit and oratorical ability throughout the trial. The prosecution won the case (Scopes's fine was later overturned on a technicality) and the anti-evolution law remained on the books. But the battle for public opinion went decidedly for the defense. Bryan's anti-intellectualism, his lack of sophistication, and his simple faith yielded unlimited scorn from the press on the scene and from educated observers throughout the nation. Darrow later castigated "ignoramuses" and "bigots" and regretted that Bryan had become "the idol of all Morondom."[40]

The Monkey Trial did grave and lasting damage to the image of those who clung to a verbally inerrant Bible. Even though states passed more anti-evolution laws and fundamentalist churches continued to grow, after 1925 millions of Americans equated fundamentalism with intolerance and ignorance. Many Protestant conservatives quietly dropped their support of the movement, fearful of being embarrassed by association. Sinclair Lewis's novel *Elmer Gantry*, published in 1927, seemed to many to describe perfectly the intellectual vacuity, hypocrisy, and dishonesty of fundamentalists.[41]

By the end of the decade, fundamentalism was in serious decline within the mainline churches, especially at the upper levels of teaching and authority. (Again, the Lutherans, still heavily ethnic and socially and theologically conservative, were exceptions to the generality.)[42] This trend accelerated when two conservative schisms rent the Northern Baptists a few years later, and J. Gresham Machen led a group of fundamentalists out of the Presbyterian Church of America.[43]

More than ever before, the liberal minority controlled the mainline denominations. They also attempted to control the media. Mainline leaders, through the Federal Council of Churches, persuaded the national radio networks to grant them a monopoly over the free time given to religious groups. They also fought successfully to deny fundamentalists and evangelicals even the right to purchase time for religious broadcasting. Only the Mutual Broadcasting System resisted, and such programs as Charles E. Fuller's "Old-Fashioned Revival Hour" and "The Lutheran Hour," sponsored by the conservative Missouri Synod, became the nation's most popular religious radio shows. (In 1944, even the Mutual Broadcasting System would cave in to mainline pressure, announcing severe restrictions on religious broadcasting and forcing evangelicals and fundamentalists to invent the method of syndicating programs on local stations. As late as 1956, mainliners were trying, unsuccessfully, to persuade radio executives to ban paid—i.e. evangelical and fundamentalist—broadcasting.[44])

As the 1920s came to a close, then, mainline churches on the whole retained their respectability. They had bent with the times; they were truly modern. Government leaders consulted with mainline leaders. The media were reasonably sympathetic. Seminary professors could boast of at least a modest regard from academia. And liberal Christians in all walks of life could enjoy a self-confidence born of the belief that the faith was in the vanguard of forces destined to bring enlightenment and progress to the world.

The Great Depression did much to cool Americans on the "religion of business" and faith in the idea of automatic progress.[45] Not unexpectedly, donations to churches plummeted during the hard times. From 1930 to 1935, the decrease in giving to the Methodist, Congregational, and Presbyterian churches was 38 percent.[46] The Episcopal Church experienced a 35 percent decline in receipts between 1929 and 1934.[47] In the dollar equivalents of the time, contributions in the Episcopal Church to missions declined from $2.25 per capita in 1930 to 96 cents in 1940.[48] In total, religious expenditures by all faiths between 1926 and 1936 dropped 36 percent, from $817 million to $519 million.[49]

Membership in the mainline churches showed a slight decrease during the period 1926–36. Overall church membership in the United States increased during the decade by only 2.3 percent.

The Empty Church

When the Federal Council of Churches promoted an evangelistic National Christian Mission, the results were highly disappointing; seventy million Americans remained unchurched. Many observers thought that the churches were losing influence. A pronouncement by leading churchmen on a major steel strike received much less attention than a similar statement nineteen years earlier.[50]

During the 1930s, Congregational, Reformed, Lutheran, and Methodist bodies united to form larger denominations. The Gallup poll found that seven in ten Americans were church members and about four in ten attended church or synagogue in a typical week—the same numbers we see today. The Bible was consistently found to be the nation's most popular book, but then, as now, comparatively few actually read it.[51]

Ultraconservatives would later claim that the Protestant churches, and in particular the mainline, were riddled with Communists and "pro-Communists" during the 1930s; that liberalism was the gateway to leftist extremism and treason. The charges do not hold up. While many mainline leaders were indeed left of center, especially during the pre–New Deal years, and some moved to the point of radicalism, very few succumbed to totalitarian ideology.

In fact, most Protestant clergy and laity were conservative during the Depression decade. The defeat of Herbert Hoover and the end of prohibition disturbed a great many Protestants. A *Literary Digest* poll conducted in 1936 showed that a majority of Protestant church members voted for Alf Landon; an astounding 78 percent of Congregationalists backed the GOP presidential candidate in the Democratic landslide. A poll of 21,606 clergymen published in 1936 showed that 70 percent of them opposed New Deal policies.[52]

Still, the misery and hopelessness of the era—25 percent of the workforce was unemployed in 1932, and a third of all American farmers lost their land in the first four years of the crisis—prompted some liberal clergy to advocate socialist remedies. The

Fellowship of Socialist Christians, for example, guided by the Union Theological Seminary professor Reinhold Niebuhr, was organized during the winter of 1930–31. (Dietrich Bonhoeffer, a young student at the left-leaning Union Seminary, thought the institution was "accelerating the process of the secularization of Christianity in America."[53]) The General Conference of the Northern Methodists adopted a report in 1932 condemning the profit motive and labeling the industrial order "unchristian, unethical and anti-social."[54] The Northern Baptist Convention said in 1932 that government "must fully exercise its sovereign right to own, control and administer property; to control private business, to coordinate economic activities, to inquire what wealth the citizen possesses, how he got it, and what he does with it."[55] The General Council of the Congregationalists passed a resolution in 1934 pledging "to work toward the abolition of . . . our present competitive profit-seeking economy."[56] Similar sentiments came from Presbyterian and Episcopal bodies.[57] In 1936, the pro-socialist United Christian Council for Democracy was created, containing Methodists, Presbyterians, Episcopalians, Congregationalists, and others.

But this activity reflected the sentiments of only a small minority of mainline members. Niebuhr's fellowship had 100 adherents at one point; the ineffective United Council was created by 85 clerics and a handful of laity.[58] One radical statement that came out of a conference of Congregationalists in 1934 expressed the views of only 130 people.[59] The leftist Church League for Industrial Democracy, created by Episcopalians, had only about a thousand members. Moreover, the General Conference of the Methodists changed its tune in 1936 and condemned socialism.[60]

Some clergy were taken in, often briefly, by the idealistic and antifascist claims of the Soviet Union. Professor Harry F. Ward of Union Theological Seminary, the Methodist clergyman J. B. Matthews, and the Episcopalian William B. Spofford Sr., editor of the *Witness*, are prominent examples. But as a careful study by

Ralph Lord Roy has shown, the Communist Party in America did not undertake a full-scale campaign to infiltrate the churches, and very few clergy (possibly as few as fifty) ever joined the Party. The influence of Communists and fellow travelers in the churches during this period and later was slight.[61]

Indeed, denunciations of socialism and communism could be heard from pulpits all across the country. Conservatives were active among the Presbyterians, Episcopalians, and Methodists.[62] The Disciples of Christ and the Lutherans took a generally moderate position. The Federal Council of Churches, the *Christian Century* (which had a mailing list of a quarter of all the ministers in America), and a great many mainline leaders supported the New Deal.[63] (Council apologists often quoted Franklin D. Roosevelt's quip in 1932 that he was "as radical as the Federal Council.")[64] In short, the vast majority of Protestant clergy and laity, including those in the mainline, retained their confidence in the traditional political, economic, and social system throughout the hard times.

The full effects of World War I and the general suffering of the Great Depression had a sobering impact on many liberal Christian thinkers. To them, liberalism's optimism, idealism, and hope for the Kingdom of God on earth seemed inadequate, superficial, and misleading. One theologian declared in 1934 that liberal theology was dead, "now fallen beneath the same sentence of doom which it so often pronounced upon older systems of theology: O irony of ironies, its 'thought-forms' have become 'outmoded'!"[65]

To the front came a number of "neo-orthodox" writers who attracted widespread attention. Absorbing the works of the European theologians Emil Brunner, Karl Barth, and Paul Tillich, Reinhold and H. Richard Niebuhr, Walter Marshall Horton, John Bennett, and others challenged some of liberalism's most basic assumptions. H. Richard Niebuhr summarized his perception of liberal theology in a single sentence: "A God without

wrath brought men without sin into a kingdom without judgment through the ministrations of a Christ without a cross."[66]

Neo-orthodox leaders sought to return to a more or less orthodox Christianity, stressing biblical revelation, original sin, the lim-
itations of human reason, the transcendence of God, and divine
judgment. Neo-orthodoxy claimed that history was more
"ironic" and "tragic" than liberals perceived it.

The British theologian Bernard M. G. Reardon observed that
with neo-orthodoxy faith "came to be seen less as a rationally
motivated act than, in Barth's own phrases, 'a leap in the void,'
possible for all men 'only because it is equally impossible for all.'
The burden of the neo-orthodox case against liberalism has been
that it has evacuated the gospel of its necessary *offence*."[67]

At the same time, the apostles of neo-orthodoxy separated
themselves from fundamentalists by rejecting biblical infallibility,
showing a deep respect for contemporary knowledge, and emphasizing the desirability of social reform. (Reinhold Niebuhr called
himself a Christian Marxist in the 1930s, and as late as 1940 supported the Socialist Party.) Sydney Ahlstrom called neo-orthodoxy "a reshaped Social Gospel." Others called it "chastened liberalism" and "Christian realism." It had its uses. "Most important
perhaps," wrote Ahlstrom, "it built bridges that opened communications not only with modernists who had all but decided that
Christianity was obsolete, but also with conservatives who had all
but decided that true Christians must repudiate modern modes of
thought and action."[68]

Still, neo-orthodoxy did not prove to be a viable middle
ground between liberalism and fundamentalism. It made a modest
impact on mainline leaders and thinkers for some thirty years before the prudence prompted by depression and war was abandoned. In the end, the liberal faith in the essential goodness of
human nature and the possibility of progress proved too powerful
to be altered permanently by the gloomy chidings of the neo-or-

thodox. Reinhold Niebuhr and his allies failed to persuade many, perhaps most, mainline church leaders of the possibility, if not the necessity, of blending the full supernaturalism of Christianity with modern knowledge and a passion for social reform.

Of course, most Christians knew and cared little about such intellectual matters. Their faith survived in spite of the professors, and their penchant for fundamentalism remained powerful. As late as 1963, 65 percent of Americans told Gallup pollsters that they believed the Bible to be literally true.[69]

Many liberal church leaders remained firmly within the boundaries of public opinion between the world wars by actively promoting pacifism. They argued, as did many, that World War I had been a gigantic, and no doubt avoidable, disaster. Several denominations earned the wrath of numerous congressmen and military officers by calling for the abolition of military training in schools and colleges. The Federal Council of Churches lobbied for disarmament. Throughout the Depression years, despite the emergence of aggressive totalitarianism or authoritarianism in Germany, Italy, Spain, and Japan, declarations favoring peace emerged from church meetings of all sorts. All wars, said the liberals, resulted from rival imperialisms, settled nothing, and should and could be outlawed.[70]

When Europe went to war in 1939, liberals split over American involvement. The editor of the *Christian Century*, thinking President Roosevelt too hawkish, worked against his reelection to a third term. Reinhold Niebuhr, on the other hand, saw resistance to fascism a Christian duty and created a rival publication, *Christianity and Crisis*, to promote his views. But with the Japanese attack on Pearl Harbor, the rift was largely healed and virtually all liberal church leaders backed their country's war effort. Some of those who had promoted pacifism and isolationism signed on in sadness, acknowledging that their rosy view of human nature had proved faulty.[71]

The mainline churches were highly active during World War II, ministering to the Japanese American evacuees from the West

Coast, distributing religious literature, helping servicepeople and their families, participating in USO programs, channeling private relief funds, and so on. The Federal Council of Churches and the National Association of Evangelicals, a fundamentalist and evangelical body formed in 1942, accredited ministers to serve as military chaplains.

In March 1942, liberal church leaders again proved that their views were well to the left of most Americans. Nearly four hundred mainline denominational leaders met at Delaware, Ohio, and attempted to formulate a Protestant response to America's involvement in the war. Their recommendations included an end to "the sovereign power of the nation-state" and the creation of a world government, economic systems that were flexible and responsive to human needs, a redistribution of the world's resources, and racial justice for all. *Time* magazine thought the conference "definitely pinko," and efforts to drum up support for the recommendations got nowhere.[72] On the other hand, mainline church leaders, Methodists in particular, used their moral and political influence to back the United Nations from its inception, a move that proved reasonably popular. Paul A. Carter has written, "The wartime and postwar championing of the United Nations by the churches was in a very real sense the cry of their pacifist conscience, transmuted."[73]

Soon after the conclusion of the hostilities, it became evident that America was headed for a religious revival—the seventh in a long series of national "awakenings" dating from 1730. Church construction data alone made the point. In 1946 the total spent was $76 million. By 1950 the figure had risen to $409 million, and by the end of the decade it had soared to over a billion dollars.[74]

Church membership rose from about 70 million to over 100 million between 1945 and 1955. In 1955 and 1958, a record 49 percent of Americans said they had attended church or synagogue in the past week. Southern Baptists added nearly 400,000 members during the first four years after the war. The Disciples of

Christ announced the largest membership gains in three decades. Catholics baptized about a million infants a year. The Methodist Church, the largest single Protestant body in the country, grew rapidly and in 1948 projected a need for nearly 3,000 additional clergy within the next five years.[75]

By 1952, 73 percent identified themselves as members of a church or synagogue, down only three points from the record set in 1947. Evangelism was underway at an astonishing pace, with as many as 60 percent of Americans reporting that they had been called upon to attend or join a church.[76]

Evangelicals and fundamentalists, highly active during the war, were thriving by the late 1940s. Their goals, said the evangelist Torrey Johnson, were "the spiritual revitalization of America" and the "complete evangelization of the world in our generation."[77] The million-member National Association of Evangelicals launched, among other things, the National Religious Broadcasting Association, the National Sunday School Association, and the Evangelical Foreign Missionary Association. By 1946, Youth for Christ had sponsored some nine hundred rallies around the country, bringing the gospel to as many as a million young people.[78]

By 1952, some 18,000 North American missionaries were serving overseas, about 44 percent of whom were sponsored by evangelical organizations. By 1960, the total number of missionaries had grown to more than 29,000, and the proportion sent by evangelicals had risen to 65 percent.[79]

In 1947, the highly influential Fuller Theological Seminary was founded in Pasadena, California. From it came the New Evangelicalism, a successful effort by conservative evangelicals to reform fundamentalism by making it more scholarly and involved with social issues.[80]

In response to an acute postwar shortage of clergy, the number of students in Protestant and Jewish seminaries by 1950 was almost double the prewar number. Catholic seminary enrollment was up by 30 percent.[81] On college campuses, denominational centers flourished during the 1950s as never before, with 1,500 full-time professional workers involved by 1963.[82] The powerful Danforth Foundation spent millions on campus ministry and the education of religiously inclined academics. In 1959, the interdenominational National Student Christian Federation was formed.[83]

Public opinion polls clearly reflected what was going on. In 1952, for example, 75 percent of Americans said that religion was "very important" in their lives. Five years later, 69 percent said that religion was increasing its influence on American life. That same year, 81 percent of Americans expressed the belief that religion could answer all or most of life's problems.[84]

Millions watched the evangelist Billy Graham and the Roman Catholic Bishop Fulton J. Sheen on television. The National Broadcasting Company commissioned, and showed repeatedly, Gian Carlo Menotti's *Amahl and the Night Visitors*, an opera about Christ's Nativity. Hollywood filled theaters with biblical epics and made *A Man Called Peter*, glorifying a devout minister who became chaplain to the United States Senate. Christian book sales boomed, and in 1953 alone six of the top eight best-sellers in nonfiction contained religious themes. Six major Protestant clergymen appeared on covers of *Time* magazine between 1951 and 1961. The theologians Reinhold Niebuhr and Paul Tillich were among several Christian thinkers who were widely read and respected. The British scholar and apologist C. S. Lewis attracted much attention, although what has been called his "uncompromising orthodoxy" did not appeal to some liberals.[85]

When asked in 1954 to explain the religious revival, 30 percent of those interviewed by Gallup pollsters attributed it to fear, unrest, and uncertainty about the future. This no doubt reflected tensions associated with the Cold War, the "undeclared" Korean War, and McCarthyism. Another 30 percent pointed to a renewal of faith and the effect of religion on military personnel during the war. Churches themselves were responsible for some of the activity, with 9 percent of those interviewed by Gallup noting an improvement in church programming and publicity.[86]

Scholars have often pointed to the respectability offered by church attendance in the 1950s. Going to church was what proper, middle-class, suburban people did on Sunday mornings. And membership in the mainline churches often signified upward socioeconomic mobility.[87] (The proportion of mainline members to the population as a whole, however, dropped steadily from 1940 to 1960, while the figures for evangelicals and Roman Catholics increased.[88]) Then, too, participation in the life of a church was directly involved in the strong emphasis upon the family current at the time. It was also connected with patriotism and the powerful feeling of confidence Americans had in their government and in virtually every major institution.[89]

Religious understanding during this decade was often shallow. Gallup discovered in 1954 that only 34 percent of Americans knew who delivered the Sermon on the Mount. Only 35 percent could name all four Gospels in the New Testament.[90]

Several church leaders at the time expressed doubts about the authenticity of the revival. Gerald Hamilton Kennedy, the president of the Methodist Council of Bishops, said of religious publications: "Most of the so-called devotional material is shallow and meaningless tripe that makes me sick to my stomach."[91] *Time* magazine declared in 1961 that the religious revival had "served up a kind of Christianity as bland and homogenized as if it came out of a suburban kitchen blender."[92] Three sociologists later suggested that people joined the mainline churches in the postwar years "seeking a more relaxed, less legalistic, less dogmatic version of the faith."[93]

Much of the faith of these prosperous, self-confident years had to do with positive thinking, self-growth, and self-realization, an emphasis that no doubt was strongest among the mainliners. Norman Vincent Peale's enormously popular writings and sermons best illustrate the point. Paul Vitz has called this version of the faith "pure selfism," occurring at a time "in which a generation of faltering Christians, bored with and skeptical of basic Christian theology and ignorant of spiritual life, accepted an increasingly humanist notion of the self that had been dressed up with superficial Christian language and concepts."[94]

The Social Gospel remained a vital part of mainline thought, and in the late 1940s and 1950s the Protestant establishment continued to endorse a variety of liberal reforms. It also backed internationalism and supported America's Cold War efforts. At times, church leaders became directly involved in current events. The Federal Council of Churches, for example, held seminars to generate support for the European Recovery Plan, and General George Marshall, John Foster Dulles, and members of Congress attended church rallies on the topic. The Commission on International Affairs, in essence the administrative arm of the World Council of Churches (created in 1948), had close ties with United Nations organizations.[95]

The Eisenhower administration, however, resisted private efforts by the prominent Methodist Bishop G. Bromley Oxnam to forge a close relationship between government and the mainline churches. The president, Secretary of State John Foster Dulles, and other Republican leaders chose to keep a respectful distance between themselves and liberal clerics.[96]

One reason for this aloofness involved persistent charges during the Second Red Scare that mainline church bodies were riddled with traitors. The McCarthyite Edgar C. Bundy, for example, called the National Council of Churches–sponsored Revised Standard Version of the Bible "subversive" and characterized Oxnam as "the Red Dean of North America." The Tulsa evangelist Billy James Hargis distributed "The National Council of Churches Indicts Itself on 50 Counts of Treason to God and Country," a pamphlet that included the charge that the old Federal Council of Churches had been responsible for the disaster at

Pearl Harbor. Joseph Zach Kornfedder estimated that there were six hundred secret Party members in the Methodist clergy and that two thousand more "were pretty close to the machine." J. B. Matthews declared in *American Mercury* that "The largest single group supporting the Communist apparatus in the United States today is composed of Protestant clergymen," a charge so outrageous that President Eisenhower protested. The *Reader's Digest*, the Hearst newspapers, the radio commentators Fulton Lewis Jr. and Paul Harvey, the American Legion, and others frightened millions by publicizing similar charges.[97]

In 1960, the Federal Communications Commission, reversing a long-standing policy, declared that radio and television stations could now use paid programming as required public service broadcasting. This virtually silenced the mainline churches, which had long been depending on free time to get their message across.[98] The failure of these churches, hardly suffering from poverty, to raise the necessary funds to keep on the air revealed a spiritual malaise that in retrospect appears tragic. Hereafter, the fundamentalists and evangelicals would have the media, growing in influence as never before, almost to themselves.

During the early 1960s, it became apparent that the postwar religious revival had passed its peak. In 1962, 31 percent of Americans told Gallup pollsters that they thought religion was losing its influence. Just five years earlier that figure had stood at 14 percent.[99]

In 1962, the Consultation on Church Union (COCU) was brought into existence by the United Presbyterian Church (USA), the Episcopal Church, the Methodist Church, and the United Church of Christ, the aim being united action and union. A Southern Baptist leader said at the time that the proposal was "an indication of weakness rather than strength. Lack of conviction led to these denominations' decline, and the decline will continue because such mergers are based on expediency and convenience."

The scholars Dean Kelley, Roger Finke, and Rodney Stark later agreed with the general evaluation.[100]

The Kennedy administration contributed to the public's increasingly temporal outlook. Insiders knew that the president was wholly cynical about religious matters, and many others noted an absence of the sort of public pieties that came, by word and deed, from Truman and Eisenhower. (One cannot imagine Ike befriending the "Rat Pack" or having a public birthday party featuring Marilyn Monroe.) Belated rhetoric about the high morality of the civil rights movement was the administration's major contribution to the nation's spiritual well-being.[101]

The United States Supreme Court played a much more significant role, and its activity in this area was greater than ever before. As James Davison Hunter has pointed out, "at the Supreme Court level, the first three-fourths of America's history as a nation witnessed only one-fourth of the religion cases while the last fourth of American history has witnessed three-fourths of the religion cases."[102]

In 1947, in *Everson v. Board of Education*, the Court had declared that the First Amendment erected "a wall of separation between church and state," an edifice that applied to the states through the Fourteenth Amendment. The "wall" phrase came from a famous letter of 1802 from Thomas Jefferson to the Danbury (Connecticut) Baptists. The Supreme Court had first put it into the legal record in 1878 when outlawing the practice of polygamy among the Mormons.

In 1948, in *Illinois ex rel. McCollum v. Board of Education*, the Court had banned voluntary "released time" in the public schools for religious instruction. This was the first time in American history that a state action had been invalidated on the grounds that it established religion.[103]

In 1961, in *Torcaso v. Watkins*, the Court declared that a state could not require public employees to believe in the existence of

God. Among the religions listed in the majority decision that did not include a belief in God was Secular Humanism. It was clear from this point on that nontheistic and secularistic ideologies were protected by the First Amendment religion clauses. The following year, the Court ruled in *Engel v. Vitale* that under the First Amendment a state could not sponsor prayers in its schools. The twenty-two–word prayer in question was nondenominational, and student participation was voluntary.[104]

The neo-orthodox *Christianity and Crisis* wondered whether the latest decision would "work so consistently in the direction of a secularization of the school system as to amount to the suppression of religion and to give the impression that government must be anti-religion. This impression is certainly not consonant with the mood of either the Founding Fathers or our long tradition of separation of church and state, which is based on neutrality and not animosity." The liberal *New Republic* commented, "By and large public schools have in recent years tried to be not only non-denominational but secular," adding approvingly that the Court decision gave "recognition to the relatively recent phenomenon of a widespread secular humanism in the country which constitutes, as it were, a new religion of its own."[105]

In 1963, in *Abington v. Schempp*, the Supreme Court struck down state-sponsored Bible reading and recitation of the Lord's Prayer in public schools. The "wall of separation" between church and state was becoming an iron curtain. Justice Tom C. Clark asserted that the Constitution required a "strict neutrality" toward religion, adding, however, that the study of religion, as opposed to religious exercises, was still permissible. Justice William J. Brennan Jr. pointed to "the vastly more diverse" population in modern America, noting the need to protect the rights of those who worshipped no God at all. In a dissent, Justice Potter Stewart suggested that there was "a religion of secularism" and that the refusal to permit religious exercises in the public schools could encourage the "establishment" of it.[106]

A great many conservatives expressed outrage over these reli-gio-phobic court decisions. Cardinal Spellman was "shocked and frightened" at *Engel*, while Billy Graham was "shocked and disap-pointed."[107] The *Wall Street Journal* commented at the same time, "If the majority doctrine stands, then anything that smacks of re-ligious instruction or the subtle imparting of a religious viewpoint in the public schools becomes suspect. Do not suppose this to be a fanciful exaggeration. . . . Already a Florida court decision has declared school observances at Easter and Christmas to be uncon-stitutional, and similar efforts are afoot elsewhere. (Poor kids, if they can't even sing Christmas carols.)"[108] The *Washington Evening Star* said of *Abington*, "God and religion have all but been driven from the public schools. What remains? Will the baccalaureate service and Christmas carols be the next to go? Don't bet against it."[109] In 1962, a Gallup poll had shown 79 percent of the public favoring religious observances in the public schools.[110]

On the other hand, *The Christian Century*, the unofficial voice of the mainline churches, strongly approved of the trend in Supreme Court decisions. In 1948, it not only agreed with the Court but went on to question the constitutionality of military chaplains. In 1962, it contended that the government "is and must remain secular," adding, "It is not secular*istic* nor is it devoted to the teaching of secularism, but it *is* separated from any religious establishment, including establishment of religion-in-general." In 1963, it argued that Bible reading in the schools could turn into "incantation" that would encourage "superstition."[111]

The Supreme Court position appeared to be reflecting a grow-ing secularism in American life, especially among elites. In higher education, for example, secularism had been growing steadily during the postwar period. The G.I. Bill and a large influx of first-generation college students had altered traditional liberal arts re-quirements and compelled institutions to offer more job-oriented courses. Modern research universities were growing, little inter-ested in theological and philosophical matters. Professors, as

William F. Buckley Jr. lamented in 1951 in *God and Man at Yale*, had grown increasingly open about their secular predilections.[112] A study by the sociologist Dean R. Hoge showed the level of religious orthodoxy among selected college and university students rising during the 1940s, reaching a high point in about 1952–55, and falling rapidly thereafter.[113]

Mainline Christian colleges, which tended, like the parent denominations, to blend into the culture, were losing their distinctiveness and much of their reason for being. Presbyterian colleges, for example, were in disarray as early as the late 1940s. Floundering about in an increasingly pluralistic educational milieu, they tried lamely to harmonize the traditional faith with current trends. Illinois College declared that it would "endeavor to hold before its students Christian ideals of life and conduct as essential to a complete personality." Trinity University proclaimed that "education at its best is essentially Christian, cultural and useful."[114]

The growth of secularism was experienced in the Catholic colleges and universities as well. From the 1930s through the mid-1950s, Catholic educators had been self-consciously countercultural, decrying secularism and stressing traditional church theology. Numerous liberal Catholics, however, sought to minimize the distinctions between their faith and society, and by the late 1950s, several institutions were attempting to emulate the "intellectual excellence" found at Harvard and Berkeley. This led inevitably to the rise of a more secular, "contemporary" outlook. Numerous Catholic scholars were eager to embrace respectability by abandoning what Monsignor John Tracy Ellis called their "self-imposed ghetto mentality."[115]

By the early 1960s, mainline seminary professors who were eager to be on the "cutting edge" and accepted by the secular universities seemed restless and bored. The Methodist Bishop Gerald Kennedy complained: "Many influential theologians of our day have moved from the ruins of a devastated Europe to the libraries of the theological schools and have carried defeatism into these sacred precincts—locking themselves up in their little cells with their egos, their textbooks, their jargon and their pessimism."[116]

Theological liberalism had grown stale. In 1961 the Episcopal Bishop James A. Pike made headlines by repeating a litany of complaints about the Bible, and eventually denied, among other things, the Incarnation, the Trinity, the Virgin Birth, and the bodily resurrection of Christ. (His fellow bishops rejected calls to try him for heresy.[117]) In 1963, a similar flap over the liberal Anglican Bishop John T. Robinson's *Honest to God* produced little that was novel or valuable.[118] Christian existentialism, which reduced theology to anthropology, had been around for many decades and was too arcane to excite. Neo-orthodoxy had peaked in the early and mid-1950s and was rapidly falling out of fashion.[119] The editor of the mainline *Christian Scholar* asked, "Whence the theological doldrums? Why is there so little intensive theological work being done today?"[120]

The time was ripe for bold new experiments. In October 1962, the Second Vatican Council opened in Rome, and within a short time there were rumors of major changes in the works. *Time* magazine exclaimed: "A new mood of liberalism is eddying through the Roman Catholic Church." A thirty-five-year-old priest-theologian from Tübingen University named Hans Kung was drawing huge and enthusiastic audiences across the country by proposing what was called "a fresh, provocative discussion of the place of freedom in the Catholic Church."[121] If monolithic and tradition-bound Rome could make a sharp turn to the left, what might the liberal Protestants do?

The rapid rise of secularism, the superficiality of the public's Christian faith, the general emptiness of theology, and the restlessness of clergy made liberal Christianity highly vulnerable to the cultural revolution that was about to break out. Following the shattering experience of the Kennedy assassination, and not long after Lyndon Johnson led the nation into the Vietnam War, the mainline churches found themselves virtually helpless to resist the Age of Aquarius. Indeed, many liberal religious leaders praised, supported, and directed the varied legions intent on transforming the world.

5

STUCK IN THE SIXTIES

In the chaotic period from 1965 to 1975, the mainline churches declined rapidly in several ways. For the first time in American history, the major church groups stopped growing and began to shrink. Then, too, religious giving in relation to inflation fell off, and new church construction declined.[1] Young, educated, middle-class men and women seemed especially alienated, in particular those who shared in the cultural upheavals.[2] Intellectuals used such terms as post-Protestant, post-Puritan, postreligious, and secular city to describe this era.[3]

A Gallup poll conducted in 1968 showed that 67 percent thought religion was losing its impact on society. A few years later, the figure had risen to 75 percent. Major reasons included the belief that the church was outdated, irrelevant, that morals were breaking down, and that people were becoming materialistic. In a 1971 Gallup survey, almost 40 percent of the Catholic and Protestant clergy under forty years of age said they had given serious thought to leaving the ministry. (Between 1966 and 1969, in the immediate aftermath of Vatican II, which "modernized" the Catholic Church, the number of nuns in America decreased by 14,000, and the number of seminarians by 30 percent. By 1976, 35,000 nuns and 10,000 priests had departed.[4]) Church-going dropped nine percentage points between 1958 and the early seventies.[5]

In sharp contrast, conservative churches continued to grow. In 1967, the Southern Baptists overtook the Methodists, becoming the nation's largest Protestant body. Data on missionary personnel reflected the change. Between 1958 and 1971, the number sent out by the Southern Baptist Convention grew from 1,186 to 2,494. The United Methodist overseas task force decreased during the same period from 1,453 to 1,175.[6]

Many thought that the success of conservative churches was explained in part by the fact that they offered clear-cut answers to religious questions and engaged in evangelization.[7] In 1972, as we have seen, Dean Kelley's *Why Conservative Churches Are Growing* pointed to the vital relationship among firm convictions, strictness, exclusivity, and growth. ("When a handful of wholly committed human beings give themselves fully to a great cause or faith, they are virtually irresistible."[8]) Then, too, the conservative churches tended to reject the new culture of the era. Roof and McKinney state: "Careful analysis of membership trends shows that the churches hardest hit were those highest in socioeconomic status, those stressing individualism and pluralism in belief, and those most affirming of American culture."[9]

Roof and McKinney might well have said "liberal American culture," for it was not the culture of the people who twice elected Richard Nixon to the presidency that excited the leadership of the mainline churches during this period. Literally thousands of examples can be cited to document the fact that liberals were caught up in the idealism, folly, and general pandemonium of the era to a far greater extent than the average person in the pews. Indeed, liberal clergy and laity often boasted of what they saw as their exceptional enlightenment and decried the inability and unwillingness of Christians in general to share in their commitment to "higher" causes.

In some cases the causes were indeed higher. The mainline churches were active in the struggle for racial equality, for example, having an impact on the civil rights movement in which they may always take pride. The Episcopal Church, the United Church of Christ, the Disciples of Christ, the United Presbyterian Church, and the National Council of Churches formed their own race relations commissions. Clergy and laity alike often took strong positions on the issue, and some marched and even faced violence to rid the nation of the ugliness of racial segregation. In 1963, a month before the Washington, D.C., demonstration led by Martin Luther King Jr., several prominent religious leaders set a precedent by being arrested in a civil rights march. The list included Eugene Carson Blake, the chief executive officer of the United Presbyterian Church, and Bishop Daniel Corrigan of the National Council of the Episcopal Church. It was generally acknowledged that the support of religious groups was crucial in passage of the Civil Rights Act of 1964.[10]

In response to racial violence in Mississippi and Alabama in 1963, for example, the General Synod of the United Church of Christ created a highly active Commission on Racial Justice. (By the mid-1980s, the commission had an annual budget of $1.1 million and a twenty-one–member staff.[11]) The Church's Office of Communication, under the leadership of Dr. Everett C. Parker, took significant steps to end racial discrimination in the broadcasting industry.[12] In 1965, the church elected its first black moderator and went on record as favoring an array of bold efforts to win racial equality.[13] A year later, the UCC joined other mainline churches in a multimillion dollar effort to stimulate the construction of low-rent housing throughout the nation.[14] In 1967 it contributed to a successful effort to pressure the Eastman Kodak Company to hire and train blacks.[15] The Rev. Robert V. Moss Jr., the UCC president, urged his denomination to "pursue relentlessly and with singleness of purpose absolute equality for the black man and his right to determine his own destiny."[16]

In 1964, the Lutheran Church in America passed a strongly worded statement endorsing racial equality, civil rights legislation, and civil disobedience. It condemned discrimination in churches, urged church publications to stress racial diversity and "the Christian's responsibility in the struggle for racial justice," and called on the "church, its congregations, synods, agencies and institutions" to "initiate and participate in efforts to bring about understanding at points of racial tension."[17]

The mainline Presbyterians, divided into northern and southern branches before their merger in 1983, took a similar stance. In 1965, the General Assembly of the Southern Presbyterian Church approved nonviolent civil disobedience by civil rights groups. Two years later it approved a strongly worded statement "repenting of discrimination" and requiring all synods to report on steps taken to end the "demonic power" of racial discrimination in church institutions. (Such boldness helped bring on a schism in 1973.)[18] Up north, the United Presbyterian Church set a precedent among predominantly white churches in 1964 by electing a black to the denomination's top office. Three years later, the church approved a new confession of faith that recognized for the first time the church's responsibility to be concerned with social problems and singled out racial integration as a special mission.[19]

In 1965, the first African American minister was named to the American Baptist Ministers Council. The general secretary of the American Baptist Convention (precursor of the present body) said, "We are making every effort to involve Negroes in all aspects of the life and work of American Baptists." Four years later, the convention elected its first black president.[20]

The Episcopal Church was on record as early as 1955 as strongly favoring racial integration. The General Convention that year declared that "discrimination and segregation are contrary to the mind of Christ and the will of God."[21] In 1959, clergy and laity organized the Episcopal Society for Cultural and Racial Unity, and partly as a result of its activism, Episcopal clergy and laity participated in marches and sit-ins during the early 1960s.[22] In 1961, The Rt. Rev. Arthur Lichtenberger, the presiding bishop of the Episcopal Church, and the national church staff issued a statement giving a theological rationale for civil disobedience. At the same time, the General Convention passed several strong resolutions condemning racial segregation.[23] In 1964, the church had a $100,000 civil rights fund, and 51 Episcopalians were at work on civil rights projects.[24] That October, the General Convention banned the exclusion of any member from worship in any parish on racial grounds.[25]

With the consecration in 1965 of the militantly liberal Bishop John E. Hines as Lichtenberger's successor, the Episcopal Church began taking even stronger positions and actions on a variety of issues, including civil rights. In 1967, for example, the General Convention announced a Special Program that included channeling $3 million during each of the following three years to African American, Native American, and Hispanic organizations. The sum included a controversial appropriation of $500,000 earmarked specifically for groups seeking "black economic and political power."[26]

In 1963, the National Council of Churches created its Commission on Religion and Race, which became highly involved in the civil rights scene, including cosponsorship of the March on Washington in 1964.[27] The NCC's Delta Ministry in Mississippi, which had a staff of fifty-five in 1966, was active in voter registration, citizenship education, welfare rights, and economic improvement for blacks.[28] In 1967, the year in which Newark and Detroit went up in flames during the "long hot summer," NCC leaders voted to invest funds in urban ghettos and ask member denominations to endorse economic boycotts of companies practicing "exploitation or discrimination."[29] In the early 1970s, the National Council had its first black president and was part of a mainline church effort to curtail corporate investments in South Africa.[30]

As the peaceful and self-sacrificing messages of Martin Luther King Jr. gave way to extreme militance, separatism, and violence in the late 1960s, some mainline clergy and laity were swept along with the increasingly radical tide. Often armed with little more than liberal pieties about the basic innocence and goodness of the oppressed, they were not prepared to deal effectively with those who sought more than racial equality.

In 1969, "black power" militant James Forman and some followers invaded a communion service at Manhattan's liberal Riverside Church. Forman read a "Black Manifesto" demanding $500 million in "reparations" from the nation's churches and synagogues in compensation for past discrimination. (He later upped the ante to $3 billion.) The preamble to Forman's document characterized the United States government as "this racist, imperialist government that is choking the life of all the people around the world." Calling the nation "the most barbaric country in the world," the preamble added, "we have a chance to help bring this government down." The document mentioned "armed struggle" if necessary.[31]

Before long, Forman was demanding, among other things, $50 million from the Lutheran Church in America, $60 million from the American Baptist Convention, $200 million from U.S. Roman Catholics, and $60 million (plus 60 percent a year of the income from all church assets) from the Episcopal Church. He wanted the National Council of Churches to disband and reassign all its assets to black development. Having disrupted a meeting of the NCC to make his point, he concluded: "People who believe in the Black Manifesto will forever be a plague upon the racist white churches and synagogues of America."[32]

The Roman Catholic Archdiocese of New York, the General Board of the Disciples of Christ, the black president of the American Baptist Convention, and several Jewish organizations rejected

Forman's demands outright. Episcopal Presiding Bishop Hines called the manifesto "calculatedly revolutionary, Marxist, inflammatory, anti-Semitic and anti-Christian."[33] Others were more positive.

The General Synod of the United Church of Christ invited Forman to address it, and Robert V. Moss Jr., the denomination's president, said that he strongly favored creating a $10 million fund. Forman, exclaimed Moss, was a "prophetic" figure.[34]

Forman appeared before the General Assembly of the United Presbyterian Church and asked that body to pay $80 million in cash to his National Black Economic Development Conference, to liquidate its assets in South Africa and turn the money over to the Conference, to give blacks 60 percent of the church's annual income, and to deed church lands in the South to poor blacks and in New Mexico to Mexican Americans. While the Presbyterians made no mention of channeling funds to Forman, they vowed to set up machinery to raise $50 million for use "in depressed areas for deprived people" and earmarked $200,000 for other minority causes.[35] (In 1971, the General Assembly voted to grant $10,000 to the Angela Davis defense committee. Davis, a black militant and avowed Communist who had been on the FBI's Ten Most Wanted list, was in prison charged with murder, kidnapping, and criminal conspiracy.[36])

An international conference sponsored by the World Council of Churches, chaired by the Democratic Senator George McGovern, urged church support for "guerrilla fighters" and "resistance movements, including revolutions, which are aimed at the elimination of political or economic tyranny that makes racism possible."[37] Sixteen black theologians meeting under the auspices of the six-hundred–member National Committee of Black Churchmen endorsed Forman's reparations demand, including its call for violence. The Methodist Bishop Joseph A. Johnson declared, "I see no possible way to change the structures of injustice except through violence." A Roman Catholic priest present at the meeting declared: "Deliberate, planned violence can be morally justified, and violence can play a role in effecting social change."[38]

A Special General Convention of the Episcopal Church yielded to intimidation by black militants and voted to give $200,000 to the National Committee of Black Churchmen. Delegates knew that the money was intended eventually to reach James Forman's Black Economic Development Conference. The Episcopal Church thus became the first denomination to respond with cash to Black Manifesto reparation demands.[39] (A large-scale "pocketbook rebellion" from the pews over this and other controversial grants to radicals prompted Presiding Bishop Hines to retire early.[40])

By mid-1971, Forman's Black Manifesto had raised only about $300,000. But indirectly, by appealing to the idealism, guilt, and fear of the white majority in the mainline denominations, the fiery demand helped generate millions. By 1971, the United Methodist Church, for example, voted to spend $4 million on various minority community efforts, over and above pre-Manifesto efforts. The Disciples of Christ doubled the $2 million previously earmarked for a "reconciliation" project. ("I thank the Lord for the Manifesto," said the black director of the Disciples' program.[41]) By 1972, the Episcopal Church had paid out some $6.5 million in grants for "minority group empowerment."[42] The extent to which these funds actually helped impoverished minorities remains to be studied, but skepticism seems warranted.[43]

Members of the mainline, like the public as a whole, were divided on the Vietnam War. The Disciples of Christ, to which Lyndon Johnson belonged, avoided a clear-cut stand on the war in 1966.[44] The Episcopal Church was never able to come up with a formal statement that either favored or rejected the conflict.[45] But not long after the massive American escalations by President Johnson and his Kennedy administration advisers, voices within the mainline began to express strong concern.

As early as June 1965, the General Board of the National Council of Churches asked the government to reappraise its Vietnam policy.[46] In 1966, the Lutheran Church in America expressed misgivings, listing six "especially troubling" aspects of the conflict that included "The steady escalation of military commitments in Vietnam and, with it, the increased danger of a full-scale war in Asia."[47] By 1967, both Northern and Southern Presbyterians were raising serious questions about American participation in the struggle.[48] The United Church of Christ had similar doubts.[49]

Critics in general argued that the United States had intervened in a civil war, that the conflict was illegal, that we were waging racial aggression against an Oriental people, that we were punishing blacks and the poor by drafting them and sending them to the front in larger proportion than their share of the population, that we were squandering billions that could be better spent at home, that we were trying to dominate the world, and so on.

By 1968, as the mood on the left became more radical, and violence at home and abroad became almost a way of life, many mainline leaders stepped up their criticism of the war. The National Council of Churches, for example, called upon the U.S. government to halt the bombing of North Vietnam and learn to think of its citizens as human beings rather than as "Congs," "Communists," or "guerrillas."[50] A year later, with half a million Americans in Vietnam, the organization voted overwhelmingly in favor of a resolution defending critics of the war, and urged that the United States withdraw all troops by the end of 1970. (When the NCC failed to "accept and hold in trust" a young war resister's draft card, the Episcopal priest Dick York walked along the officers' table, splashing red paint on their papers, and shouted into a microphone, "The blood of the Vietnamese is upon you!"[51])

By 1970, in Sydney Ahlstrom's words, "the nation's sense of unity had fallen to its lowest point since 1861."[52] Eugene Carson Blake, the general secretary of the World Council of Churches, told the General Assembly of his fellow United Presbyterians that Christians all over the globe, with very few exceptions, thought America morally wrong in Vietnam. They based their position in part, he said, on a belief that "the United States is as hypocritical and self-righteous as the U.S.S.R. and is proving itself morally bankrupt in the world scene."[53] The House of Bishops of the Episcopal Church asked the U.S. government "to cease immediately and finally the bombing of the people and country of Vietnam; and to withdraw all American forces . . . by December, 1971."[54] The American Baptist Convention called on President Nixon "to get Americans out of the conflict in Southeast Asia," and in mid-1971 sought withdrawal by the end of the year.[55]

In early 1972, a research unit of the National Council of Churches condemned ten Protestant denominations (including all of the mainline churches) for having investments associated in any way with military production.[56] Soon, the General Board of the NCC initiated a huge peace rally, representing Protestants, Roman Catholics, Eastern Orthodox, and Jews. A formal statement condemned the war and President Nixon, and called for immediate U.S. withdrawal from Vietnam and the cessation of all aid to Indochinese governments.[57]

Later that year, the United Presbyterians, the United Church of Christ, the American Baptist Convention, the National Conference of Churches, and several Catholic and Jewish organizations were expressing support for a variety of war dissenters.[58] The General Board of the National Council of Churches, the United Presbyterian Church, the United Church of Christ's Executive council, and the United Methodists' Board of Christian Social Concerns filed friend-of-the-court briefs in a federal lawsuit, challenging the legality of the war.[59] At year's end, the National Council of Churches asked member bodies to provide relief funds for North Vietnam as well as South Vietnam.[60]

In 1973, the Disciples of Christ endorsed amnesty for draft evaders.[61] The American Baptist Convention gave an award to the antiwar activist William Sloane Coffin Jr.[62]

Of course, serious Christians could be found on both sides of the most controversial war in our history. On the right, many cheered the effort to defend allies and halt the spread of communism. That had been the basis of American foreign policy since World War II. Proponents were also convinced that dissenters prolonged the war and aided the enemy. The arguments continue.

On the whole, however, mainline opposition, tainted as it sometimes was with extremism and anti-Americanism, appears sensible and just. The prolonged conflict was pointless (we were often fighting the people we came to save) and deadly beyond expectation. It corrupted the United States with division, drugs, rage, and despair. We were censured all over the world.

Christians, Protestant and Catholic, cried out for peace, and in this case it was their moral duty. In 1995, Robert McNamara, one of the war's architects, finally admitted as much, saying that American involvement in Vietnam was "terribly wrong."

It is easy to see that now, as we have restored relations with Vietnam and observe that the "dominoes" did not fall in Southeast Asia, causing the whole region to become Communist. But millions of Americans understood the essential futility and immorality of the conflict at the time and took steps to stop it. Some of them belonged to and lead the mainline churches.

The struggles in this period over women's rights were also highly divisive, perhaps especially among the most thoughtful Christians. In much quoted Galatians 3:28, St. Paul had declared men and women equal in baptism. But elsewhere in the Bible, in particular the writings of St. Paul, women were declared and assumed to be subordinate to men.[63] Christianity, like Judaism, was patriarchal.

In Scripture, God chose to reveal Himself in the form of a male. Jesus called God his father and said he was the Son of God. While he showed considerable sensitivity toward women, he chose male disciples. From the beginning, Christians had practiced their faith under male leadership.

The steady advance of democracy during the nineteenth century, however, began to alter this view slightly. Women spoke up at revival meetings, Free Will Baptists had female preachers, and in 1853 the Congregationalists ordained a woman. Women played major roles in the temperance and abolition movements, and proved themselves effective in leading the women's suffrage campaign. Women served as foreign missionaries after the Civil War, attended Bible institutes, and worked in churches in many capacities.

In the twentieth century, evidence mounted, especially during wartime, that women could handle any intellectual challenge and responsibility. When permitted, many excelled in theological studies. So why should they be excluded from the clergy?

In the civil rights climate of the 1960s, it was increasingly difficult to limit the role of women in churches—at least liberal Protestant churches. Mainline seminaries had tended for many decades to see the Bible, certainly selected portions of it, as a product of its time and place. That was St. Paul, not God, speaking harshly about women, professors said. (St. Paul exclaimed at one point that his teaching on the subject came directly from God.[64]) And as for the two thousand years of church tradition—well, look how long slavery had been sanctioned by Scripture. Besides, Protestants rejoiced in their freedom, often thinking themselves liberated from the past. Truth evolved, many liberals believed; the Holy Spirit was constantly guiding discerning Christians—i.e., themselves—into new and better avenues of understanding.

The issue was complicated because women themselves were divided about their goals. There were nonfeminists, more or less content to live in a traditional way; moderate feminists, who wanted fairness and equality of opportunity; and radical feminists, who sought power above all, and often made little effort to disguise their contempt for traditional institutions and moral values. The historic Christian faith was among the radicals' prime targets. In the heat of the Age of Aquarius, many mainline Protestants failed to distinguish one group of women from another. Those furthest to the left and making the most noise (and thus receiving the most attention in academia and the media) were assumed to speak for all women.

Theological arguments for and against the ordination of women were plentiful, if often opaque.[65] Some, like the Roman Catholic hierarchy, preferred not to debate at all, contending that the issue had long been settled. The Orthodox and many Protestant fundamentalists tended to agree.

In practice, pro-ordination arguments centered largely around the currently popular issue of equal rights. Sooner or later, in one way or another, proponents would ask a trenchant question: Are you or are you not in favor of discriminating against women? It could cause even the most formidable conservatives to sputter, change the subject, or lapse into embarrassed silence. Very few reasonable men wished to be seen as persecutors of women. Discrimination of all sorts was against the law in the secular world. The professional schools were filling up with women; even the military academies were admitting them. And no one wanted to be written off as a "male chauvinist pig."

Name-calling proved to be a powerful device for achieving victory. To be in favor of a male-only clergy caused one to be branded a sexist, a fundamentalist, a reactionary. The best label traditionalists could pin on their opponents was "trendy," pretty weak stuff in the war of words. And when reason and rhetoric proved inadequate, feminists used demonstrations, boycotts, tantrums, and tears to get their way.[66]

By 1971 the only mainline body to hold out was the Episcopal Church—some of whose members believed in the Catholic and Orthodox concept of episcopacy and the priesthood. But after vigorous feminist campaigning, illegal ordinations, a suit for sex discrimination, and prodding by liberal bishops, the Episcopalians opened the priesthood to women in 1976.[67] All resistance soon faded. Without a Bible or a church tradition to provide, in their judgment, dependable spiritual or ethical authority, most liberal Protestants went along with the flow of events in the secular world.[68]

In 1977, New York City's liberal Episcopal Bishop Paul Moore ordained the denomination's first openly committed homosexual priest of either sex. The Rev. Ellen Barrett said that her relationship with her lesbian lover "is what feeds the strength and compassion I bring to the ministry."[69]

The National Council of Churches elected its first woman president, Cynthia Wedel, in 1969.[70] Two years later the American Baptist Convention and the United Presbyterians chose women leaders.[71] (Women of the American Baptist Convention, which had long had female clergy, threatened a floor fight at the annual meeting if a woman was not elected president.[72]) In 1978, a study showed that the enrollment of women in seminaries in the United States and Canada had increased 118.9 percent since 1972. While women comprised only 4 percent of all ordained Protestant clergy, they made up 20 to 50 percent of the enrollment in some major American divinity schools.[73]

Not surprisingly, liberal Protestant churches tended to side with radical feminists on the most volatile issues of the day. Before 1973, for example, the United Methodists, United Presbyterians, American Baptists, and the United Church of Christ were pro-choice on abortion. After *Roe v. Wade*, they were joined by the Disciples of Christ and the Episcopal Church.[74]

When an amendment was introduced in Congress in mid-1973 to restrict the availability of abortions, the American Baptist Churches, the United Church of Christ, and the United Methodist Church joined the American Civil Liberties Union, the National Organization for Women, and the National Women's Political Caucus in opposition.[75] By year's end sixteen Christian and Jewish religious organizations had formed the National Religious Coalition for Abortion Rights. The list included the American Baptists, the United Church of Christ, the United Methodist Church, and the United Presbyterian Church (USA).[76]

In 1972, the United Methodist Women (UMW) gave $10,000 to eight women's liberation action groups and proclaimed that its purpose was to "bridge gaps between church women and the women's movement." The UMW's *Response* magazine soon published such radical feminists as Mary Daly and Rosemary Radford Ruether. It was the beginning of a long and continuing relationship between the powerful and well-funded (giving totaled $37,926,300 in 1992) Methodist group and a wide variety of radicals. At a 1982 UMW assembly, Dr. Hazel Henderson invoked Gaia, the Greek earth goddess, who, before human beings came along, "managed the biosphere very well by herself."[77]

There was also much support among mainline leaders for the Equal Rights Amendment and "unisex" language. In 1980, the National Council of Churches, which often worked closely with the National Organization for Women and other feminist groups, sponsored an "inclusive language" translation of the Bible. Some radical feminists disapproved because the translators had not gone far enough: Jesus continued to be called "the Son of God."[78]

A year later, at a meeting of feminists sponsored by the NCC, God was addressed as "Mother" in the prayers and the liturgy. Dr. Elizabeth Bettenhausen of Boston University's School of Theology questioned whether "the whole of Christianity has been a religion to reinforce male dominance."[79]

In 1983, the NCC released a lectionary that showed how powerful the radicals in the women's movement had become in a short time. God was now the "Father [and Mother]" or "[Mother and] Father." The Deity was addressed as "Sovereign One" but never as "Lord." Instead of the "Son of Man," Jesus was called "Child of God." The aversion to the masculine pronoun "himself" was such that one verse read: "Christ humbled self." The strongly profeminist committee that made the translation, headed by a Lutheran (whose own denomination, the Lutheran Church in America, rejected the book), complained that old Bible language about God the Father "has been used to support the excessive authority of earthly fathers."[80]

In the Episcopal Church, there was considerable sympathy among theologians, church leaders, and liberal interest groups for such efforts. The new Book of Common Prayer released in 1979 contained several examples of "inclusive language" and contained a daily lectionary that omitted scriptural references to the subordination of women (as well as to sexual immorality and sodomy).[81] A 1982 hymnal altered the language of most of its contents in deference to feminist demands. "Good Christian men, rejoice," in the popular Christmas carol, became "Good Christian friends, rejoice."[82]

In 1984, the Episcopal Cathedral of St. John the Divine in New York City displayed a four-foot bronze statue of the Crucifixion featuring a Christa, not the Christus, complete with undraped breasts and rounded hips.[83] The conservative writer Florence King later declared that the Episcopal Church, to which she belonged, became "a non-church the moment it committed this blasphemy."[84]

At the 1994 General Convention of the Episcopal Church, a service was held opposing sexism. It included a litany celebrating numerous women that omitted mention of the Virgin Mary. Forgiveness was asked "especially for our prejudices against women who have disabilities or whose racial identity or sexual orientation is different from our own." At one point in the service, the bishop of western North Carolina apologized for having offended women by calling God "Father."[85]

The Statement of Faith of the United Church of Christ, revised in 1977 and 1981, uses inclusive language.[86] The United Methodist Book of Worship, approved in 1992, contains rites using nonsexist language such as "God, our Father and Mother." A revision committee headed by Bishop Susan Morrison made several efforts to display God's motherly aspects, including a reference to God as "like a Bakerwoman" and "our grove, our lover, our well."[87] The Presbyterian Church's *Book of Common Worship*, released in 1994, scrupulously avoids the use of the masculine pronoun in references to God and, in some cases, to the Son of God.[88]

The homosexual rights movement of the 1960s also made a strong impact on the mainline churches. To be opposed to the equal treatment of gays and lesbians in all areas of life, the argument went, was to be a bigot, a "homophobe." The issue, proponents said, was about fairness, equality, and love. They also employed tactics, such as the disruption of religious services, used by civil rights advocates and radical feminists.

But unlike the drive for the equal rights of women, this crusade failed to convince the majority of clergy and laity in the mainline churches. Scripture was unequivocal in its condemnation of sodomy, and church tradition had from the beginning been at least officially hostile.[89] Even more important was the lack of sympathy the general public revealed toward homosexuals (who were probably between 2 and 2.5 percent of the population).[90] The average American might well be tolerant of homosexual orientation, which some thought genetically based, but homosexual activity usually found defenders only on the extreme left. In the mainline churches, such support often proved significant.

In 1972, the United Church of Christ ordained William Reagan Johnson of San Francisco, the first professed homosexual to be so honored by any mainline church. (At the time, there was no formal church policy on the question, ordinations being under the supervision of local associations of churches.) When asked if he could be a good minister without a wife, Johnson replied "I don't really feel I need a wife. I hope some day to share a deep love relationship with another man."[91]

The following year, a gay liberation lobby was at work attempting to win acceptance of homosexuality from the National Council of Churches.[92] In 1975, the NCC, the United Church of Christ, the Unitarian Church, and many local Quaker chapters passed civil rights planks that defended the rights of homosexuals, without addressing the question of whether homosexuality was a sin.[93]

Two years later, as we have seen, the self-declared lesbian Ellen Barrett was ordained in the Episcopal Church. William Johnson, who had been traveling across the country since his ordination talking about sexuality and homosexuality, was pleased. "We are two," he said. "That's progress." Johnson added, "I see women's liberation and gay liberation as movements of the Holy Spirit. I really believe God is trying to break through again to teach us something we missed before."[94]

In 1977 the new president of the United Church of Christ, The Rev. Dr. Avery Denison Post, pledged to support homosexual demands. "When scripture is used to fuel a mission against people or to build a case for the denial of human rights or civil liberties to those people, then scripture is in my opinion being misused."[95]

Six years later, the General Synod of the United Church of Christ formally endorsed the ordination of homosexuals.[96]

Still, no mainline church has officially endorsed homosexual behavior. When a gay church, the Universal Fellowship of Metropolitan Community Churches, applied for membership in the National Council of Churches, successful objections were raised by American Baptists and the Lutheran Church in America, among others.[97] When the effort was altered years later to include only "observer" status, as many as twelve churches were allegedly ready to leave the National Council, causing the request to be denied.[98]

And yet, as we have seen, homosexual conduct has many defenders in the mainline leadership. Many less prominent clergy and laity are also sympathetic, especially among the radical feminists. The Women's Ministry Unit of the Presbyterian Church (USA), for example, gave financial grants to Presbyterians for Lesbian and Gay Concerns, the National Organization for Women, and the Religious Coalition on Abortion Rights in 1990.[99]

In many mainline seminaries there is a great deal of support for gays and lesbians. The Episcopal Church's General Theological Seminary, for example, endorsed a policy that permitted a lesbian professor to live in faculty housing with her female lover. Bishop Craig B. Anderson, the seminary's dean and president, declared that GTS "has been and continues to be supportive of gay and lesbian persons."[100] (A major exception is the leadership of the Princeton Theological Seminary, which has actively supported the Presbyterian Church in its opposition to ordaining practicing homosexuals.[101]) This stance, surely in part a reflection of attitudes dominant in secular colleges and universities, may in time, of course, result in the emergence of more liberal mainline policies.[102]

Homosexuals have also made strong inroads into the publishing world, where religious books sympathetic to their cause have become routine. In 1993, for example, HarperSanFrancisco brought out *Jesus Acted Up: A Gay and Lesbian Manifesto* by the gay activist and former Jesuit priest Robert Goss. The book is "A daring celebration of Jesus' solidarity with society's outsiders that confronts church homophobia head-on as a betrayal of Jesus' liberating message." The opening line on the full-page ad in the publisher's catalogue: "Jesus is as queer as you and me."[103]

Theology in this period followed the leftward trend of the mainline leadership and the secular liberal elite in general. Great names departed—C. S. Lewis (1963), Paul Tillich (1965), Emil Brunner (1966), Karl Barth (1968), Reinhold Niebuhr (1969), Harry Emerson Fosdick (1969)—and no one of comparable stature replaced them. In the mid-1960s, Harvey Cox's *The Secular City* and Joseph Fletcher's *Situation Ethics* attracted many liberals because of their leftist sympathies and rejection of the supernatural. Liberation theology, black theology, and feminist theology appealed to predictable interest groups. Five principal "Death of God" theologians, who meant different things by the phrase, fascinated journalists briefly.

In 1966, James McCord, the president of Princeton Theological Seminary, said that he thought the growing involvement of churches in the secular world had produced a theology emphasizing "the God of the present."[104] Bill Coats has observed: "Theological identities were forged along political not personal lines. Sin was associated with political enemies (the capitalist class, men, whites, straights, Western imperialists) and not the self. Salvation became the equivalent of justice, the overthrow of one's political enemies."[105]

By the end of the 1960s, liberal Protestants (and many liberal Roman Catholics) had virtually abandoned the idea of heresy.[106] In 1970, The Rev. Dr. George E. Sweazey, the spiritual leader of the United Presbyterian Church, reported hearing from a seminary president that "theology today is in a shambles—that's the long and the short of it." And to the people in the pews, Sweazey said, it seems at times that "all the certainties" are "coming loose."[107]

On liberal seminary campuses during these years, orthodox Christianity was often not a top priority. Langdom Gilkey of the University of Chicago Divinity School reported in 1966, "The younger men don't even raise the issue of the Virgin Birth or Original Sin. They're discussing the existence of God. And if there's no God, you don't have to argue about any of the other doctrines."[108]

Moreover, the intellectual and spiritual quality of liberal seminary students appeared to have dropped. A special committee created to study the Episcopal Church's ministerial education program found in 1967 that roughly 43 percent of church seminary students had college averages of C+ or lower, and that more than half had come to theology after having tried some other occupation. Most students, the committee reported, found chapel so boring and irrelevant that they frequently skipped services.[109]

A Rockefeller Foundation report of 1976 observed sharp declines in overall quality at the seminaries of the "Big Five": the divinity schools at Harvard, Yale, Chicago, Vanderbilt, and New York's Union Theological Seminary. Training had lost much of its scholarly rigor: elective courses had proliferated and language requirements and basic courses in the Bible, church history, and doctrine had vanished. The schools provided "general education for those interested in a diffuse variety of religious studies, personal quests for the meaning of life, social activism and pastorally oriented behavioral science." The study found that chapel attendance had declined radically and that student manners "are more relaxed, sex freer and acquaintance with drugs often more than theoretical." Most telling, perhaps, was the finding that a surprising number of graduates dropped out of organized religion altogether.[110]

In keeping with the times, mainline churches hosted an assortment of silly services. When Richard York was ordained an Episcopal priest in 1968, for example, he wore a psychedelic chasuble decorated with yarn balls and tinkling bells. The Berkeley, California, church was decked out with gas-filled balloons and banners, and a rock group provided hymn settings. The sermon was entitled "God Is Doing His Thing."[111]

In 1971, seven thousand people jammed into New York City's Episcopal Cathedral of St. John the Divine for the *Hair Mass*, a service commemorating the third anniversary of the Broadway opening of the popular musical. The event had everything: braless women, hot pants, a rock band, balloons. One family munched on hamburgers, malts, and french fries during the service. The Harvard theologian Harvey Cox gave the sermon. Over 2,500 received Communion, including several Jews.[112]

The highly popular rock musicals *Jesus Christ Superstar* and *Godspell* were also blended with religious services at times. At New York City's Fifth Avenue Presbyterian Church in 1971, a minister smilingly baptized a baby "In the name of the Father, the Holy Ghost, and Jesus Christ Superstar."[113]

The first religious service of ordination ever held by a major denomination in which women assumed all the principal roles took place in 1972. The Rev. Davida Fay Crabtree, a radical feminist, became a minister in the United Church of Christ. Her stole was embroidered with wildflowers, church symbols, and peace and social action symbols.[114]

A year later, at a meeting of the General Synod of the United Church of Christ, a communion service featured a Dixieland band and singing, clapping, and dancing in the aisles in a mass version of an airlines commercial. The carrying on was such that few took notice when two gays, hand-in-hand, marched onto the platform to protest that their concerns had not been addressed by the convention.[115]

Any sort of rite could turn bizarre. At St. Clement's Episcopal Church in Manhattan in 1972, an environmental theater baptism service featured photos of the Kennedy brothers and Martin Luther King Jr., a man shaving in an open bathroom singing "We Shall Overcome," three nude young people playing kazoos and splashing in a plastic wading pool, an actor performing a bathtub scene from a play, and incense. Worshipers received greetings of "love" and a palmful of mud upon entering. At the baptism, candidates were daubed with Magic Marker in the sign of the cross. Afterward, the congregation hoisted the three newly baptized people (one was a three-year-old) onto their shoulders and paraded around the room.[116]

Weddings were conducted in parks, on beaches, and on mountaintops. One Methodist minister in California enjoyed sitting and chatting with couples about their lives, concluding by casually telling them that they were now married. "We're married?" asked one happy pair. "You've blown our minds." Not to be bested by the mainline, a minister from the Universal Life Church conducted a service in 1969 in which he and the couple before him were nude. The proceedings concluded with the solemn declaration: "You're married as long as you dig it."[117]

The Roman Catholic Church had more than its share of such frolic, all sorts of experiments being made in churches often stripped of their visible ties to the past. A "Hippie Mass" in Davenport, Iowa, in 1969, for example, featured a priest, Father James

Grubb, who "pauses as he says the Mass, cocks his head, and smiles approvingly at the ear-piercing, modern sounds that pour from the gyrating rock-musical group beside him at the altar." At another mass, the Offertory and Our Father were "performed" by a female dancer. One "liturgical" song—the Beatles' "With a Little Help from My Friends"—bothered a monsignor because it referred to drug use. Father Grubb wore gaily decorated burlap vestments, taught feminism and encouraged rebellious nuns, reveled in media attention, and began experimenting in drink, drugs, and sex to show parishioners that he was "with it." (He later repented so completely that he returned to the Latin Mass.)[118]

In the late 1960s, a leftist, interdenominational "underground church" began to appear throughout the country, touted by the likes of the Episcopal priest Malcolm Boyd, an author (*Are You Running With Me, Jesus?*) and nightclub performer, and the Milwaukee civil rights agitator Father James Groppi. This movement wanted to drastically reform organized religion, divesting it of rigid structure, authoritarianism, ritual, and dogma. Advocates took strong and predictable positions on race, sex, poverty, and war.

The Rev. John Pairman Brown, an underground proponent and professor at Berkeley's Episcopal Church Divinity School, exclaimed: "we intend to surface as a nucleus of Church union and renewal, in the hope that what we represent will melt the denominations from the bottom up."[119] Boyd told a National Council of Churches meeting in 1967: "There's a new Christian movement springing up in this country when many are saying that the church is believed to be dying. And this revolution is taking place largely unknown to official church leadership."[120]

Of greater significance was the Jesus Movement of the early 1970s. While adopting countercultural lifestyles and commitments to peace and "social justice" causes, adherents seemed more interested in supernatural religion than radical politics. This movement involved tens of thousands of mostly young people who joined an assortment of small, interdenominational, and often highly evangelical churches, organizations, and communes—from The Way Word coffeehouse in New York's Greenwich Village to the Christian Surfers in Encinitas, California. (One convert to the latter said he sought Christ after he found the perfect wave in Hawaii and did not experience happiness.)[121]

A "Sweet Jesus Rock Concert" at Stanford University in 1971 drew eight thousand. The Jesus People sponsors almost had rebellion on their hands when one evangelist told the crowd to "abstain from sexual immorality, and that means abstain except in marriage." The evangelist reported, "We're finding this is the last area people want to give up."[122]

Jesus shirts (Jesus is my Lord), bumper stickers (Smile, God Loves You), posters, buttons, Jesus wristwatches, records, clothes, even a "Jesus cheer"—"Give me a J, give me an E. . ."—were all part of the excitement. Various show business personalities got involved, often producing best-selling records and books. Few were more zealous than the singer-actor Pat Boone, who baptized more than two hundred converts in his own swimming pool in a single year.[123]

Maureen Orth in the *Whole Earth Catalog* shed light on the origins of this fervid movement. "The first thing I realized was how different it is to go to high school today. Acid trips in the seventh grade, sex in the eighth, the Viet Nam War a daily serial on TV since you were nine, parents and school worse than 'irrelevant'— meaningless. No wonder Jesus is making a great comeback."[124] Bishop James Pike's youngest son, Christopher, told a similar story, describing how he was converted by a college campus evangelist after a life devoted to drugs, television, and Eastern religion.[125]

Of course, many sophisticated people thought the entire Jesus phenomenon absurd. But there were prominent Christians who thought otherwise. Billy Graham said in 1971, "If it is a fad, I welcome it."[126] The Episcopal priest Robert Terwilliger of New York City's Trinity Institute commented: "There is a revival of religion everywhere—except in the church."[127]

In fact, there were charismatic and "Neo-Pentecostal" movements within the Episcopal, Presbyterian, and Lutheran churches in the early 1970s. There were probably more than 200,000 Roman Catholic charismatics in this country.[128] But these Christians were a distinct minority, and in the mainline churches they lacked virtually any impact on denominational leaders and decision-making bodies.

The "Jesus freaks" and the underground church soon went the way of long sideburns, peace signs, and bell-bottom pants. The cults, sects, and Eastern religions that were fashionable in some circles, and never statistically significant, received very little attention once the Vietnam War became history.[129]

By the late 1970s, the country was moving to the right. This caused much frustration among liberals, who condemned the "age of greed" and thought they were witnessing unprecedented corruption. The historian Christopher Lasch growled, "Self-preservation has replaced self-improvement as the goal of earthly existence. . . . The happy hooker stands in place of Horatio Alger as the prototype of personal success."[130]

The shift in the public mood increased as people became increasingly concerned about the decline in the nation's moral and cultural standards. Evangelicals were responsive to the trend, linking Christian orthodoxy with conservative politics. They had dropped their inhibitions about engaging in politics when they gained media respect and attention with "born-again" Jimmy Carter in the White House.

In late 1979, the sociologist Wade Clark Roof noted that religious liberals were falling behind the times. "Those who are affirmative and walking with confidence are the conservatives."[131] Harry Siefert, a retired professor of religion at the School of Theology at Claremont, California, looked at plummeting membership in the mainline churches and wrote, "There is little evidence that liberal churches are looking forward or offering specific programs appropriate for present and future generations."[132]

By the 1980s evangelicals were a major force in the Republican Party, and in the 1990s they seemed more powerful than ever. In 1995, the neoconservative leader Irving Kristol predicted that the movement would conquer the GOP, likening it to the powerful religious awakenings of the eighteenth and nineteenth centuries.[133]

Many mainline leaders and theologians, along with liberals in general, reacted angrily to the conservative tide. Some returned to biblical criticism as a vehicle for attacking the transcendent faith of their foes in the culture wars. In *Meeting Jesus Again for the First Time*, for example, Marcus Borg portrayed Jesus as a feminine, multicultural figure, stripped of the supernaturalism some scholars were now saying had been invented by later followers. Jesus now fit the needs of the left in its struggles against "reactionaries." As one reader put it, "Since Jesus confronted the conventional wisdom of his day, he can be employed in our contemporary struggle against hierarchy, exclusivity, patriarchy, imperialism, consumerism, meritocracy and individualism."[134]

Liberation theology, black theology, and especially feminist theology remained popular in the mainline seminaries, continuing to transform the study and practice of the faith into the polemics of socialist revolution, lesbian emancipation, ethnic and racial distinctiveness, radical environmentalism, and the like. Process theology, which began to attract attention after World War II and was important by this time, appealed to some interested in dense philosophical thought and eager to challenge orthodox Christianity. Postmodernism, a gospel of moral and cultural relativism popular in academia, was implicit if not explicit in much contemporary theology. By the mid-1990s, winds from the far left had blown powerfully in the liberal Protestant denominations for at least three decades.

In political and cultural matters, mainline leaders largely preferred to remain happily locked into the ideology of the Vietnam War years. Now closely linked to the Democratic Party, which had itself been overtaken by the far left in 1972, they tended, for example, to attack anti-Communist American foreign policy, to defend the welfare state, and to back anything supported by leftist blacks, radical feminists, homosexual activists, and groups like the American Civil Liberties Union that were actively attempting to keep religion (especially the "right-wing" variety) and biblical moral standards out of American public life.

Thus the charge that mainline liberals are "trendy" does not hold up. "Stuck in the Sixties" is a more accurate epithet. Liberals are fond of saying that the only permanent thing in modern life is change, and they often portray themselves as pragmatists. In fact, they have absorbed an ideology that essentially remains the same. Not public opinion, not even election results, can shake the left's commitment. The congressman Richard Armey devised a relevant epigram: "Conservatives believe it when they see it. Liberals see it when they believe it."[135]

The penchant for "stuckness," as theologians would be tempted to call it, was illustrated when Bishop Edmond Browning became the presiding bishop of the Episcopal Church. With this selection, the bishops (who choose the PB) presented a map for the church to follow with roads that ran in only one direction.

During the John Hines years, 1965–74, a great many Episcopalians were less than pleased by the church's endorsement and financial support of various social causes. Membership, perhaps coincidentally, dropped from 3,616,000 in 1965 to 3,445,000 in 1971. It seemed, moreover, that the church was falling apart. Church school enrollment declined 24 percent, confirmations were down 26 percent, infant baptisms 21 percent, and adult baptisms 44 percent. Hines called himself "the worst administrator of any Episcopal Presiding Bishop in history" and, as we have seen, stepped down before his twelve-year term expired.[136]

His successor was Bishop John M. Allin of Mississippi, the most conservative of the candidates. The election marked what *Time* magazine called an "Episcopalian Backlash."[137] But Allin's tenure was generally unhappy. The church continued to move leftward and Allin, a gentle man, could do little about it.

In 1985, the bishops selected Bishop Edmond Lee Browning to be the next presiding bishop. Browning, who had once held a post in the church headquarters in New York City, was a solid citizen in the left wing of the church. He had adamantly favored women as priests and bishops, sought use of the National Council of Church's unisex lectionary, argued for the ordination of practicing homosexuals ("I would hope we are not frozen in any kind of set belief about homosexuality"), and actively opposed the nuclear arms race. On other social and political issues, his outlook was entirely predictable. "Peace and justice causes," he said, "will be a high part of my agenda."[138]

At the same time, Gallup pollsters reported a wide gap between the people in the pews and the Episcopal Church leadership. Among the laity, 78 percent did not think it the church's place "to be an agent of political change in the United States"; and 76 percent thought the church should concentrate on "worship and spiritual matters" more than on political issues.[139]

Browning soon showed that he lacked any interest in what the pollsters found, or even in what the General Convention of the Church decided; his "agenda" was paramount. Under the presiding bishop's guidance, the church lurched further to the left. Two revealing Browning appointees: The Rev. Canon Linda Strohmier, a gay and lesbian activist (who has spoken of God as "the god" and "it") as the church's evangelism officer, and Thomas K. Chu, a member of the gay and lesbian lobby group Integrity, as the national staff officer for Young Adult and Higher Education Ministries.[140]

Browning's zeal, as we have seen, was not unusual among mainline leaders. In his circle of mainline peers he stood out in no particular way. The activities of the National Council of Churches in recent years perhaps best illustrate the penchant of liberal Protestants to follow an ideological line engraved in stone in the days of Ringo Starr and George McGovern.[141]

In 1981, the NCC began to call itself "a community of Christian communions which, in response to the gospel revealed in the Scriptures, confess Jesus Christ, the incarnate World of God, as Savior and Lord." At the same time, however, the NCC leadership showed itself as interested in left-wing political and social positions as it was anything else.

In midyear, the NCC Governing Board publicly expressed total opposition to the new Reagan administration's policies, the first time the board had taken such a step since the council's founding in 1950. "In [the Reagan] vision of America the fittest survive and prosper, and there is little room for public purpose since it interferes with private gain. Compassion is a weakness in the competitive struggle of each against all." The board also went on record favoring permanent-residence status for illegal immigrants who had been in the United States for a "reasonable period of time," opposing military aid to El Salvador, and requesting an immediate "nuclear freeze" with the Soviet Union.[142]

Later that year, the Methodist Bishop James Armstrong of Indiana was elected president of the National Council of Churches. His record included participation in campaigns for civil rights, peace in Vietnam, disarmament, hunger relief, and abolition of the death penalty. He vigorously opposed the right-wing Moral Majority, and in particular The Rev. Jerry Falwell. "One, he is not Biblical. Two, his sexism and rigid legalism dehumanize the very persons for whom Christ lived and died."[143]

That November, a reporter for the liberal *Christian Century* noted the NCC's intolerance of the pro-life position and its "predictability, its lethargy, its penchant for passing too many peace-and-justice resolutions of doubtful efficacy." She also observed the organization's nervousness about its public image, citing a new

$90,000-a-year budget item for an "interpretation department" to help explain the NCC's work to its own member churches and the general public.[144]

In early 1982, the Missouri Synod Lutheran pastor Richard Neuhaus and the Methodist minister Dr. Ed Robb attacked the council in a public debate for its political partisanship. Both charged that the liberal churches were less willing to criticize human rights violations in Marxist countries than they were to denounce the errors of capitalist nations. Robb cited "a long list of N.C.C. resolutions criticizing pro-American governments in Latin America and Asia." In response, Dr. Arie Brouwer, a member of the council's Governing Board, said that critics of the council were "obsessed" with the threat of Marxist totalitarianism and charged that Robb was one of those conservatives who "uses Christianity" to promote political agendas.[145]

In early 1983, the Institute on Religion and Democracy, run by Robb, produced a 100-page booklet documenting the claim that the foreign policy of the council and other liberal Protestant bodies "often leans in some significant ways toward the Marxist-Leninist left." The *Reader's Digest* and CBS's *60 Minutes* pursued the story. Much evidence substantiated the general claim, although the sums of money involved were relatively small. Others joined the fray, including the *United Methodist Reporter*, which found a clear pattern of left-wing bias in hundreds of NCC political statements over a five-year period. James Wall of the *Christian Century* said that council staffers often supplied answers "filled with romantic revolutionary rhetoric."[146] Kenneth Woodward of *Newsweek* observed that the council's "collective voice has become as predictable as an evangelist's altar call."[147]

In 1985, following Reagan's reelection and further assaults by conservative critics, the NCC declared itself willing to mend its ways. The council now advertised its new emphasis on prayer, worship, and evangelism. The General Secretary Arie R. Brouwer said that the flesh of the council was "weak—and deeply wounded" by attacks.[148] By the late 1980s, contributions from member churches had dropped 50 percent from 1975 (reflecting hard times in the mainline more than intellectual dissent), and the staff had been cut from 187 twenty years earlier to 61.

But in fact little changed. In 1990, the NCC Governing Board condemned celebrations of the 500th anniversary of the landing of Columbus, stating that "reflection and repentance" were appropriate. The aftermath of Columbus's "discovery," said the resolution, brought "invasion, genocide, slavery, 'ecocide' and the exploitation of the wealth of the land."[149] Soon, in a sharp break with national public opinion, the NCC expressed vigorous opposition to the Persian Gulf War.

In mid-1991, the Greek Orthodox Church suspended its ties to the National Council of Churches. Citing liberal positions taken on abortion and homosexuality, Archbishop Iakovos said, "We cannot play anymore with 'Christianity'—in quotation marks. Christ is not a playboy." In a newspaper interview, the archbishop, an ecumenical leader and former head of the World Council of Churches, decried "the new morals and the new ideas." But he believed that in time the tide would turn back toward a more biblically based faith. "I feel and I see some signs that Christianity will rediscover its soul."[150]

Even though the NCC had by this time lost much public credibility, it pursued its agenda with customary passion. In 1991, it joined the left in opposing the nomination of the conservative Clarence Thomas to the United States Supreme Court.[151] In 1992, NCC officers joined twenty-three church leaders in criticizing George Bush and the Republican Party for mentioning God during the political campaign. A letter issued by the NCC said that "any partisan use of God's name tends to breed intolerance and to divide." The general secretary, The Rev. Joan Brown Campbell, said in the letter: "We deplore the suggestion that to be fully franchised one must not only be Christian but espouse a particular understanding of life in Christ."[152]

The Empty Church

In early 1993, a delegation from the National Council met with Vernon Jordan, the chair of President-elect Clinton's transition team. The United Methodist Bishop Melvin Talbert, a delegate, employed his best "libspeak" to express the group's delight with a Democratic victory and eagerness for a voice within the administration. "Our commitment is not to draw attention to ourselves but to address issues and concerns that impact the lives of the diverse groups and persons in this nation who have been marginalized, especially during the past 12 years." Talbert praised "the signs of inclusiveness manifest in the cabinet appointments " and hoped that Clintonites would present "a vision for an inclusive community" to the nation and the world.[153]

Soon a larger NCC delegation was invited to Washington to meet the new chief executive. Presiding Bishop Edmond Browning was on hand, as was General Secretary Joan Brown Campbell. Not in thirty years had the liberal Protestants been so warmly received in the White House. One delegate, in the words of an observer, grumbled that their previous exclusion was part of a "Reagan-Bush strategy to discredit mainline church leaders in order to remove them from the national debate and bolster the Reagan-Bush domestic and foreign policy agendas."

Clinton dished out some platitudes and assured his visitors they would participate in future high-level administration meetings. James M. Wall, writing in the *Christian Century*, predicted a close relationship between the president and the National Council and praised the president's "openness to this rich source of moral and spiritual wisdom." No talk here about the separation of church and state. Wall said also he was confident that "the concerns of African-American, Hispanic and Asian-American church leaders resonate with the Clinton agenda of empowering minorities."

The delegation left council position papers for the White House staff to ponder, including an endorsement of universal government health care. Indeed, council experts on health care were already at work assisting Hillary Rodham Clinton's task force on the topic.[154]

In 1995, fifteen leaders of the National Council of Churches met with the president for forty-five minutes, extolling his social policies and calling him "the guardian of the nation." At the end of the meeting, the visitors "laid hands" on Clinton and prayed that he would be "strong for the task" of defending welfare state spending against congressional Republicans. The conservative columnist Cal Thomas commented:

> Perhaps that's why so many of the mainline churches would be more properly labeled "sideline" churches. They, and others for whom politics and government have become the way of salvation, have squandered their moral power on a lesser and weaker kingdom that eventually will pass away and is incapable of changing people's hearts.[155]

6

RENEWING THE MAINLINE

As we have seen, the plight of the mainline churches has undergone considerable scrutiny in recent years. Partisans have explored a variety of possible explanations, often expressing the desire not only to understand the problems but to rectify them. If the American people have largely lost interest in the history and meaning of denominationalism, there are still many who cherish the traditions of their churches and do not relish their disappearance. Even should there be a future union of mainline denominations, as liberals have often sought, advocates of this superchurch have wondered what might be done to make it a success.

There are those, too, who seek to understand the mainline malaise as an insight into the nature of contemporary America. Some of these investigators have been especially interested in probing the relationship between the shift in public morals over the past thirty years and the decay of liberal Protestantism.

The challenge has been made more complex for all concerned because while the mainline churches have declined in every way, national church attendance has apparently remained steady, conservative churches have blossomed, and the religious faith of the American people has stayed at extraordinarily high levels.

Denominational leaders, scholars, journalists, and concerned members of local congregations have been asking for years: What has gone wrong with the mainline, and what is to be done? Let us begin by considering three major explanations for the declining membership that demand consideration.

It has long been observed that cities corrupt morals and encourage religious skepticism. In recent years, numerous scholars have contended that urbanism has been a powerful force in the decline of supernaturalism. Harvey Cox, in the highly influential book *The Secular City*, declared that "cosmopolitan confrontations of city living exposed the relativity of the myths men once thought were unquestionable."[1] Sociologists have argued that the general outlook in cities is permissive, flexible, pluralistic, and sophisticated.[2]

There is some truth here, as we saw when discussing fundamentalist objections to the rise of urban culture in the 1920s. But a broader examination presents a more complex picture. As the sociologist Roger Finke and Rodney Stark have pointed out in *The Churching of America*, the growth of cities actually increased religious participation, in part because of the accessibility of many churches. Moreover, Protestant churches were more successful in urban areas than in the countryside. Mainline churches prospered in part because the Social Gospel was more popular in cities than in rural areas. By 1926, 83.5 percent of Episcopalians, 71 percent of Northern Presbyterians, 69.3 of Congregationalists, and 68.6 of Northern Baptists lived in urban areas.[3]

In the 1920s, despite all the rhetoric surrounding the Scopes Trial, fundamentalism was largely an urban movement, with its strength in the northern and eastern sections of the nation.[4] In recent years, biblically conservative interdenominational churches have grown rapidly, and their typical location has been in major metropolitan centers.[5] As Robert Wuthnow has observed of the evangelical movement, "Its leaders came from large urban congregations and included seminary and college professors with good educations and skills in publishing and broadcasting."[6] America's cities are filled with churches representing an astonishing variety of denominations. Consult the telephone book for Chicago, Pittsburgh, Los Angeles, or Atlanta to see the point illustrated vividly. In short, cities are not in themselves responsible for the deterioration of liberal Protestantism. Vital religion is present in all of our urban areas.

It has also been thought that as people become more educated (or at least acquire more diplomas), they are less likely to be believing Christians. Wade Clark Roof, in a study of baby boomers, concluded that education more than anything else contributed to a growing split "between the more conventionally religious and the more secular sectors of the population."[7] Since education levels have risen dramatically in recent decades, and the mainline churches tend to attract people from the middle and upper ranges of the socioeconomic scale, the attrition among liberal Protestants appears to be understandable and predictable.

It is true that the importance of religion tends to decline with rising education levels. Finke and Stark observed the "corrosive effect of scholarship on religion" well before the American Revolution."[8] Wuthnow has carefully described the close relationship between high educational levels and liberal religious and social attitudes, especially since the 1960s.[9]

Gallup pollsters discovered, for example, that only 66 percent of college graduates believe that Jesus is God or the Son of God. While that figure remains far higher than one would find among comparably educated Europeans, it trails the general population of the United States by a considerable margin. Only 22 percent of college graduates describe themselves as born-again Christians. Nineteen percent of college graduates say that religion is not at all important to them. That figure is 11 percent among high school graduates and 9 percent among those who did not graduate from high school.

On the other hand, college graduates are no less likely than other groups to regard themselves as "a religious person." They are more likely than those with less education to be church members and to attend church in a given week. College graduates are no less likely than anyone else to want religious training for their children and are actually more likely to provide it. Those with at least some college background are more likely than others to take part in Bible study or prayer groups outside of church.

Gallup concluded: "College graduates treat religion with more skepticism and intellectualism, but they are far from hostile to religion. Education changes the form and focus of religious practice, but it is not an enemy of faith."[10]

In a national study of Presbyterian baby boomers, researchers concluded that "the amount of formal education has no bearing on how active one is in church. . . . Our fundamentalists, for example, were as well educated as any of the other groups in the sample. Most of those who lost their faith, or who adopted unorthodox opinions, did so *before*, not after, going to college."[11]

In short, the mainline churches are not dying simply because their members and potential members have spent too many years in school. Very few people who leave their churches cite lack of intellectual respectability among their reasons. Pride, indifference, alternative religions, and a wide assortment of diversions may keep some of the educated from Christianity, but the faith itself, as history richly reveals, is not a natural enemy of intellect. Most college graduates in our time still seem to understand that.[12]

Many liberals, as we have seen, also argue that "outdated" worship services (the "Sister Act" thesis), stodgy morality, and overly conservative social positions keep people at home on Sundays. Mainline churches, it is said, suffer from being insufficiently attentive to the spirit of the sixties. Rock music services, AIDS Sundays, special collections for Latin American revolutionaries, sermons on environmental funding, feminist theology, gay marriages—the "cutting edge," we are assured, will attract millions, especially the young.

The study of Presbyterian baby boomers found "virtually no

support" for the theory that people left their church because it had become "socially irrelevant." Indeed, most of those surveyed knew "little or nothing" about the policies promoted by their denominational leaders. For them "the church" meant their local congregation. Moreover, the study found a great variety of opinions among baby boomers. "Most of them have mixed views on controversial issues. . . . active baby boom mainliners tend to be liberal on one issue and conservative on another."[13]

Roof found that baby boomers strongly preferred churches to be tolerant about "lifestyle issues." On the other hand, he discovered much concern about the nation's decaying moral order, with special attention being paid to the family and the school. A commanding 70 percent of those surveyed favored a "return to stricter moral standards."[14]

When Gallup pollsters asked people why they left church, only 19 percent cited "Moral Teachings on Sex and Marriage Too Narrow," a single point above "Poor Preaching." Only 13 percent cited "Dislike Traditional Form of Worship." Twelve percent said "Church Unwilling to Work for Social Changes." The leading reason (38 percent) cited was "Too Much Concern for Money." As for churches and political issues, mainline Protestants, by a vote of 56 percent to 37 percent, said that churches should keep out of politics entirely. That figure was exactly the same expressed by the American people as a whole.[15]

Clergy and laity often disagree about this, however. A majority (61 percent) of Episcopal priests surveyed by Gallup said that the church should give equal emphasis to "worship and spiritual matters" and to "social and political issues." But 76 percent of the laity said that worship and spiritual matters should be the top priority.[16]

Gallup speculated that young people may be staying away from churches because of their teachings on sex. "To most Americans, 'religion' is associated with sexual restraint. But sexual restraint is not a message that young and single people want to hear."[17] And yet in mainline churches where virtually any sort of conduct is condoned, young people still stay away. The reverse tends to be true in evangelical churches with strict moral demands. When adults of all ages were asked, only 28 percent of the unchurched and 17 percent of the churched said they would welcome a greater emphasis by churches on sexual freedom in the future.[18]

When Gallup asked people in 1992 for reasons they attended church less frequently, only 8 percent said they disagreed with church policies and teachings. A mere 1 percent gave as their reason that the churches were too old-fashioned. Heading the list were "Have no time, too busy" (19 percent) and "Conflicts with work, study schedule (14 percent)." Most of the reasons given were practical. As many people (4 percent) said "Move around too much, new to community" as said "Atheist, non-believer."[19]

In 1991, the Presbyterian Church (USA) sponsored two surveys among the nation's unchurched. Both studies revealed that more than 60 percent of those polled stayed away from church because of work/school commitments, "Just a habit/Lazy/Just don't," and "No time." Most of those interviewed were not hostile to religion, and many showed a willingness to return. But church attendance just didn't seem important.[20]

And with that, we are getting at the heart of the problem facing the mainline denominations. Numerous polls and studies point to an important fact: great numbers of people stay away from churches simply because they do not see them as relevant to their lives. Liberal Protestantism in particular has become so secularized and indistinct that it cannot compete successfully with an abundance of causes and activities that many find more valuable. The great majority of Americans still cling to the Christian faith, or at least a watered-down version of it, but many fail to see good reasons for committing themselves to a mainline church.

Consider the alternatives of modern life. Occupations, neighborhoods, athletic teams, hobbies, and ethnic groups can provide a sense of personal identity and pride. Political parties and organizations work to create the "good" society. All sorts of community groups offer friendship and opportunities for service to others. Professional counselors are available to help with personal and family problems. Schools, the media, computer networks, concerts, and lectures entertain, inform, and educate. They also supply ample quantities of liberal ideology for those in need of it.

Weigh the benefits: Sunday with the family at the beach or in church listening to a sermon on AIDS; working for overtime wages or enduring pious generalities about "dialoging," "inclusiveness," and "sharing and caring"; studying for exams or hearing that the consolations and promises of the Bible are not "really" or "literally" true; entering a race to raise funds for disadvantaged children or sitting through pleas for federal health insurance; shopping at the mall or hearing about the wickedness of anti-abortion demonstrators; reading the newspaper or being harangued about racism and sexism.

But what about Jesus Christ, whom 84 percent of Americans believe to be God or the Son of God? The church can certainly present Him in a distinctive way. Conservative and evangelical churches preach the timeless and ever useful gospel, opening hearts and minds to the supernatural, amending lives, and satisfying the spiritual hunger of millions.

The mainline churches? Thousands of their parishes still present the traditional and authentic Christian message. But all too often, believing so little of the orthodox faith, liberal Protestants offer merely what can be found elsewhere in secular society. The sociologist Daniel V. A. Olson has observed, "the religious subculture of mainline denominations is based on a shared identity that is only marginally distinct from mainstream culture. . . . identity expectations are relatively indistinct from those of most citizens. . . . many of their value concerns and interests are served by other secular institutions."[21]

Americans are a practical people and a great many of them fail to be convinced that the mainline churches are worth their time.

Liberal Protestantism, in its determined policy of accommodation with the secular world, has succeeded in making itself dispensable.

In fact, the vast majority of Americans are not convinced that going to any church is necessary to be a good Christian.[22] Roof found that baby boomers saw religion "less in doctrinal or ecclesiastical terms, and much more in personal meaning terms, and often in vague and generalized terms." People frequently said merely that they tried to lead a good life and follow the Golden Rule. Said one Presbyterian dropout, "I feel if you do your part of what matters to you, whatever it is, if you sincerely believe in something, whatever it can be, and if you can make just a little bit of difference, then I think that you've done something worthwhile."[23] A local Rotary club or Moose lodge could teach that sort of pap as well as a church.

The study of the Presbyterian baby boomers concluded that for many dropouts, "It's simply that church does not seem very important to them. . . . They are 'too busy,' and they have a myriad of other commitments. Above all, they see no real point in getting involved." The authors concluded that the major problem is the mainline's spiritual enervation. "Somehow, in the course of the past century, these churches lost the will or the ability to teach the Christian faith and what it requires to a succession of younger cohorts in such a way as to command their allegiance."[24]

Gallup found that almost half of those who said they left church after moving their residence said simply that they "never got around to looking for a new church." Very few of these people were invited to attend a mainline parish. This is highly significant since about half of those approached to join a church respond favorably. Gallup reports: "The vast majority of evangelizing in the United States is done by conservative and evangelical churches."[25]

Roof found that of the baby boomers who grew up as conservative Protestants, 80 percent remained within that religious tradition. In contrast, only 65 percent of those raised in the mainline churches still identified themselves in this way. More than a third switched, 17 percent of them to conservative Protestantism. Those who dropped out of organized religion altogether could explain their actions only in generalities such as "Church didn't seem relevant," "I was bored," and "I developed other interests."[26]

And so the mainline churches wane—disheartened, aging, increasingly irrelevant, all too often satisfied to serve as a sort of sanctimonious echo of National Public Radio or the left wing of the Democratic Party. For a variety of reasons, many liberal Protestants, especially church leaders, have endorsed a view of reality and a way of life that have helped produce a society that is cracking up. And they have become part of the problem.

However tragic, there is nothing new about this. History is filled with examples of Christians who have pursued worldly goals at the expense of the "foolishness" of the gospel. The Reformation was a reaction to such a state of things, and Protestantism quickly proved vulnerable to the same temptations. William H. Willimon has written: "the persistent problem is not how to keep the church from withdrawing from the world but how to keep the world from subverting the church."[27]

Looking at American history, Finke and Stark have described an "endless cycle" in which sects become churches, churches grow increasingly secular and lose their organizational vigor, and new sects are founded to restore a supernatural faith. The losers in this cycle are those ecclesiastical bodies that have grown worldly, failing to satisfy members most in need of the sacred. In short, Finke and Stark contend that when a church becomes a mainline body, it begins to wilt. And out of secularism comes revival.[28] The "Seven Sisters" of today's mainline Protestantism are thus, in this provocative view of things, on the inevitable road to oblivion. It is the price they must pay for failing to resist the world, one of Christianity's sternest commands.

The German theologian Wolfhart Pannenberg has written: "the Protestant mainline churches are in acute danger of disappearing. I expect they will disappear if they continue neither to resist the spirit of a progressively secularist culture nor try to transform it."[29] But a commitment to transform and convert must be grounded on something deeper than religious skepticism, moral relativism, and this morning's *New York Times* (the newspaper and its imitators being liberal Holy Writ).

Here we are at the root of things: the submission of liberal Protestantism to a secular gospel rests upon a failure to accept the essentials of the Christian faith. Alasdair MacIntyre once observed, "Theists are offering atheists less and less in which to disbelieve."[30] The first and most critical step in halting the slide of the mainline churches is the restoration of their commitment to orthodox theology. Everything else depends upon that.[31]

It is also the great stumbling block. To begin with, the recapture of orthodoxy requires faith in an all-powerful God who was and is capable of the miraculous. Christianity without miracles is dead, and its Founder and the Apostles madmen. That is true no matter how many fine paragraphs about "symbolic truth" and the like are spun by seminary professors eager to escape the supernatural.

The basic assertion on which the faith rests, as St. Paul made clear in I Corinthians 15:16–19, is a miracle: the bodily resurrection of Jesus Christ. There are many sound arguments for its plausibility. But ultimately, like the Incarnation, the Transfiguration, the Ascension, and numerous other awesome elements in the story of Jesus Christ, it is historically incredible and must be accepted on faith. From that acceptance, we are told, flows grace. Believers begin to be transformed from within.

The New Testament scholar George Eldon Ladd concluded a detailed study of the resurrection with: "In the end, I accept the biblical witness to the resurrection not because of logical proof or historical reasoning, but because of an inner quality of the gospel, namely, its truthfulness. It so overpowers me that I am rendered willing to stake the rest of my life on that message and live in accordance with it. My faith is not faith in history but faith in the God who acts in history."[32]

Fundamentalism is not a requirement of orthodoxy. The Scriptures most certainly bear certain traits of their time and place. We need not, for example, accept as fact the vindictive, bloodthirsty, and often contradictory behavior of Jehovah described by the early Hebrews. As the Bible scholar William Neil has explained, the Jewish idea of the character of God developed over time, the ruthless superman becoming the God of mercy, righteousness, and love. "The most significant and far-reaching advance ever made in the field of religion was when Israel harnessed morality to religious faith." It was "the uniqueness of their contribution to humanity."[33]

In the New Testament, we need not deny inconsistencies in, say, stories of the death of Judas Iscariot or of the resurrection of Jesus.[34] Had the accounts been exactly alike, their reliability would be far less convincing. As the New Testament scholar I. Howard Marshall notes, "the Gospels do not profess to give us a chronological account of the ministry of Jesus, nor do they profess to tell us everything in detail just as it happened."[35] The Bible translator J. B. Phillips wrote of the New Testament, "It is not magical, nor is it faultless: human beings wrote it. But by something which I would not hesitate to describe as a miracle there is a concentration upon that area of inner truth which is fundamental and ageless. . . . it is the *truths* which are inspired and not the words, which are merely the vehicles of truth."[36]

The difficulty is, of course, to know what is essential belief. Fortunately, we do not have to invent a standard. The early church produced the Apostles' and Nicene Creeds as sufficient statements of the Christian faith, and no better guides to the essentials have ever been produced. Rooted solidly in Scripture and affirming the major facts of Christ's life, death, and resurrection, the creeds contain that which orthodox followers of the faith have always accepted. Many Christians believe more, but none should believe less.

To repeat, faith in the authority and power of Christ involves more than reason. It is a response of the whole person to One whose claims ring true, whose teachings shatter and inspire, whose promises answer the longings of the heart, and whose continuing presence is the staff of life.

Many liberals quickly dismiss such a historic and supernatural view of the faith as "archaic," "naive," and the like. The German New Testament scholar Rudolf Bultmann, for example, considered such an approach sheer folly. Bultmann, who had a huge following among American biblical scholars after World War II, claimed that virtually nothing reliable could be known about Jesus. He rejected the Virgin Birth and the Resurrection, among other things, as primitive nonsense. The early church, in his view, invented most of the sayings ascribed to Jesus. In "demythologizing" the New Testament and translating it into "existential" language, Bultmann sought to make the faith meaningful to modern men and women.[37]

In 1981, the General Synod of the United Church of Christ adopted a "Statement of Faith" as an updating of the creeds. Written in unisex language, it omitted the historic triadic form of the Trinity, skimmed over traditional doctrinal matters, eliminated many references to miraculous events in the Bible accounts, and rejected the exclusiveness of Christian truth. The apologist Roger Lincoln Shinn wrote that the document better met the needs of modern, scientifically minded people, being "less rigid, less authoritarian." Its use was optional and unbinding. Indeed, everything about the Statement, Shinn declared proudly, was permissive.[38]

The resistance to orthodox theology is understandable. Its return to the mainline churches would seriously alter or destroy an assortment of "gains" won by the religious left. It would require, to begin with, a serious reconsideration of much contemporary scholarship, biblical criticism in particular. Experts of an orthodox persuasion can be found to undertake the task; differences between schools of thought, after all, usually have as much, if not more, to do with preconceptions about the nature of things as about scholarly credentials. (If you believe, as did Bultmann, that miracles are impossible, for example, that faith greatly influences your research and conclusions.) Distinguishing the solid advances in knowledge from speculation and polemicism is a necessary, albeit difficult, first step in restoring the viability of the traditional, supernatural faith.

It seems likely that many seminaries, in the grips of radical feminists, political activists, multicultural relativists, and the like, will have to be sidestepped in this process. To repeat, religious scholars are often loath to lend credibility to the supernatural; it isn't scientific, reputable, sophisticated, progressive. They do not wish to be identified with "foolishness." They reject the idea that people in the first and second centuries might have better understood the faith than modern liberals. They are often amused by the quantity of belief and trust exhibited by unlettered men and women at any time.[39]

In 1976, evangelical Episcopalians were forced to create their own seminary, bypassing ten others, to provide students with orthodox Anglican teaching. (Today, Trinity Episcopal School for Ministry attracts more financial support than any other Episcopal seminary.)[40] Orthodox Christians throughout the mainline may well have to do likewise. It is essential not only to recover the truths of the ancient faith but to train clergy to preach and live them. It is the clergy, let us remember, who have taken the lead in the accommodation of Christianity to the modern world.

These new institutions must devote themselves to rigorous spiritual formation as well as scholarship. An active prayer life, for example, has always been a vital part of the lives of those in the forefront of the authentic faith. Prayer, wrote J. V. Langmead

Casserley, "is the highest act of the human spirit, for man is most of all himself when what he does is most completely penetrated and sustained by the power and grace of God."[41] Such thought is old-fashioned, biblical, orthodox—and thus, to many in the mainline, subversive.

Radical feminists are especially determined to move far beyond the pale of the traditional faith. Elizabeth Schussler Fiorenza, at Harvard Divinity School (where women make up 60 percent of the student body), is one of many scholars at work on a feminist reinterpretation of the New Testament. Prof. Sallie McFague of the Divinity School of Vanderbilt University, whose *Models of God* won the American Academy of Religion Award of Excellence in 1988, passionately opposes the masculine imagery of God portrayed in Scripture and wants to get rid of all "our safe havens, called dogmas and orthodoxy."[42] Margaret McManus of the Center for Women and Religion at the Graduate Theological Union, in Berkeley, California, said in 1992 that women's ordination was just the beginning and that equality was no longer the prime consideration. "The issue is transformation of our religious institutions."[43]

The transformation is being pursued internationally. Daphne Hampson, a "post-Christian" Systematic Theologian at St. Andrew's University, described by Naomi Goldenberg of the University of Ottawa as "one of Europe's finest feminist theologians," said in 1992: "We should describe God in our own terms, drawn from our own day and age and not keep looking to the past. I don't think women should be looking at the Bible at all. As long as they do they are promoting patriarchal literature."[44]

In November 1993, 2,000 women and 85 men, including leading staff members of the Presbyterian and Methodist denominations, attended a "ReImagining 1993" conference in Minneapolis. The event was sponsored by local churches and underwritten by a $65,000 grant from the Presbyterian Church (USA). Additional funding came from the National Ministries of the American Baptist Church, the Division of Congregational Ministries of the Evangelical Lutheran Church in America, the Board of Homeland Ministries of the United Church of Christ, the Women's Division of the United Methodist Church, and several orders of Catholic nuns.

The conference featured a veneration of "Sophia, Creator God," a workshop on belly dancing, addresses by self-identified lesbians, a downgrading of the Atonement ("I don't think we need folks hanging on crosses and blood dripping and weird stuff. . . . We just need to listen to the god within"), and rites from other religions such as the American Indian tobacco ritual.[45] The Rev. Kathi Austin Mahle, cochairwoman of the steering committee that planned the event, said of participants, "We wanted women who were doing cutting-edge theology."[46]

A prayer used in Minneapolis at a Sunday communal "blessing of milk and honey" read in part:

> Our maker Sophia, we are women in your image. . . . With the hot blood of our wombs we give form to new life. . . . With nectar between our thighs we invite a lover, we birth a child; with our warm body fluids we remind the world of its pleasures and sensations. . . . We celebrate the sweat that pours from us during our labors. We celebrate the fingertips vibrating upon the skin of a lover.

This was recited by individual women, except for the vibrating fingertips line, which was read by two women together. At the conclusion of the meeting, Melanie Morrison of Christian Lesbians Out Together (CLOUT) received a standing ovation as she invited lesbian, bisexual, and transsexual women to join hands in a circle on stage.[47]

The United Methodist Bishop Earl G. Hunt commented, "When the church seems to be losing its struggle with powers and principalities, weird things begin to happen."[48]

Some years ago, a British evangelical alliance produced a report containing a basic truth that warrants repeating: "In the last analysis there is only one distinction to be made; that is, between those who believe in the essentials of the Gospel and those who do not. This fundamental distinction is drawn sharply in the New Testament, as sharply as the difference between darkness and light, death and life."[49]

With a solid theology in place in the renewed mainline, sound morals should follow. There again, the resistance will be fierce, for Christian and secular morality are very often at odds. William H. Willimon has portrayed the Christ-centered church as "a political and ideological monkey wrench thrown into the culture."[50]

The moral standards are different because the ultimate goal is different. As the orthodox Episcopal priest Gale D. Webbe has written, "no human soul can ever be really alive to God without first being dead to this world." Christians are interested in much more than just what most people call "the good life." Webbe observes: "The Gospel counsel is un-American."[51]

Christian conduct, of course, has differed widely in different times and places. But the guiding principles of the faith are unshakable. Orthodox Christians, obeying Scripture and tradition, will seek to do their best for their fellow human beings, especially the helpless, the broken, and those dismissed by the world (on the left and right) as "losers." Malcolm Muggeridge once observed, "We become forgetful that Jesus is the prophet of the losers' not the victors' camp, the one who proclaims that the first will be last, that the weak are the strong and the fools are the wise."[52] After the love of God comes love of neighbor; that's what the faith is about.

More specifically, these Christians—these odd and disturbing people—will make every effort, for example, not to worship anything (including self) other than God, live for wealth or power, engage in illegal conduct, violate marriage vows, sanction abortion as a means of contraception, place their careers ahead of their spouses and children, exploit the poor (for money or for votes), condone violence and pornography, discriminate against anyone, cause needless suffering to any living creature, succumb to despair, or take great pride in their spiritual and charitable achievements. Jesus was especially critical of the Pharisees.

For their beliefs and efforts, orthodox Christians will often be despised. A common charge against them is that they are rigid and narrow. In some things they are indeed. They follow One who said, "Enter by the narrow gate; for the gate is wide and the way is easy, that leads to destruction, and those who enter by it are many. For the gate is narrow and the way is hard, that leads to life, and those who find it are few."[53]

The pursuit of such a theology and morality does not require a denigration or rejection of reason and science. It is still entirely possible for orthodox Christians to welcome the expansion of knowledge and to be grateful for advances that have improved and lengthened our lives. The internationally acclaimed physician William Foege was proud to announce to an audience of fellow Lutherans in 1995 that he had participated in efforts leading to the eradication of Guinea Worm disease and river blindness, which had plagued millions of Africans for untold centuries. He considered his scientific efforts an integral part of his faith.[54]

As Christian intellectuals have long illustrated, the faithful need not be unthinking and reactionary. Arthur Michael Ramsey, a brilliant Christian intellectual and future Archbishop of Canterbury, wrote: "For 'all things were made by Him,' and all honest endeavor in science, in philosophy, in art, in history, manifests the Spirit of God."[55] Richard John Neuhaus has observed that "it is within religion—more accurately, it is within the Christian understanding of reality—that everything finds its role. In that understanding, nothing that is true or good or beautiful can be excluded."[56]

Orthodox Christians must, however, be prudent—cautious about the claims of scholars and secularists to make humankind the exclusive arbiter of truth; distrustful of those who would make intellectual or aesthetic activities the primary focus of existence; critical of all who see life on this planet as an end in itself rather than just the beginning.

How much of what is widely accepted by educated people in our time should the serious Christian endorse? One general answer to that extremely complex question is: that which is undeniably true, and little else. As much as possible, Christians should draw the line at solid evidence—as difficult as that frequently is to determine—and be ever wary of advocates interested primarily in promoting an ideological agenda.

Basic, verifiable scientific findings about nature, for example, pose no problem. But conclusions from these facts advocating the banishment of God from creation and from human life need not be swallowed. One can admire the many contributions of the social sciences while remaining highly skeptical of, say, Sigmund Freud, Alfred Kinsey, and Margaret Mead, whose shoddy research methods and secular preconceptions have been recently exposed by scholars.

Christians may respect Bible scholarship but need not endorse theories designed to rationalize and dismiss the faith. Reviewing the radical John Hick's book *The Metaphor of God Incarnate: Christology in a Pluralistic Age*, Mother Mary Jean of the Episcopal Community of St. Mary observed: "This is a strange way to do scholarly biblical criticism: Throw out the evidence that doesn't fit your dogmas."[57]

The task of seeking the true, the good, and the beautiful becomes especially hard when you confront the arts and humanities, now dominated by postmodern polemicism. Writing of the discipline of history, Gertrude Himmelfarb observes that the very ideas of truth, knowledge, and objectivity—even facts—are commonly derided and dismissed by professionals. The ideology has reached the point in academia as a whole, Himmelfarb reports, that a feminist scientist has declared Newton's *Principia* to be so permeated with "gender symbolism, gender structure, and gender identity" as to be nothing less than a "rape manual."[58]

The writer Lisa Schiffren has observed that "the culture of liberalism—multiculturalism, amorality, radical feminism—has left our society so soiled and frayed that it is hard to see how it will mend."[59] In such a culture, from the Fox television network to the Harvard University Press, Christians must be more cautious than ever about what purports to be truth.

The acceptance of the fullness of Christian orthodoxy requires, perhaps above all else, a radical humility—a denial of personal pride, an emptying of self demanded repeatedly in Scripture and by the church over the centuries. In the Psalms we learn that God "leads the humble in what is right, and teaches the humble his way."[60] Jesus spoke of the necessity of having a childlike faith, at one point telling his squabbling disciples: "Truly, I say to you, unless you turn and become like children, you will never enter the kingdom of heaven. Whoever humbles himself like this child, he is the greatest in the kingdom of heaven."[61] St. Paul urged the Christians at Ephesus to "be imitators of God, as beloved children," and "lead a life worthy of the calling to which you have been called, with all lowliness and meekness."[62]

Of course, such appeals have rarely been welcome. In church history, no less than in other areas of the past, serious humility has been all too rare. In all walks of life, power, fame, luxury, and learning have a tendency to poison selflessness.

Modern American men and women, many of whom are basking in wealth, freedom, opportunity, good health, and entertainment, do not rank humility among their basic values. Indeed, the whole Western way of life runs in the opposite direction. And when you are determined to be "modern," "progressive," and "broad-minded," the ancient pleas can seem especially hollow. Sin, too, can be a formidable barrier. Bishop James Pike, a flagrant adulterer at the height of his popularity with liberals, was no more interested in humility than he was in the creeds.[63]

But radical humility is vital. Gale D. Webbe has called it "the hardest of all virtues to acquire" and "the foundation-stone of the spiritual building."[64] There is no other door through which to enter the full and orthodox Christian faith, the "scandalous" faith of the creeds, and the high moral standards that flow naturally from it.

Grasping this truth, and referring to the basics of the faith, the Episcopal Bishop John W. Howe said recently, "As I look at what is happening in our beloved church, and in most of the churches, I find myself wondering how it is that things so simple that a child can grasp them easily are increasingly beyond the comprehension of bishops, theologians, and other leaders in the church."[65]

With a renewed faith and morality in place, what might also be required to rejuvenate the mainline churches? Here we revisit Dean Kelley, whose book *Why Conservative Churches Are Growing* has won widespread acclaim.

Kelley's thesis, it will be recalled, was that a strong church is exclusive and strict. His definition of strictness includes absolutism, conformity, and fanaticism. Members must give a successful conservative church, he says, "absolute and unswerving allegiance; be willing to work, suffer, and die for it; abandon all competing activities, allegiances, and responsibilities in its favor; tell its Good News tirelessly and unself-consciously to strangers; wear its stigmata of humiliation on their bodies; submit to its strictures, conformities, and disciplines; go where they are sent and do what they are told." Only a small minority of people are capable of such zeal, Kelley believes, "Perhaps one in a hundred or one in a thousand."[66]

While he understands that all this is unlikely to appeal to people in the middle and upper levels of the socioeconomic scale, Kelley argues that declining liberal churches must take major steps in the direction of the most successful conservative churches in order to survive. "For all practical purposes, there is no means by which the deterioration of social strength in a given organization can be slowed or arrested except by a reassertion of strictness."[67] The mainline, he says, has become distinguished for its "placidity, decorum, and tolerance—i.e., sterility," and has failed to meet the spiritual needs of a nation reeling with social disorders.[68]

Kelley stresses the importance of possessing a compelling teaching about the ultimate purpose and destiny of humankind. He calls such teachings "meanings." A liberal himself, Kelley rarely mentions Christian theology, but when he does he worries about intolerance. "Even the most gentle, humble, and loving Christians must divide the world into those who confess Christ as Lord and those who don't."[69]

Mainline churches with orthodox theology would indeed be required to stress the unique importance of Jesus Christ. Out of this claim, to be sure, have come evils of every sort in the past. But in the spirit of love that is vital to the faith, and in the humility that must accompany all claims to knowledge about God, reinvigorated mainline churches would have to show tolerance and respect for all religions. Pope John Paul II, who has traveled the world promoting peace and understanding, and Mother Teresa, who loves and serves the dying in a Hindu nation, could be used as models on this score. Fanaticism, cruelty, and contempt for others are not necessary components of a religious revival; indeed, they are counterproductive and self-destructive.

Orthodox theology in itself contains intellectual and moral demands that would restore a large measure of strictness to the mainline. Requiring acceptance of the undiluted faith, long the practice in Christendom, would create a climate of exclusivity, mutual purpose, and community, and so would demands for purity of life.

The moral component of an orthodox faith would contribute in an extraordinary way to the restoration of strictness. Many people have difficulties with the most basic theology; many struggle with even the simplest Bible stories. But everyone can understand pleas for personal integrity, marital fidelity, sensitivity and respect for others, and so on. The lessons are taught most effectively, of course, by example.

High moral standards would set mainline Christians apart, helping them to live in peace and love and to witness to others in a way that is now often difficult. Kelley found that "no strong religious movement ever got far on a diffident, believe-and-let-believe approach."[70] Prosperity eludes churches in which anything goes and nobody cares.

In 1994, teenage Southern Baptist youth made headlines when 100,000 of them publicly pledged to avoid sex before marriage. One fifteen-year-old girl said of the True Love Waits campaign, "I hope it says we don't have to be like the generation before us. We can set new standards."[71] Can one imagine such a concept catching fire in, say, the Episcopal Church?

Gallup tells us what most Americans desire from churches. Christians want "to deepen their relationships to Jesus Christ" and learn about the Bible. "They also want their churches to help them learn how to put their faith into practice; to shed light on the important moral issues of the day; to help them learn how to serve others better and to be better parents. Americans understand that for their faith to be meaningful, it must be real and have a real impact on their day-to-day lives."[72]

There are other ways of contributing to a necessary sense of strictness. Requiring sacrificial financial giving and large quantities of time and energy have proved effective. The pastor of a Lutheran church in Seattle made this proposal in 1995: "Reintroducing what is hard hitting—like the wrath of God, penance, fasting, and self-mortification—will go a long ways toward ending the Lutheran blues."[73]

Finke and Stark observe: "People tend to value religion on the basis of how costly it is to belong—the more one must sacrifice in order to be in good standing, the more valuable the religion." The mainline denominations as they now are, the two scholars argue, rank low in costs and benefits, prompting many people eventually to lose interest and go elsewhere.[74]

Rejuvenated mainline churches must also become engaged actively in evangelism. With an orthodox faith that has equipped them with a distinctive and all-important message, and a commitment of members to lead exemplary lives, this basic Christian activity should be more natural than it now is. When was the last time a member of the United Church of Christ knocked on your door with a pamphlet? Do Methodists reach you by telephone as often as credit card solicitors?

And when strangers show up on Sunday morning, how are they treated? I have attended Episcopal churches in which not a single person even said hello, let alone invited me to return. Gallup reports that "Americans are, in fact, the loneliest people in the world" and strongly desire their churches to provide a sense of community.[75] Many conservatives know this and have prospered accordingly. Said one member of an extremely successful interdenominational church in a Milwaukee suburb: "All the preachers get the word across and people care about you here."[76]

The renewed mainline churches must become deeply involved in the media. Their current near-silence is a scandal, and is surely a reflection of their worldliness and lack of commitment to the authentic faith. But the lassitude must be shaken off if parishes are to grow and become beacons of spiritual light.

Millions (half the population at one time or another) watch televangelists and send them hundreds of millions of dollars annually. Gallup found that almost half of viewers attend church once a week or more, and that 68 percent of them had tried to encourage someone to believe in Jesus Christ. Billy Graham has used radio and television successfully for decades, preaching the gospel to more people than anyone else ever has. Pat Robertson runs a highly successful television network. The Faith and Values Network (a model of bad religious broadcasting) reaches 24 million subscribers. Conservative Roman Catholics have the Eternal Word Television Network, available to 39.6 million American homes and broadcasting twenty-four hours a day to Europe, Africa, and Central and South America. By mid-1995, there were twenty-three religious cable networks.[77] Fundamentalist radio and television stations abound throughout the country. There is spiritual energy at work on at least the fringes of the media. The mainline can and should compete effectively.[78]

Moreover, the mainline should join conservative churches in objecting to the way networks and major stations neglect and abuse (especially by blasphemy) the Christian faith.

Studies have shown an overwhelming bias against religion by media leaders. In one survey of the East Coast media elite, 86 percent said they seldom or never attended religious services, and 50 percent listed their religion as "none."[79] In 1990, the conservative Media Research Center published an extensive study of the media, documenting a powerful left-wing and secular bias.[80]

The television critic Howard Rosenberg has wondered why networks have failed to create at least an occasional dramatic series with a church theme, observing that "you see more hookers, rapists and serial murderers on TV than clerics." He asks, "If religion is boring, why is it important to so many people?"[81] The television journalist Bill Moyers commented, "Just about every other human endeavor is the subject of continuing coverage by the media, even to the point of saturation." But there is "no room in the inn" for religion as a "crucial force in American life. So most Americans remain religiously illiterate."[82]

In the newspaper world, religious journalism is shunned, and those who do find work in the field occupy the bottom rung of the status ladder. The Marquette University journalism professor Bill Thorn has noted that religious coverage is "mostly shallow, insipid and uninformed." Marvin Olasky of the University of

Texas's journalism school has blasted the press for shunning and trivializing religion, declaring that such deprecation "separates it from society. This is irresponsible of the press."[83]

The movie critic Michael Medved has described the modern film industry's antireligious bias in detail, calling it "positively pathological." In his book *Hollywood vs. America: Popular Culture and the War on Traditional Values*, published in 1992, Medved recalls a producer who simply could not accept the fact that nearly half the American people participated in religious services each week. "If all those people really go to church," he snorted, "then how come I don't know a single one of them?"[84]

In late 1995, Andrei Codrescu, a commentator on National Public Radio, criticized some Christians for contending that all believers will go to heaven and that nonbelievers are destined for hell. On the popular program *All Things Considered*, he said: "The evaporation of 4 million [people] who believe in this crap would leave the world a better place." NPR officials apologized but would not allow a two-minute response by Ralph Reed, the head of the Christian Coalition, which had objected to the remarks. Codrescu also apologized, "for the language, but not for what I said."[85] The story quickly disappeared, leaving one to ponder the severity of the reverberations in the media had the attack been aimed at the left instead of the right.

Suppose a rejuvenated mainline added its considerable weight to the struggle against neglect and bias in the media, doing so not as liberals or conservatives but as concerned Christians, eager for accuracy and fairness. The result might convince millions that the faith was relevant, formidable, even necessary. Some of those moved by the facts might join a mainline church.

The renewed mainline churches could take numerous tips from fast-growing and successful conservative bodies. They might, for example, consider a ministry to men—that minority of the population that seems almost by nature to be the most resistant to religious involvement.[86]

The interdenominational Promise Keepers movement, started in 1991, is filling stadiums all across America with men eager to add spiritual meaning to their lives. They worship together, listen to speakers, share testimonies about their struggles in the faith, participate in prayer sessions and small group sessions, and have a "sharing time" when they can talk about God working in their lives. The seven promises they pledge to keep include honoring and worshiping Jesus Christ; practicing "spiritual, moral, ethical and sexual purity"; building "strong marriages and families through love, protection, and biblical values"; and "reaching beyond any racial and denominational barriers to demonstrate the power of biblical unity."

A postal worker recalled, "I went to Indianapolis last year. It was great: 62,000 men worshipping God, singing His praises together. It showed me that men can be spiritual, that holding hands and praying together is OK and doesn't make you less of a man." A pastor said, "I think there's a real revival going on in America today, and this is part of it. Many men have been confused about their roles in the church and in the family. They have their priorities of work and home out of whack. This is the spirit of God waking them up. I've seen men separated from their wives reconcile after attending a conference. I've seen a son and his father reconcile. I've heard of men going to their bosses to confess unethical behavior."[87]

The president of Promise Keepers declared, "We are seeing a great awakening, a huge hunger among men who want to learn to live successfully in today's world."[88] In 1995, more than 600,000 men were expected to attend these sessions.[89]

Critics of the Promise Keepers movement say it is trying to "turn back the clock" to a "Father Knows Best" value system, and they dismiss it as basically a white, suburban Republican movement. Feminists have been especially critical. The Rev. Priscilla Inkpen, a United Church of Christ minister in Boulder, Colorado, claims that Promise Keepers is a dangerous attempt to reverse gains made by women. "Those guys have done nothing but figure out another way to stay on top."[90] Annie Laurie Gaylor, cochair of the national Feminist Caucus (and a board member of the Freedom From Religion Foundation), said in early 1996: "The thought of all these men having meetings in sports stadiums because they think they have a problem with women gives me the willies. It reminds me of Nazi Germany. They're not saying, 'Heil Hitler', they're saying 'Jesus' instead."[91]

Where do the mainline churches stand on the Promise Keepers? (The United Methodist Board of Discipleship chose neither to endorse nor to denounce the movement.[92]) Where might they stand if renewed? Is Promise Keepers too "touchy-feely" for a great many middle- and upper-middle-class mainline members? Given the current popularity of hugging and kissing during worship services, and the success of such programs as Cursillo and Marriage Encounter, that seems doubtful. Still, if true, the mainline churches could invent a similar program with a lower emotional level. It is not beyond their intellectual or financial means. It is a question of will—which ultimately is a question of faith.

Renewed mainline churches should also take immediate steps to stem the flight of their own young people. This is a complex topic, for youth often exit at an early age. There is also what Gallup calls the "life cycle effect" in which people tend to leave the church in their late teens and early twenties and begin to return in their late twenties, especially once they have married. "In general, religious interest and activity increases with age."[93]

But steps could be taken to alter this process. We know that there is an enormous desire throughout the country for religious education. One study found that "Almost all parents want religious education for their children, and most want to get it in Sunday schools . . . everyone stresses moral education and character education alongside the more cognitive elements of learning about the Bible and church teachings."[94] If schools and colleges shun religion, making it seem odd and disreputable, churches can devise high-caliber youth programs, classes, and specially designed worship services to teach the faith and encourage sound morals. Many conservative churches have done this successfully.

In contrast, mainline churches all too often lack effective Sunday schools, offer nothing special for adolescents, and think they are being "cool" in the eyes of twentysomethings by preaching the use of condoms and urging easy abortion policies. Mainline college and university religious centers are very often among the most left-wing places in town. (A Gallup poll published in early 1996 showed the religious involvement of college freshmen at an historic low.[95])

The failure of churches to reach out effectively to young people has had profound social ramifications, contributing to the apathy, demoralization, and violence of modern youth culture. The moral relativity taught in many liberal churches has also been destructive. The Brown University educational expert William Damon has stressed the importance of firm convictions, guiding principles, and clear expectations for the healthy development of young people. The root of the plight of contemporary youth, he writes, "is the culture's failure to provide children with what they need for their spiritual growth."[96]

The renewed mainline may well wish to build elementary and secondary schools, Christian alternatives to the rapidly disintegrating public institutions. Enrollment in the some ten thousand evangelical Protestant schools in the 1990s is climbing at an estimated 10 percent a year. Voucher systems, giving parents the right and the funds to choose the schools their children attend, may well enhance this growth.

Such schools can be devoted both to Christian principles and to overall academic excellence. Love Christian Academy in Nanuet, New York, for example, prides itself on the extremely high test scores of its students. It is a school where 127 of the 135 students are black. (An estimated 75 percent of Christian schools are interracial.) At Delaware County Christian School in Newtown Square, Pennsylvania, 10 percent of the graduating class in 1991 were National Merit finalists (compared with less than 1 percent of graduating seniors nationwide). Pastor Clinton Utterbach, whose three-thousand–member Pentecostal church has spent $7 million on Love Christian Academy, said in 1994: "There's nothing that I perceive about Christianity that forces you to be second class."[97]

There are now more than two hundred all-black Christian day schools in urban areas throughout America, and their numbers are growing. The schools sometimes meet in store fronts.[98] Mainline churches contain vast areas of unused space, particularly in the often huge urban parishes. Schools could be started there—if the mainline cared enough about young people.

Mainline churches might also prepare instructional materials to assist the half million families educating their children at home. The McGuffey Readers, first published in 1836 and still in use in some circles, are surely not the last word in Christian education.

If television chooses to ignore or ridicule Christianity, the mainline churches could counter with their own programs aimed at young people of all ages. Why not an educational program like *Sesame Street* with a Christian bent? Why not Christian talk shows and cartoons? (In 1995, the Lutheran Church–Missouri Synod produced an animated Christian Christmas story as part of an on-going evangelism effort. Young people learned that the real Christmas gift is "a Savior which is Christ the Lord."[99]) Why not a series of dramatic programs based on true stories that make the startling, indeed revolutionary point that God is alive, at work, and in love with humanity. Because the media dwell almost exclusively on disaster and suffering, these stories of "Good News" might attract sizable audiences.

Renewed mainline churches could certainly do more to satisfy the spiritual needs of college students. Special efforts could be made, for example, to appoint chaplains who are believers striving to lead holy lives. Awards and financial gifts could be given to those institutions that had not officially or in practice (in the name of diversity, of course) declared orthodox Christianity anathema.

But could the mainline denominations afford such activity in a time of shrinking budgets? They are not impoverished. The Methodist Church brought in $3.3 billion in 1993, and, as we have seen, gives away tens of millions of dollars a year. The Episcopal Church received $1.6 billion in 1993. Its resources are such that the presiding bishop did not even notice the theft of $2.2 million by an appointee who lived in extreme luxury. (The woman in question blamed her actions in part on sexism.[100])

The Biblical Witness Fellowship observes how missionary funds are spent in the United Church of Christ:

> Of the approximately $13,000,000 spent by the World Board and $39,000,000 spent by the national agencies annually, a huge percentage is used to send religious professionals to meetings with other religious professionals, sustain a confusing complexity of boards/agencies/commissions/councils/etc., produce volumes of religious paperwork that few people read, and sustain an often radically liberal political agenda which only a minority of UCC members know about or support.[101]

If the mainline churches pooled their resources and talents, funds at least to begin urgently needed evangelization would appear. Again, it is largely a question of will. A renewed mainline would desperately want youth in the fold—for the sake of the lives and souls of those young people, for the present and future vitality of the Christian faith, and for the welfare of a nation reeling from juvenile violence, crime, ignorance, and apathy. Vigorous and vital youth programs led by churches that challenge the assumptions and actions of the secular world could change the lives of millions and help alter the perilous course of our civilization.[102]

Renewed mainline churches will also accelerate their social and charitable activities. Liberals are correct in emphasizing the importance of soup kitchens, fund-raising for starving nations, aid for immigrants and migrant laborers, shelters for battered women and pregnant mothers, and the like. Moreover, the public wants churches to be engaged in such activities. Gallup reports: "A plurality of Americans today believe organized religion is not concerned enough about social issues."[103]

The mainline could follow the lead of others. What might the media report about religion that is positive, asks the Media Research Center? "In 1992, Catholic Charities USA spent $1.7 billion on serving 14 million people, feeding 8 million and sheltering an estimated 285,000, and Catholic Agencies are the single largest private provider of health services to AIDS sufferers." And conservative Protestants do their share. For example, "Operation Blessing, the humanitarian arm of Christian Broadcasting Network, has donated $67.7 million to help the poor since 1978, and that figure rises to $363.7 million with leveraged giving and matching gifts from churches in the U.S. and abroad."[104] Christian churches are meant to be dynamically compassionate.

Political activism is more controversial. The sociologist James Davison Hunter warns: "The temptation for churches, synagogues, denominations, and other religiously based organizations is to conflate public life with politics. When yielded to, as they all too often are, the pursuit of political power and the wielding of political influence become the dominant way in which religious bodies define themselves and their mission in the social order." In 1950, there were sixteen major religious lobbies in Washington, D.C. By 1985, the number had grown to at least eighty and has increased since then.[105]

But political action can obviously be important. We should have learned by now that if churches will not work to make this a better world, the chances of evil flourishing are greatly enhanced. And of course political activism is often closely intertwined with social and charitable activities. Church lobbyists, for example, might well try to gain tax advantages for worthy causes, promote legislation that helps the family, and urge Congress to reform welfare laws that trap and destroy minorities.

The issue is what to advocate, not advocacy itself. The standard churches use should always be the orthodox faith, not simply what the editors of *Newsweek* or Senator Ted Kennedy think moral and just. Richard John Neuhaus has written, "Christians as Christians (and not simply as people of goodwill), have a responsibility to advance a social vision derived from biblical teaching."[106]

Some issues are extremely complex: the minimum wage, capital punishment, the federal deficit, the environment, public housing, affirmative action, school vouchers, specific military engagements, and so on. Churches need to deliberate at length about such matters and pray even more before taking official positions. To be fair, the deliberations should involve as many members as possible, not just church bureaucrats and activists. Gallup reports: "One thing that millions of Americans clearly want from their churches is more influence for the laity, the people in the pews."[107]

Christians working together can accomplish much. In 1993, for example, a multifaith coalition of liberal, conservative, and religious groups worked successfully to push the Religious Freedom Restoration Act through Congress. This measure, signed by the president, counteracted a 5–4 decision by the Supreme Court and placed the responsibility on the government to justify any legal curtailment of traditional religious practices that might technically violate the law. It was a victory for small religious groups and a defense of religion against the power of the state.[108]

One thing more should be said about the clergy in the renewed mainline. In a revitalized church they would be equipped with a message about faith and morals that would help them compete with their conservative and evangelical counterparts. They should be personally orthodox and working hard at holiness. But to prosper they will have to possess additional qualities and skills. There are orthodox clergy in and outside the mainline today whose churches are as feeble as the worst run by liberals, and the responsibility for this state of affairs often rests squarely with the person in the pulpit.[109]

A pastor should possess an attractive personality. That sounds like mere common sense, but all too often problems begin here. He or she must show concern for others, learn names, socialize, shake a lot of hands, smile a lot. I have known clergy who give members and visitors the impression that they might as well not exist. Muttering a reluctant greeting, failing to speak, turning away almost disdainfully to sustain a show of clerical dignity and reserve—that will not wash in Peoria. The same is true of strutting, preening, and all sorts of self-serving fussiness. Loftiness is not necessarily saintliness. As we have seen, Americans do not go to church to be patronized, ignored, and rejected. As for clergy who are just painfully shy, they should seek help to overcome their handicap.

Clergy should try to treat the laity with the same respect and affection they expect to receive. (The Golden Rule!) The people who come to church on Sundays are not by definition, as some clergy think, the enemy. Some might even become, if at all encouraged, friends.

Clergy must reveal professional competence. Sermonizing comes immediately to mind, for an amazing number of pastors are "rhetorically challenged." Again, common sense is a guide.

Sermons should be carefully prepared. A specific, helpful message should be contained; serious Christians cannot thrive for long on a strict diet of bland generalities. I have sat through hundreds of sermons based largely if not exclusively on the repetition of religious clichés. At Christmas Eve and on Christmas morning 1995, I listened to sermons by two Episcopal Church bishops that together could not have taken an intelligent adult Christian five full minutes to prepare. "Winging it" should be unacceptable in a renewed mainline church.

Sermons should last no longer than twenty minutes. I have often heard ten minutes of material expanded into the forty-minute and up range, leaving every sensible person who is still awake exhausted and irritable. Some veteran members of churches with long-winded pastors have mastered the art of sleeping with their eyes open. This is obvious when cameras zoom in on members of congregations listening to televangelists. Some of the faithful appear to be zombies.

(Imagine the acting ability of Puritans, who regularly endured sermons of two hours and more. One scholar estimates that in a lifetime the average Puritan listened to nearly fifteen thousand hours of sermonizing.[110] Perhaps these churchgoers chose not to believe in Purgatory because they thought they had already been through its equivalent.)

Above all, sermons should teach the faith. What man of you, said Jesus, "if his son asks him for bread, will give him a stone? Or if he asks for a fish, will give him a serpent?"[111] Sermons should offer Christians more than stones and serpents.

Some congregations go for years, even decades, without instruction and consequently suffer from spiritual anemia. How many mainline laity today could speak knowledgeably for thirty seconds on, say, the Atonement, baptism, the Eucharist, or a single saint? How many could even define "sanctification"?

For that matter, how many could describe the heritage of their denominations? In several decades as an Episcopalian, in churches all across the country, I have heard fewer than a half-dozen sermons in a regular Sunday service that dealt in a meaningful way with the Anglican tradition. If mainline Christians know more about professional sports or soap operas than about their religion and their church, it is at least in part because they have not been taught.[112]

Pastors should also have some solid training in counseling, organizational skills, finance, and church growth. Seminaries free from the current concentration on leftist dogma could devote more time to the advancement of basic proficiencies.

Clergy in the renewed mainline must be active for the faith. They should regularly call on parishioners; visit hospitals, nursing homes, and jails; answer letters promptly; carefully prepare worship services; knock on some doors. They should study (not just read) something. I have known clergy of several denominations to devote the better part of their lives to physical exercise, domestic chores, civic groups, hobbies, television, hanging out with pals, and drinking. In no other profession, except for the professoriate, is the temptation to be lazy as easily indulged.

Gallup reports that "Almost one in five among the unchurched cites a bad experience with a pastor as a major reason for no longer attending church."[113] A renewed mainline, if it is to succeed, must have clergy who are inspired, able, and on the move.

Finally, how difficult will it be to renew the mainline? An abundance of evidence suggests that the task is extremely formidable. For one thing, as we have seen, many liberal Protestants, especially at the leadership levels of the mainline churches, are pleased with the current situation. They are proud of their conduct, see themselves in the vanguard of even new and more progressive change, and are convinced that membership declines are dropping off and may even have been beneficial. Three liberal sociologists who studied Presbyterians observed that they found few ready to reverse "a century of mainline Protestant creativity."

> The Protestants are proud of their colleges and universities, of their fellow members who are community and world leaders, of their religious leaders who espouse ecumenicity, racial justice, openness, and critical thinking. Protestantism has a rich heritage of liberation, intellectual achievement, and political leadership. Its young people are the best and the brightest, the most capable of leadership in tomorrow's world. It's a pity they don't go to church, but, well, worse things could happen."[114]

These sociologists share the belief of most liberals that efforts to restore orthodox theology would be futile. "The formulations of the past will not suffice. Rather, new bases of authority claims must be generated. This is an urgent task for Protestant theologians today." One possibility, they contend, successful in fast-growing baby boomer churches in Southern California, would be to profess biblical authority and stop at that. "Understandings of heaven and earth, God and history, could be left to individual resolution, and clergy would acknowledge tacitly that they have little compelling to say on these matters." The sociologists talk of "journey theology," "faith walks," and religion that "assumes no single religious authority, permanent identity, or boundaries."[115]

What about biblical morality? The sociologists are not encouraging. The best they can create is a generality that implies at least a large measure of moral relativism: "The churches could emphasize thoughtful and responsible Christian moral living in twentieth- and twenty-first-century America." Contemporary saints could be our guides. "Examples today are Archbishop Desmond Tutu and ex-president Jimmy Carter. Anyone observing them and listening to them feels their moral power."[116] Many in the mainline, especially in leadership positions, would agree.

It is extremely unlikely that efforts to renew the mainline churches will start from the top down. Meaningful reform will no doubt have to come, as it has in the past, from the rank and file.[117] The "faithful remnant," described in Scripture, consists of those who will not kneel to Baal or to any other substitute for the One at the heart of existence. These believers will face, as always, great labor, frustration, and persecution—the latter often coming at the hands of fellow Christians who claim to be tolerant and inclusive.

Few if any basic compromises may be expected in the struggle. To simplify only slightly, the clash is between two fundamentally different views of life: one based on the supernatural and the other on humanity itself. One is rooted in the gospel, the other in modernity. We are either under the guidance of a living and loving God who has revealed Himself to us and has told us, at least in general terms, how to live and die, or we are alone on an indifferent and dangerous planet, forced to devise truth for ourselves.

The battle, as we saw briefly in chapter one, is underway. Small groups within almost all the mainline denominations are at work attempting to change the course of things. They hold conventions and worship services, publish an assortment of materials, create formal and informal employment networks, attend denominational meetings, write letters to establishment publications, and in general do everything in their power to restore orthodox faith and morals to their churches. Examples from three denominations will suffice.

The Good News movement of the United Methodist Church has roots that go back to 1967. With a national office in Wilmore, Kentucky, the organization is supported financially by some twelve thousand of the faithful. Its bimonthly magazine, *Good News*, is mailed to some sixty-five thousand Methodists.[118] (In 1994, the church reported having 8.5 million members.) Evangelical renewal groups, sympathetic with the Good News effort, meet all across the country.

In 1994, conservative Methodists created the Confessing Movement. A promotional flyer described the reasons why:

> Some United Methodists elevate their private experience to the position of judge and arbiter of Christian faith. Others exchange the historic faith for political, therapeutic, sexual, or gender-based ideologies with religious veneers. This abandonment of classical Christianity is occurring in a church that has nearly lost its immune system with regard to false teaching—in a church that appears fearful of, and perhaps unwilling to face, even a minimal level of doctrinal discipline.[119]

By early 1995, more than thirteen thousand had become associated with the movement.[120] A conference in Atlanta in April attracted more than nine hundred. Keynote speaker Dr. Mark Horst declared: "Tonight we gather to recall the United Methodist Church to remember and reclaim and reignite its doctrinal heritage." Countering fears that the movement was divisive, Horst said, "The really deep division which has rocked the Church . . .

is the division between those who want to throw out the classical faith of the Church and those who do not."[121]

Few Church leaders were impressed; only six active and retired bishops gave their support. (There are 49 active bishops.) Later in 1995, one liberal critic charged in the pages of *Christian Social Action* that the Confessing Movement was "demonstrably anti-ecumenical" and challenged members to demonstrate that they were "not also anti-women, anti-poor and anti-gay."[122]

Lutherans for Religious and Political Freedom was underway even before the ELCA was created in 1988. Some orthodox Lutherans were deeply disturbed by attacks on the authority of Scripture and by an assortment of anti-American foreign policy statements. The new ELCA gave liberal church leaders a bureaucracy and an authority to better pursue their agenda, increasing the challenge for the small group of conservative Lutherans.

For several years the organization's bimonthly publication had a paid circulation of just over two thousand, and virtually all the work was done by a board of fifteen people. (The ELCA reportedly has nearly 4 million members.) Group leaders played a role in the rejection of the report on human sexuality that enraged a great many church members. But on the whole, the organization's impact was minimal.

Liberal church leaders treated Lutherans for Religious and Political Freedom with a mixture of silence and contempt. When the group's founder, David Carlson, left for a nondenominational church, the establishment publication, *The Lutheran*, paired his photograph with that of a pastor who had been charged with a sex crime.[123]

In June 1989, several hundred traditionalists of the Episcopal Church met in Fort Worth, Texas, to create the Episcopal Synod of America (ESA), the culmination of a variety of conservative groups formed since the 1960s. Bishop Clarence C. Pope Jr., of the Diocese of Fort Worth, gave the opening address.

The secular press is primarily interested in the vexing symptoms of our problem—the ordination of women to the presbyterate and episcopate, problems related to practicing homosexuality, the dangerous and seemingly unstoppable influence of radical feminist theology, questions related to how we shall address God, the authority of the Bible, the nature of tradition, marital fidelity, and personal morality, as examples.

But at the heart of the crisis, he said, was

the loss of respect for the authority of Holy Scripture and the embracing of a worldview that ignores history. Under these circumstances both Scripture and tradition are treated as personal possessions to be tried on from time to time. If they fit the current fad of the age, then all well and good—but if not, then toss them aside for more exciting vesture.[124]

Only 18 (of more than 200) bishops, one-third of whom had jurisdiction, initially supported ESA, and that number soon dropped.[125] The organization's leadership was weak. Its ranks failed to include more than 1.5 percent of the church's active membership. Within a few years, ESA had seriously disintegrated and scores of orthodox clergy, some of the brightest and holiest people in the denomination, had left the Episcopal Church. A large number of their colleagues had succumbed to liberal pressures to conform.

As these examples illustrate, there is good reason to be pessimistic about the ability of orthodox mainliners to reform their denominations. The laity, however conservative, remain largely uninformed and uninterested. Clergy, formed by the seminaries, often ambitious, and eager to avoid clashes with feminists and other strident members of their congregations, tend to conform to liberal demands. And as we have seen, the liberal leadership of the mainline remains firmly stuck in the sixties—far more eager to win the approval of the *Washington Post* and the National Organization for Women than to appear faithful to writings, creeds, and traditions from the "dead" past.

The United Church of Christ reformer David Runnion-Bareford states flatly that people of his mind will not be successful in the struggle with mainline liberals in the UCC, and that conservatives will have to go elsewhere. A serious exodus began in 1991, he says, after efforts to work with ruling liberals proved futile. (Runnion-Bareford's journal, *The Witness*, noted in August 1995 that since 1992 the UCC had lost an average of 42 churches and 27,500 members a year.[126]) Within the next decade, he thinks, many orthodox Christians from several denominations might unite.[127]

The Rev. John Eby, a traditionalist in the American Baptist Church, says that he is optimistic one day and pessimistic the next. In September 1995, he was one of forty Baptist pastors who met in Pomona, California, to step up their reform efforts, deciding to hire a full-time director and organize at the grassroots level. People are leaving in droves, he says, and the exodus has somehow to be stopped.[128]

The Rev. Robert Miller, associate editor of the *Presbyterian Layman*, believes that denominationalism as we know it today will soon be a thing of the past. "The whole emphasis will increasingly be on local churches and smaller regional groupings." Miller's evangelical magazine, with a circulation of 520,000 and a readership of 1.2 million, has contributed greatly, he believes, to the growing gap between the liberal rulership of the Presbyterian Church (USA) and the people in the pews. "We are helping make the transition to whatever form happens next."[129]

The Rev. Sam Edwards, who heads the ESA, is gloomy about the future of his denomination: "Institutionally, the Episcopal Church is collapsing into the vacuum of amorality that its leadership has fostered and its membership has been willing to tolerate." He has no qualms about the nature of the liberal opposition: "it is fierce, implacable, amoral, heartlessly sentimental, and totalitarian." And yet Edwards believes that all things are possible with

God, and that, if it be His will, the Church might yet be rescued from heresy, sin, and oblivion.[130]

The Methodist Jim Heidinger, who is more hopeful, uses the analogy of the Soviet Union: an empire led by aging bureaucrats who ruled by intimidation and lacked popular support suddenly, unexpectedly collapsed. That could be the fate of the liberal establishment, he believes.[131]

There is no law of history decreeing the victor in this struggle. The liberal notion of a clock that can move only "forward"—that is to say, in a liberal direction—is merely self-serving. Writer Digby Anderson has pointed out that the Victorians turned the clock back in the late 1800s by reversing the spiritual and moral slide brought on by the Enlightenment. "By the end of the century they had substantially reduced crime, halved illegitimacy, and produced a complex, powerful, and sophisticated moral order. And not only a moral order but a moral understanding and language. Virtue had been lost. Virtue was restored." Anderson concludes: "The problem does not lie with the clock. Its hands can be moved in either direction. The problem is whether men want to turn its hands back, want to do so enough to suffer the consequences."[132]

It is too early to forecast the fate of the mainline churches with any certainty. They may, of course, be renewed. But there are at least two other possibilities. Plans are underway, under the banner of the Consultation on Church Union (COCU), to unite mainline churches in a loose sense—there will not be a merger of existing organizations—early in the next century. Should that happen, in what one wag has called the mating of dinosaurs, the denominations might remain as they are, continuing to shrink individually but together appearing, at least for a time, large and influential. In the new alliance, further shifts to the left can be expected as church bureaucrats strive for authority commensurate with larger membership numbers.

The United Church of Christ, for one, is determined that the new "Churches in Covenant Communion" will carry its ideological banners. The Twentieth Synod of the UCC, meeting in the summer of 1995, approved the COCU proposal but stated that the UCC would not be compelled to baptize in the name of the Father, Son, and Holy Spirit (a "sexist" formulary). The United Church of Christ also appended to its acceptance a note stating that the ordination of gay, lesbian, and bisexual persons was a gift the UCC was bringing to COCU.[133]

Some mainliners are unenthusiastic about a COCU alliance. Catholic-minded Episcopal bishops, for example, are leery about a mutual recognition of ministries that does not require the reordination of Protestant clergy to insure apostolic succession. When the Christian Church agreed to be one of the "Churches in Covenant Communion," in September 1995, members of the evangelical Disciples Renewal expressed deep concern, in part because of the UCC position on the ordination of practicing homosexuals, which, they feared, would be approved and encouraged by COCU.[134] The power of dissenters to derail dreams of a liberal Protestant superchurch remains to be seen.

Perhaps the mainline churches will continue to exist, within or outside COCU, but not as Christian churches. On the horizon, at least in some chic quarters, are blends of New Age religion that include rock crystals, "channeling," earth/goddess worship, and Gnosticism, an ancient heresy that denied the biblical account of the life of Jesus, said that matter is evil, and claimed that truth comes from within the individual.

The veteran religion writer Russell Chandler said in 1994, "Now, New Age has gone mainstream. It's also had a growing influence in mainline churches."[135] Kosmin and Lachman report, "An inevitable friendship has developed between the New Age followers and the adherents of smaller pre–Christian European religious traditions, the neopagans and the Wiccans, or witches."[136] Maurice Smith, an expert on New Age, commented, "If I had to put my finger on one reason New Age is popular, it is the belief that you are God, and therefore can determine what is right and wrong. . . . New Age is the ultimate do-it-yourself religious system."[137]

Should the mainline churches choose to remain as they are, separate or united, or descend into witchcraft and the like, their survival in the long run seems extremely doubtful. They could sputter on for decades without orthodox Christianity, of course, appealing to an assortment of professors, radical feminists, and vegetarians. But their appeal would be increasingly minimal.

The continuing moral and cultural disintegration of American society will clearly have an impact on the struggle over the future of the mainline churches. The political scientist James Q. Wilson reports: "Surveys I have taken, and others I have read, indicate that the single most widespread concern of middle-class Americans is over the decay of values—evidenced by crime in the streets, juvenile delinquency, public lewdness, and the like but going much beyond these manifestations to include everything that suggests that people no longer act in accordance with decent values and right reason."[138]

Malcolm Muggeridge has observed: "The movement away from Christian moral standards has not meant moving to an alternative humanistic system of moral standards as was anticipated, but moving into a moral vacuum."[139] Millions of Americans today are reconsidering the role of religion in this country, questioning the desire of many liberals to have a "religion-free" culture.

In mid-1995, a gang in Milwaukee repeatedly raped a fourteen-year-old girl in the early hours of the morning. The attackers were between eleven and fourteen years of age. The eleven-year-old, who carried a handgun during the incident, was the ringleader. A shaken columnist from the local liberal newspaper asked, "Has it really come to this?"[140]

A short time later, a twelve-year-old in New York City was shot dead in a dispute with a sixteen-year-old over twenty-five cents. A neighbor of the victim said, "parents need to get kids into church again and teach them about the Bible. The children need God in their lives again."[141] This is simplistic, of course, for we do not know exactly how to change human character for the better.[142] Still, it is clear from experience that the neighbor's formula would be a major step in the right direction.

In July 1995 President Clinton asked publicly: "Don't you believe that if every kid in every difficult neighborhood in America were in a religious institution on weekends——a synagogue on Saturday, a church on Sunday, a mosque on Friday—don't you really believe that the drug rate, the crime rate, the violence rate, the sense of self-destruction would go way down and the quality and character of this country would go way up?" The editors of the *Wall Street Journal* commented, "If Ronald Reagan had said that about the social worth of simple religious belief in 1982, they would have laughed him off the TV screens. This is 1995, and no one's laughing anymore."[143]

When John Henry Newman led an effort in the early nineteenth century to revive the Church of England spiritually, it is said that he placed these words beneath a picture of Oxford University hung in his room: "Can these dry bones live?"[144] That is precisely the question we must ask of the liberal Protestant churches as we approach a new millennium.

To survive and prosper as Christian churches, the mainline denominations need to rethink and redesign their current operations in numerous ways. To begin with, there must be a greater emphasis on theological orthodoxy, an openness to the spiritual power promised in Scripture and amply described by saints throughout church history. Without such a commitment, renewal will be impossible.

Renewed mainline churches must be active, missionary-minded, demanding, disciplined, distinctive. Informed faith, personal holiness, and social concern should be top priorities—pathways to the eternal life that is, after all, the very point of our existence. If the faith be true, C. S. Lewis reminds us, "There are no *ordinary* people. You have never talked to a mere mortal. Nations, cultures, arts, civilization—these are mortal, and their life is to ours as the life of a gnat. But it is immortals whom we joke with, work with, marry, snub, and exploit—immortal horrors or everlasting splendours."[145]

As we have seen, there are critics of the mainline churches who predict their demise. David Mills, a resistance leader in the Episcopal Church, has written, "Barring divine intervention on a scale not seen since the parting of the Red Sea, they will predictably and inevitably collapse." Mills sees their mortal illness as part of a larger picture of the decay of Christendom in the West stemming from the collapse of shared beliefs and unexamined assumptions about the nature of truth. "Such also is Rome, seen as a whole; that is, as including Hans Kung and Rosemary Radford Ruether as well as Pope John Paul II. Such will be Orthodoxy as well, when those churches have more fully been infected by modernity and the cultural ghetto that has so far protected them has finally turned into a suburb."[146]

There is indeed cause for pessimism. But in my judgment, the possibility of self-transformation remains alive. If enough mainliners become sufficiently informed and concerned, I believe, they have a chance of reviving and invigorating their churches. With determination and energy, for example, elections can be won. Liberals, let us remember, are a minority—a fact they prefer to conceal. Zealous leftists who took over several labor unions in the 1930s and 1940s were eventually ousted by the rank and file (to be sure, with the help of the United States Congress). In the mainline, a full-scale struggle would be fierce, and the orthodox forces would have to be much larger and more committed than they are now. David Mills reminds us that in the mainline "liberals inevitably fight longer and harder and yell louder than orthodox believers, who have better things to do, like care for their families and evangelize the lost."[147]

Liberal bureaucracies can be dismantled. The most effective way to achieve this is through the power of the purse strings. That process is already underway, as we have seen, as laity leave and reduce their pledges. One way to stop the flow of liberal propaganda from headquarters is to make it too expensive to publish.

New leadership can reform seminaries. And the process of finding and electing orthodox leaders can be hastened by the protestations and selective donations of concerned clergy and laity. A determination by enough church members not to fund the promoters of heresy, immorality, and general kookiness could have a profound impact. Failing that, new seminaries can be founded. The success story of Trinity Episcopal School for Ministry has already been noted.

Renewed mainline churches would be vital and vigorous, commanding the loyalty, obedience, respect, and self-sacrifice of orthodox Christians. That vision might inspire the majority of mainliners to go to work to save their spiritual homes. But it might also fail to be grasped, permitting the liberal Protestant churches to proceed on their steady slide toward complete irrelevance.

NOTES

Chapter 1. Confused and Helpless

1. Sometimes the Reformed Church of America appears on such lists instead of the Lutherans. One important study divides the mainline denominations into liberal and moderate categories. The Episcopal, Presbyterian, and United Church of Christ churches are termed liberal, while the Methodists, Lutherans, Disciples of Christ, Northern Baptists, and Reformed churches are called moderate. See Wade Clark Roof and William McKinney, *American Mainline Religion: Its Changing Shape and Future* (New Brunswick, N.J., 1987), pp. 81–90, 110–47. There is value in this distinction. Episcopalians are clearly more liberal than Baptists, for example. But the overall similarities among the churches, in my judgment, warrant usage here of the standard terminology. See also William R. Hutchison, "Protestantism as Establishment," in William R. Hutchison (ed.), *Between the Times: The Travail of the Protestant Establishment in America, 1900–1960* (Cambridge, 1989), pp. 4–6. For a valuable list of mainline characteristics, see Peter W. Williams, *America's Religions: Traditions and Cultures* (New York, 1990), pp. 333–34.

2. Barry A. Kosmin and Seymour P. Lachman, *One Nation Under God: Religion in Contemporary American Society* (New York, 1993), pp. 43, 257–63. In 1974, the University of Chicago's National Opinion Research Center came up with very different findings. Dividing American whites into seventeen ethnic and religious backgrounds and scoring them by educational attainment and family income, the center found that the Episcopalians, the

213

highest WASP group, ranked only sixth, behind American Jews, then Irish, Italian, German, and Polish Catholics. See the analysis by James Webb in *Wall Street Journal*, June 5, 1995. On data from the 1980s, see Kosmin and Lachman, *One Nation Under God*, p. 256.

3. Ibid., pp. 43, 253, and data from the researcher Albert Menendez as reported by Richard John Neuhaus in "While We're At It," *First Things*, May, 1995, p. 86.

4. See William R. Hutchison, "Past Imperfect: History and the Prospect for Liberalism," in Robert S. Michaelsen and Wade Clark Roof (eds.), *Liberal Protestantism: Realities and Possibilities* (New York, 1986), pp. 65–82.

5. I Thessalonians 2:13, Galatians 1:8–10, Ephesians 4:14, inter alia.

6. The same conditions may be witnessed in Britain and Sweden. See "Moralization and Demoralization: A Moral Explanation for Changes in Crime, Disorder and Social Problems," in Digby Anderson (ed.), *The Loss of Virtue: Moral Confusion and Social Disorder in Britain and America* (New York, 1992), pp. 3–13.

7. *Wall Street Journal*, November 19, 1994; "To Boldly Go . . . ," *National Review*, December 5, 1994, p. 16. One study shows that three out of four Americans believe the nation is suffering from moral decay; 84 percent wish that moral values more often guided government policies. Amitai Etzioni, "The Politics of Morality," *Wall Street Journal*, November 13, 1995.

8. Os Guinness, *The American Hour: A Time of Reckoning and the Once and Future Role of Faith* (New York, 1993), p. 29.

9. *Wall Street Journal*, December 28, 1994.

10. Paul C. Vitz, *Psychology as Religion: The Cult of Self-Worship* 2d ed. (Grand Rapids, Mich., 1994), p. 167.

11. George Gilder, "Breaking the Box," *National Review*, August 15, 1994, pp. 37–38.

12. Cited by Cal Thomas in *Milwaukee Journal*, August 1, 1993.

13. Peter Mullen, "Enough is Enough!," *National Catholic Register*, September 5, 1993, p. 1.

14. *Los Angeles Times* story in *Milwaukee Journal Sentinel*, June 14, 1995.

15. William J. Bennett, *The Index of Leading Cultural Indicators* (Washington, D.C., 1993). The quotation is from p. ii. Total federal, state, and local spending on the welfare system in 1993 amounted to $325 billion. "Lies, Damned Lies, and Welfare Reform," *National Review*, July 11, 1994.

16. Michele D. Wilson and Alain Joffe, "Adolescent Medicine," *Journal of the American Medical Association*, June 7, 1995, p. 1657.

17. *Milwaukee Journal Sentinel*, July 10, 1995. Still, FBI data show a decrease in crime in recent years.

18. *Wall Street Journal*, November 9, 1994. In the year ending June 30, 1995, the prison population grew by almost 9 percent, the largest increase on record. *Milwaukee Journal Sentinel*, December 4, 1995.

19. *Wall Street Journal*, October 29, 1993.

20. *Milwaukee Journal Sentinel*, June 7, 1995. For comparative historical data from the United States and Europe, see Gertrude Himmelfarb, *The Demoralization of Society: From Victorian Virtues to Modern Values* (New York, 1995), pp. 222–24. "In teenage illegitimacy," she points out on page 224, "the United States has earned the dubious distinction of ranking first among all industrial nations."

21. *Milwaukee Journal*, August 30, 1994. Clifford D. May of the *Rocky Mountain News* soon pointed out, however, that the Census Bureau data revealed that 72.8 percent of all American children lived with married parents. This figure included the widows, widowers, and divorced people who had remarried to re-create traditional nuclear families. Ibid., September 7, 1994.

22. *Wall Street Journal*, December 28, 1995.

23. Ibid., April 25, 1995.

24. *Chicago Tribune*, July 18, 1994; E. J. Dionne in the *Washington Post*, September 13, 1994.

25. Meg Greenfield, "The Real 'Character Issue,'" *Newsweek*, May 23, 1994, p. 46.

26. "Prayer in Schools: Our Readers Respond," *Parade Magazine*, January 1, 1995, p. 14, in *Milwaukee Journal*, January 1, 1995.

27. *Milwaukee Journal Sentinel*, May 22, 1995. Another nationwide poll released later that year reported that 76 percent of those questioned said they rarely or never trusted "government to do what is right." Ibid., August 1, 1995. This degree of public cynicism toward government is unprecedented in polls.

28. William Murchison, *Reclaiming Morality in America* (Nashville, 1994), p. 122.

29. William M. Newman, "The Meanings of a Merger: Denominational Identity in the United Church of Christ," in Jackson Carroll and Wade

Clark Roof (eds.), *Beyond Establishment: Protestant Identity in a Post-Protestant Age* (Louisville, Ky., 1993), pp. 296–307. The quotation is from p. 305.

30. Kenneth L. Woodward, "Dead End for the Mainline?" *Newsweek,* August 9, 1993, p. 46.

31. *Foundations Daily,* September 2, 1994. This was a publication of the Episcopal Synod of America.

32. Robert Wuthnow, *Christianity in the 21st Century: Reflections on the Challenges Ahead* (New York, 1993), pp. 39–40.

33. "Cautious Methodists," *In Trust* (Autumn 1993): 24.

34. Mark Tooley, "Madness in Their Methodism: The Religious Left Has a Summit," *Heterodoxy,* May 1995, p. 6.

35. Kenneth B. Bedell (ed.), *Yearbook of American and Canadian Churches 1996* (Nashville, 1996), pp. 250–56. In the "Inclusive" category, the Disciples of Christ cite 937,644, the Episcopal Church lists 2.5 million, the Lutherans claim 5.2 million, and the Presbyterians use 3.7 million. The 1994 data on the Episcopal Church came from *The Episcopal Church Annual, 1996* (Harrisburg, Pa., 1996), p. 19. The Church has roughly the same number of active members as it had in 1945!

36. Bedell (ed.), *Yearbook of American and Canadian Churches,* pp. 252, 255–56.

37. The standard date of 1850 has been corrected in Roger Finke and Rodney Stark, *The Churching of America, 1776–1990: Winners and Losers in Our Religious Economy* (New Brunswick, N.J., 1992), pp. 110–13. There are nearly 500,000 churches, temples, and other places of worship in the United States, and at least 2000 denominations. See George Gallup, Jr., *Religion in America, 1996* (Princeton, 1996), p. 5.

38. See Dean R. Hoge, Benton Johnson, and Donald A. Luidens, *Vanishing Boundaries: The Religion of Mainline Protestant Baby Boomers* (Louisville, Ky., 1994), pp. 4–8.

39. Woodward, "Dead End for the Mainline?" p. 47. See Wade Clark Roof, *A Generation of Seekers: The Spiritual Journeys of the Baby Boom Generation* (San Francisco, 1993), pp. 177–78. And yet six in ten people under the age of thirty tell Gallup pollsters that they are members of a church or synagogue. "Church Membership Continues to Show Remarkable Stability," *emerging trends,* March 1995, p. 4.

40. Cf. Finke and Stark, *The Churching of America,* p. 8.

41. "United Methodists Show Age, Says Survey," *Christian Century,* July 5–12, 1995, p. 673.

42. Roof and McKinney, *American Mainline Religion*, pp. 152–54.

43. Quoted in Woodward, "Dead End for the Mainline?" p. 47.

44. John L. Ronsvalle and Sylvia Ronsvalle, *The State of Church Giving Through 1993* (Champaign, Ill., 1995), pp. 24, 28, 36.

45. *Wall Street Journal*, July 7, 1995.

46. *Milwaukee Journal Sentinel*, May 29, December 26, 1995; Michael Gazzaniga in "Legalizing Drugs: Just Say Yes," *National Review*, July 10, 1995, p. 46.

47. See "Bottom Lines," *In Trust* (Summer 1993): 25; "Bottom Lines," ibid. (Spring 1994): 21–22. Still, in 1994, donations to religions totaled $58.87 billion, making it by far the top charitable priority. Gifts to education, for example, came to $16.71 billion. *Wall Street Journal*, May 25, 1995.

48. "Presbyterians Delay Action on Gay Ban," *In Trust* (Autumn 1993): 23.

49. *Milwaukee Journal*, December 17, 1994.

50. Ibid., June 12, 1993.

51. *Milwaukee Journal Sentinel*, May 2, 1995; "Council Cuts Budget $2.45 million for '95–'96," *Episcopal Life* (December 1995): 5.

52. P. A. Crow, "National Council of Churches of Christ in the U.S.A.," in Daniel G. Reid et al., *Dictionary of Christianity in America* (Downers Grove, Ill., 1990), p. 799.

53. Roof and McKinney, *American Mainline Religion*, pp. 150–51.

54. George Gallup Jr. and Jim Castelli, *The People's Religion: American Faith in the 90's* (New York, 1989), p. 259.

55. Ibid., p. 141. See also p. 263.

56. See Finke and Stark, *The Churching of America*, p. 167.

57. *The Episcopal Church Annual, 1996*, pp. 29–30.

58. Robert Wood Lynn, "'The Survival of Recognizably Protestant Colleges': Reflections on Old-Line Protestantism, 1950–1990," in George M. Marsden and Bradley J. Longfield (eds.), *The Secularization of the Academy* (New York, 1992), p. 171.

59. *Washington Times*, March 29, 1994. See Kosmin and Lachman, *One Nation Under God,* pp. 190–92. This study found that only 18 percent of members in the United Church of Christ and 23 percent of Episcopalians were Democrats.

60. In contrast, 48 percent called themselves conservative or somewhat conservative. Telephone poll conducted by Greenberg Research for the Democratic Leadership Council, released on November 17, 1994, by the

Roper Center for Public Opinion. Cf. Gallup and Castelli, *The People's Religion*, p. 224.

61. John C. Green, James L. Guth, Lyman A. Kellstedt, and Corwin E. Smidt, "Murphy Brown Revisited: The Social Issues in the 1992 Election," in Michael Cromartie (ed.), *Disciples And Democracy: Religious Conservatives and the Future of American Politics* (Grand Rapids, Mich., 1994), p. 51.

62. Stanley Hauerwas and William H. Willimon, *Resident Aliens. . .* (Nashville, 1989), p. 38. Cf. Thomas Sieger Derr, "Continuity and Change in Mainline Protestantism," in Richard John Neuhaus (ed.), *The Believable Future of American Protestantism* (Grand Rapids, Mich., 1988), pp. 50, 56–57, 61–62, which challenges the link between religious and political liberalism within the mainline. On the other hand (p. 66), we read: "The mainline tends to have a liberal social agenda, while much of the evangelical grouping is markedly to the right."

63. *Milwaukee Journal*, June 4, 1992.

64. Woodward, "Dead End for the Mainline?" p. 48.

65. Tooley, "Madness in Their Methodism," p. 6.

66. Interview with David Runnion-Bareford, December 13, 1995.

67. Interview with James V. Heidinger II, December 18, 1995.

68. Leonard R. Klein, "Lutherans in Sexual Commotion" *First Things* (May 1994): 35. The Evangelical Lutheran Church in America sets racial and sexual quotas for members of committees and assemblies at the churchwide and synodical levels. See Edgar R. Trexler, "Bishops Affirm Quotas, *The Lutheran*, March 1995, p. 33.

69. Interview with David Carlson, December 13, 1995.

70. W. Clark Gilpin, "The Theological Schools: Transmission, Transformation, and Transcendance of Denominational Culture," in Carroll and Roof, *Beyond Establishment*, p. 194.

71. Manfred T. Brauch, "Let Us Now Praise Foolishness," *In Trust* (Spring 1994): 5.

72. Thomas C. Oden, "Measured Critique or Ham-handed Trivia?," ibid., pp. 24–25. See his *Requiem: A Lament in Three Movements* (Nashville, 1995), a powerful indictment of contemporary theological education. Cf. Donald E. Messer, *Calling Church and Seminary into the 21st Century* (Nashville, 1995), a predictable liberal response by the president of a Methodist seminary.

73. Hauerwas and Willimon, *Resident Aliens*, pp. 166, 170.

74. *Washington Times*, April 21, 1994.

75. Ibid.

76. Ibid.

77. Richard L. Tafel, "And From My Lips Will Come What Is Right," *Harvard Magazine*, July/August, 1991, p. 12. For more on the left at Harvard Divinity School, see John Hinton, "Ivy League Theology," *Academic Questions* (Spring 1993): 37–45, and Jendi Reiter, "God And Womon at Harvard," *Heterodoxy*, June, 1992, p. 12. See also Ari L. Goldman, *The Search For God at Harvard* (New York, 1991), a book that unintentionally documents the worst of what conservative critics have said about HDS. See especially pages 275–83.

78. Hinton, "Ivy League Theology," *Academic Questions* (Spring 1993): 42.

79. Paul Wilkes, "The Hands That Would Shape Our Souls," *Atlantic Monthly*, December 1990, p. 74. For more on contemporary seminary students, see Christopher R. Seitz, "Pluralism and the Lost Art of Christian Apology," *First Things* (June/July 1994): 17–18; "Enrollments Up a Little," *In Trust* (New Year 1993): 26; Melinda R. Heppe, "Women Seminarians Prefer Theology," *In Trust* (Easter 1993): 4–5; Melinda R. Heppe, "Changing Concepts of Leadership," *In Trust* (Summer 1994): 6–7.

80. Melinda R. Heppe, "Changing Concepts of Leadership," *In Trust* (Summer 1994): 6.

81. Many seminarians (one female student in six) have experienced failed marriages. Some suffer from a variety of psychological problems. Wilkes, "The Hands That Would Shape Our Souls," p. 61.

82. Melinda R. Heppe, "A Significant Responsibility: New Faculty Reflect on Finding a Balance," *In Trust* (Summer 1995): 17.

83. Tafel, "And From My Lips Will Come What Is Right," p. 12.

84. Seitz, "Pluralism and the Lost Art of Christian Apology," 17–18.

85. Interview with Dan Baumgarten, December 16, 1995. Baumgarten is a 37-year-old moderate who estimates that as much as a third of the Princeton faculty is conservative.

86. "Life At Nashotah House," *Nashotah House Catalogue 1995–1996*, pp. 6–11. The quotation is from p. 7.

87. While Nashotah House has admitted women since 1969, it does not acknowledge the priesthood of women and will not permit them to function sacerdotally. This is part of the seminary's more than 150-year tradition

of faithfulness to the Catholic heritage, the source of much of the institution's current difficulties within the Episcopal Church.

88. A leading official of the Disciples of Christ estimates that 90 percent of the denomination's 36 regions would not favor the ordination of practicing homosexuals. There is no denominational policy. Interview with Donald Manworren, January 2, 1996.

89. William F. Willoughby, "UCC: A Libertarian Stance on Sexuality," *Christian Century*, August 3–10, 1977, p. 676.

90. *Milwaukee Journal*, June 14, 1994.

91. In contrast, 109 bishops signed a statement in 1994 affirming an orthodox statement on morality. For a good summary of recent developments, see Robert Randolph, "Revival or Decline?" *Evangelical Catholic* (March/April 1995): 1, 8–13.

92. *The Episcopal Church Annual, 1996*, p. 94. For examples of the influence of lesbians in the caucus, see "Women's Caucus Targets Patriarchy," *The Living Church*, October 22, 1995, p. 7. At times the caucus has worked closely with Integrity, an influential church organization devoted to expanding homosexual rights.

93. John Shelby Spong, *Rescuing the Bible From Fundamentalism: A Bishop Rethinks the Meaning of Scripture* (San Francisco, 1991), pp. 116–19.

94. The Yale historian Boswell died of complications from AIDS late that year.

95. *New York Times*, February 8, 1996.

96. *Milwaukee Journal Sentinel*, December 18, 1995. Of course, AIDS is not to be taken lightly. A study published in 1995 reported that one in every 92 young American men, ages 27 to 39, may have been battling the AIDS virus in 1993. The study's author, a health analyst at the National Cancer Institute, estimated that between 630,000 and 897,000 people were infected as of the first month of that year. Ibid., November 24, 1995.

97. *The Episcopal Church Annual, 1996*, p. 80.

98. Editorial, "In This Corner," and "Resolutions Adopted by General Convention," *The Living Church*, September 25, 1994, pp. 2, 7; *Foundations Daily*, September 2, 1994.

99. Murchison, *Reclaiming Morality in America*, p. 53.

100. Klein, "Lutherans in Sexual Commotion," pp. 31–38.

101. *Milwaukee Journal*, July 3, 1993.

102. William H. Willimon, *What's Right With the Church* (San Francisco, 1989), p. 59.

103. Mark A. Noll, "The Lutheran Difference," *First Things* (February 1992): 36.

104. See Theodore McConnell, "Why George Bush Should Become a Baptist," *The Living Church*, February 16, 1992, pp. 11–12.

105. K. L. Billingsley, "PC Goes to Church," *Heterodoxy*, May-June 1993, p. 15.

106. "Events And People," *Christian Century*, July 24, 1991, p. 712.

107. Robert Bezilla (ed.), *Religion in America: 1992–1993* (Princeton, 1993), p. 75.

108. Cited in Richard John Neuhaus, *The Naked Public Square: Religion and Democracy in America*, 2d ed. (Grand Rapids, Mich., 1986), p. 243.

109. Ibid., p. 73. For a 1987 poll confirming this general point, see James Davison Hunter, *Culture Wars: The Struggle to Define America* (New York, 1991), pp. 116–17.

110. "Firing Frenzy?" *Christian Ministry*, May-June, 1994, p. 5. In a 1995 poll conducted by the Times Mirror Center for the People and the Press, 55 percent gave high ratings to the character of the nation's religious leaders. *Milwaukee Journal Sentinel*, May 22, 1995.

111. William R. MacKaye, "Out of Bounds: The Call to End Sexual Misconduct in the Churches," *In Trust* (Autumn 1993): 8.

112. Ibid.

113. Bob Libby, "New Laws Provide for Stronger Response to Clergy Misconduct," *The Living Church*, September 18, 1994, p. 7.

114. *Milwaukee Journal*, January 27, 1995.

115. *National Catholic Register*, February 21, 1993; March 20, 1994; *Milwaukee Journal*, January 23, 1995.

116. Barbara Brown Zikmund, Adair T. Lummis, and Patricia M. Y. Chang, "Second Preliminary Report of the Ordained Women and Men Study," Center for Social and Religious Research," Hartford Seminary, October, 1995, pp. 8–9.

117. David L. Miller, "Is There Any Word From The Lord?," *The Lutheran*, March, 1995, p. 9.

118. John B. Cobb Jr., "Faith Seeking Understanding: The Renewal of Christian Thinking," *Christian Century*, June 29–July 6, 1994, p. 642.

119. Frank C. Strasburger and Robert Cain, "Why the Young Ones Have Gone: Two Responses," *Plumbline, A Journal of Ministry in Higher Education* (November 1994): 20–21.

120. Thomas Day, *Why Catholics Can't Sing: The Culture of Catholicism and the Triumph of Bad Taste* (New York, 1990), p. 69.

121. Quoted in Woodward, "Dead End for the Mainline?" p. 47.

122. Interview with James V. Heidinger II, December 18, 1995. For the poll, conducted by Wright State University scholars, see Michael Sigler, "Methodism Unmasked: Official Survey Reveals Membership Still Conservative," *Good News* (November/December 1990): 15–19.

123. Kosmin and Lachman, *One Nation Under God*, pp. 191, 193.

124. Klein, "Lutherans in Sexual Commotion," p. 31.

125. "Centrist Backlash," *In Trust* (New Year 1994): 23. A poll of Episcopalians taken in 1994 by the church's independent weekly magazine, *The Living Church*, revealed strong opposition to the blessing of same-sex marriages, the ordination of practicing homosexual persons, and the mandatory acceptance of women as priests—major planks in the left's platform. See "Voices of Episcopalians," *The Living Church*, June 12, 1994, p. 13.

126. "It's All The Rave," *The Living Church*, November 27, 1994, p. 7.

127. Rosemary Radford Ruether, *Women-Church: Theology and Practice of Feminist Liturgical Communities* (San Francisco, 1988), pp. 273–74.

128. Church review by Daniel Sack in *Anglican and Episcopal History*, March, 1995, p. 113.

129. Patricia Wainwright, "The Gospel in Rock 'n' Roll," *The Living Church*, April 2, 1995, p. 9.

130. Chris Fouse, "Don't Underestimate Our Youth!" *Foundations*, March/April, 1994, p. 5.

131. Editorial, "Show and Tell," *The Living Church*, June 20, 1993, p. 9.

132. Letter of Alexander Seabrook in ibid., April 9, 1995.

133. Donald E. Miller, *The Case for Liberal Christianity* (San Francisco, 1981), pp. 15, 19.

134. *Milwaukee Journal*, May 3, 1994.

135. Donald A. Luidens, "Numbering the Presbyterian Branches: Membership Trends Since Colonial Times," in Milton J. Coalter, John M. Mulder, and Louis B. Weeks (eds.), *The Mainstream Protestant "Decline"* (Louisville, Ky., 1990), p. 64.

136. Charles S. MacKenzie, "Deformation of the Church," in Stanley Atkins and Theodore McConnell (eds.), *Churches on the Wrong Road* (Chicago, 1986), p. 30.

137. Neuhaus, *The Naked Public Square*, pp. 19, 110. When asked how often public issues or political candidates were discussed during your church service, only 9 percent told Gallup "often." Forty-three percent said "occasionally" and 46 percent said "never." "Political Discussions at Church?" *emerging trends*, April 1995, p. 4.

138. Noll, "The Lutheran Difference," p. 37.

139. "Who Belongs to the Religious Right?" *emerging trends*, April 1995, pp. 1–2.

140. Grover G. Norquist, "Hate Trick," *American Spectator*, September 1994, p. 62; *Wall Street Journal*, November 28, 1994. By mid-September 1995, the coalition had 1.7 million members, 1,700 chapters, and links with more than 75,000 churches. Editorial, ibid., September 14, 1995.

141. Ibid., July 19, 1994. Still, coalition members represented only 15 percent of registered Republicans, and their turnout at the polls in November 1994 was only 22 percent of the total GOP turnout. Letter from Michael Cudahy in ibid., March 2, 1995.

142. *Milwaukee Journal*, July 14, 1994.

143. *Milwaukee Journal Sentinel*, April 14, 1995.

144. Roof, *A Generation of Seekers*, p. 177.

145. Quoted in Hunter, *Culture Wars*, p. 145.

146. James Hitchcock, *What Is Secular Humanism? Why Humanism Became Secular and How It Is Changing Our World* (Ann Arbor, Mich., 1982), p. 17.

147. Roof and McKinney, *American Mainline Religion*, pp. 159–61.

148. Dean M. Kelley, *Why Conservative Churches Are Growing: A Study in Sociology of Religion* (Macon, Ga., 1986), p. xxii.

149. Roof and McKinney, *American Mainline Religion*, p. 20.

150. Finke and Stark, *The Churching of America*, p. 1. See also pp. 245–50.

151. This was true especially of members who felt involved in decision making and were comfortable with the leadership's handling of finances. Giving was highest among members of the Assemblies of God, with annual per capita contributions of $628. Presbyterians gave $611, Baptists $550, Lutherans $415, and Catholics $160. Assembly of God members are expected to tithe, and there is a similarly strong emphasis among Baptists.

Catholics, Lutherans, and Presbyterians have lower, if any, expectations. See Dean R. Hoge, Charles Zech, Patrick McNamara, and Michael J. Donahue, "Description of Congregations and Laity in the 1993 American Congregational Giving Study," the first of four preliminary study reports available through Professor Hoge.

152. Kosmin and Lachman, *One Nation Under God*, p. 197. There are evangelicals in many denominations, including the mainline. Gallup reports that 57 percent of Baptists, 32 percent of Methodists, 29 percent of Lutherans, 27 percent of Presbyterians, and 14 percent of Episcopalians say they are "born-again" Christians. Gallup and Castelli, *The People's Religion*, p. 93. About 20 percent of all evangelicals, Kosmin and Lachman report, are black.

153. *Milwaukee Journal*, April 23, 1994.

154. See, for example, Richard N. Ostling, "The Church Search," *Time*, April 5, 1993, pp. 44–49.

155. Daniel V. A. Olson, "Fellowship Ties and the Transmission of Religious Identity," in Carroll and Roof (eds.), *Beyond Establishment*, pp. 32–51.

156. *Milwaukee Journal*, April 23, 1994.

157. Ronsvalle, *The State of Church Giving Through 1993*, pp. 24–29.

158. David F. Wells, *No Place for Truth, or Whatever Happened to Evangelical Theology?* (Grand Rapids, Mich., 1993), pp. 12, 131, 134.

159. Address by The Rev. Roger Jack Bunday, December 21, 1995, at All Saints' Cathedral, Milwaukee.

160. Interview with Robert Miller, December 27, 1995.

161. Roof and McKinney, *American Mainline Religion*, pp. 112–13. The Methodists have 13 percent college graduates, the Lutherans 12 percent, and the Disciples of Christ 11 percent. The "no religious preference" category has 25 percent.

162. Interview with Jeffrey Wallen, December 9, 1995.

163. Interview with David Carlson, December 13, 1995.

Chapter 2. Consumer Christianity

1. Robert Kelley, *The Cultural Pattern in American Politics: The First Century* (New York, 1979), p. 39.

2. See Dumas Malone, *Jefferson the Virginian* (Boston, 1948), pp. 106–9,

237, 274–80; Daniel J. Boorstin, *The Lost World of Thomas Jefferson* (New York, 1948), pp. 119–66.

3. Marvin Meyers (ed.), *The Mind of the Founder: Sources of the Political Thought of James Madison* (Indianapolis, 1973), pp. 14–15.

4. M. E. Bradford, *Founding Fathers: Brief Lives of the Framers of the United States Constitution*, 2d ed. rev. (Lawrence, Kans., 1994), p. xvi.

5. Robert H. Bork, "What to Do About the First Amendment," *Commentary* (February 1995): 23–24.

6. Terry Eastland (ed.), *Religious Liberty in the Supreme Court: The Cases That Define the Debate Over Church and State* (Washington, D.C., 1993), pp. 71–72. Cf. Jon Butler, *Awash in a Sea of Faith: Christianizing the American People* (Cambridge, Mass., 1990), pp. 257–68.

7. *Milwaukee Journal Sentinel*, December 23, 1995.

8. Ibid., July 13, 1995.

9. Barry Schwartz, *George Washington: The Making of an American Symbol* (New York, 1987), pp. 7, 194.

10. *Zorach v. Clauson*, 343 U.S. 306, 312 (1952).

11. Alexis de Tocqueville, *Democracy in America* (New York: 1945), I, 308. Cf. Butler, *Awash in a Sea of Faith*, pp. 289–91.

12. See Roger Finke and Rodney Stark, *The Churching of America, 1776–1990: Winners and Losers in Our Religious Economy* (New Brunswick, N.J., 1992), pp. 87–104, 117–23.

13. Quoted in Alice Felt Tyler, *Freedom's Ferment: Phases of American Social History From the Colonial Period to the Outbreak of the Civil War* (New York, 1962), p. 239.

14. Roy P. Basler (ed.), *The Collected Works of Abraham Lincoln* (New Brunswick, N.J., 1953), VI, 155–56. Cf. Butler, *Awash in a Sea of Faith*, pp. 293–95.

15. Russel Nye, *The Unembarrassed Muse: The Popular Arts in America* (New York, 1973), p. 32.

16. George M. Marsden, "The Soul of the American University: A Historical Overview," in George M. Marsden and Bradley J. Longfield (eds.), *The Secularization of the Academy* (New York, 1992), p. 11.

17. *Church of the Holy Trinity v. United States*, 143 U.S. 457, 465, 471 (1892).

18. Sydney E. Ahlstrom, *A Religious History of the American People* (New Haven, Conn., 1972), p. 804.

19. William W. Sweet, *The Story of Religion in America* (New York, 1950), p. 402.

20. *United States v. Macintosh*, 283 U.S. 625 (1931).

21. Robert Wuthnow, *The Restructuring of American Religion: Society and Faith Since World War II* (Princeton, 1988), pp. 3–5.

22. George Gallup Jr. and Jim Castelli, *The People's Religion: American Faith in the 90's* (New York, 1989), p. 36.

23. *Christian Faith in Action: Commemorative Volume, The Founding of the National Council of the Churches of Christ in the United States of America* (New York, 1951), pp. 19, 147.

24. "The Most Important City," *Time*, July 4, 1960, p. 38.

25. Martin E. Marty, *Pilgrims in Their Own Land: 500 Years of Religion in America* (New York, 1985), p. 404.

26. *Zorach v. Clauson*, 343 U.S. 306, 313 (1952).

27. "The Supreme Court," *Time*, June 28, 1963, p. 13.

28. "Protestants," ibid., December 6, 1968, p. 104.

29. Thomas Sowell, *Inside American Education: The Decline, the Deception, the Dogmas* (New York, 1993), passim.

30. Thomas C. Reeves, "Partisan Revelry at the Advocacy Conference," *Academic Questions* (Fall 1995): 53–57.

31. Dinesh D'Souza, *Illiberal Education: The Politics of Race and Sex on Campus* (New York, 1991), p. 229.

32. Richard Bernstein, *Dictatorship of Virtue: Multiculturalism and the Battle for America's Future* (New York, 1994), p. 9.

33. "Religion and the Court 1995: A Symposium," *First Things* (December 1995): 25.

34. Ibid., p. 32.

35. The plea was rejected by a federal court. See Linda Chavez in *Milwaukee Journal Sentinel*, December 23, 1995.

36. Interview with Bozell in *National Catholic Register*, April 24, 1994; Media Research Center Report No. 4, "Faith in a Box: Television and Religion," March 24, 1994, passim. This report also shows that when characters on prime time dramas and sitcoms are shown to be religious, the portrayals are overwhelmingly negative.

37. *Wall Street Journal*, March 31, 1994.

38. Richard John Neuhaus, "A Word on 'The Competition,'" *First Things* (June/July 1993): 60.

39. Letter by Jerome F. Winzig in ibid., March 7, 1995.

40. Ibid., September 22, 1994.

41. Arianna Huffington, *The Fourth Instinct: The Call of the Soul* (New York, 1994), pp. 107–8.

42. Edward Farley, "The Tragic Dilemma of Church Education," in Parker J. Palmer, Barbara G. Wheeler, and James W. Fowler (eds.), *Caring for the Commonweal: Education for Religious and Public Life* (Macon, Ga., 1990), p. 142.

43. "People Think Religion Can Solve Today's Problems," *emerging trends*, March 1996, p. 4.

44. Gallup and Castelli, *The People's Religion*, pp. 4, 20.

45. Ibid., pp. 4, 17, 45, 63–64, 66, 73, 90, 102, 140. The concluding quotation is on page 90.

46. Ibid., pp. 14, 47. The only major nation to score higher was India, with 81 percent.

47. "The Importance of Religion Intensifies as People Grow Older," *emerging trends*, March 1995, pp. 4–5.

48. "Those who state no religious preference are more likely to be young, male, well educated and to live in the Northeast or the Pacific Coast region." The "nones" in effect make up the fourth-largest denomination in America, their numbers being ahead of Lutherans, Presbyterians, Episcopalians, Jews, Mormons, members of the Orthodox Church, and members of smaller Protestant sects. Gallup and Castelli, *The People's Religion*, p. 118.

49. "Judeo-Christian Faith Still Dominates Religious Preference in America," *emerging trends*, May 1995, p. 4.

50. Gallup and Castelli, *The People's Religion*, pp. 123, 131.

51. Ibid., p. 116.

52. Barry A. Kosmin and Seymour P. Lachman, *One Nation Under God: Religion in Contemporary American Society* (New York, 1993), pp. 2–5. In 1994, Gallup reported the number of adult atheists and agnostics at 3 percent. Gallup, *Religion in America, 1996,* p. 25.

53. "Judeo-Christian Faith Still Dominates Religious Preference in America, *emerging trends,* May 1995, p. 4.

54. "Church Membership Continues to Show Remarkable Stability," ibid., March 1995, p. 1.

55. Robert Bezilla (ed.), *Religion in America: 1992–1993* (Princeton, 1993), pp. 10, 18, 22, 36, 55, 66. Another study published in 1991 revealed that 86.5 percent of all new immigrants declared themselves Christians, 1.8 were Jewish, and the rest stated no religion or did not respond. The study leader said that "most immigrants are in the mainstream of the Judeo-Christian culture." Terrance Dunford, "Higher Education Confronts the 'New Demographics,'" *Academic Questions* (Winter 1991–92): 13.

56. Finke and Stark, *The Churching of America*, p. 15.

57. Cited in Ostling, "The Church Search," *Time*, April 5, 1993, p. 47.

58. Quoted in Edward T. Oakes, "Evangelical Theology in Crisis," *First Things* (October 1993): 38.

59. *USA TODAY*, April 1, 1994; "Nine Persons in 10 Believe in Heaven (But Fewer Expect to Get There)," *emerging trends*, February 1995, p. 2.

60. "Saying Grace Before Meals Still a Common Practice," ibid., May 1994, p. 2.

61. "Both Students and Parents Approve of School Prayer," ibid., March 1995, pp. 2–3. Sixty percent of teens favored prayer in the public schools.

62. "People Believe Religion Is Losing Its Impact but Not Its Relevance," ibid., April 1995, p. 5.

63. *Milwaukee Journal*, September 17, 1994.

64. Ibid., September 21, 1994.

65. "Both Students and Parents Support School Prayer," *emerging trends*, February 1995, p. 1.

66. "Religion Index Hits Ten-Year High," *emerging trends*, March 1996, p. 1.

67. George Gilder, "Breaking the Box," *National Review*, August 15, 1994, p. 40; *Wall Street Journal*, February 6, 1995. The latter article also describes the boom in Christian music and assorted merchandise, sold increasingly in the major retail outlets.

68. *Milwaukee Journal*, July 25, 1994.

69. Ibid., July 19, 1993.

70. *Wall Street Journal*, May 26, 1993.

71. Richard John Neuhaus, "Pluralism and Wrong Answers," *First Things* (June/July 1994): 72–73.

72. See Kosmin and Lachman, *One Nation Under God*, pp. 158, 166–67.

73. *Washington Times*, March 29, 1994.

74. *Syracuse Herald-Journal*, October 24, 1992.

75. David C. Stolinsky, "America: A Christian Country?" *New Oxford Review* (July/August 1994): 21.

76. About 1.8 percent of the population aged 15 or over receive communion on an average Sunday. See George Austin, "The Last Word," *Foundations* (September/October 1995): 16.

77. Alan D. Gilbert, *The Making of Post-Christian Britain: A History of the Secularization of Modern Society* (London, 1980), p. 9.

78. Bezilla (ed.), *Religion in America*, pp. 23–24; Gallup and Castelli, *The People's Religion*, pp. 73–79.

79. Jacques Barzun, *God's County and Mine. . .* (New York, 1954), p. 107.

80. George Weigel, "Talking the Talk: Christian Conviction and Democratic Etiquette," in Michael Cromartie (ed.), *Disciples and Democracy: Religious Conservatives and the Future of American Politics* (Grand Rapids, Mich., 1994), p. 86. C. S. Lewis once observed privately, "The very *kind* of truth we are often demanding was, in my opinion, never even envisaged by the ancients." W. H. Lewis (ed.), *Letters of C. S. Lewis* (New York, 1966), p. 287.

81. *Milwaukee Journal*, January 23, 1995.

82. Carl E. Braaten, "Protestants and Natural Law," *First Things* (January 1992): 24.

83. Quoted in *Catechism of the Catholic Church* (Liguori, Mo., 1994), p. 475.

84. C. S. Lewis, *Mere Christianity* (New York, 1960), p. 19. For interesting illustrations of the natural law, see C. S. Lewis, *The Abolition of Man* (New York, 1955), pp. 95–121.

85. Allan Bloom, *The Closing of the American Mind* (New York, 1987), p. 39.

86. Letter by Robert P. George in *First Things* (April 1995): 7. A book edited by George, *Natural Law Theory: Contemporary Essays* (New York, 1995), is of exceptional value in weighing the case for this point of view.

87. David Martin, "Making People Good—Again: The Role of Authority, Fear and Example," in Digby Anderson (ed.), *The Loss of Virtue*, p. 232. For a brilliant defense of natural law by a distinguished social scientist, see James Q. Wilson, *The Moral Sense* (New York, 1993), esp. pp. 225–51.

88. Martin, "Making People Good—Again," in Anderson (ed.), *The Loss of Virtue*, p. 233.

89. *Catechism of the Catholic Church*, p. 474.

90. See J. Budziszewski, "The Problem With Communitarianism," *First Things* (March 1995): 23–24.

91. John T. McNeill (ed.), Library of Christian Classics (Philadelphia, 1960), *Calvin: Institutes of the Christian Religion*, II, 1504. See Braaten, "Protestants and Natural Law," *First Things*, pp. 20–26, and Carl F. H. Henry, "Natural Law and a Nihilistic Culture," ibid, January 1995, pp. 54–60. Henry points out, however, that there are differing views among scholars about Calvin's acceptance of natural law. Many contemporary evangelicals reject natural law and rely on Scripture alone.

92. Martin Luther King Jr., *Why We Can't Wait* (New York, 1963), pp. 84, 99.

93. *Milwaukee Journal*, October 6, 1994.

94. Robert Wuthnow, *God and Mammon in America* (New York, 1994), p. 58.

95. See Bezilla (ed.), *Religion in America*, pp. 66–67.

96. Gallup and Castelli, *The People's Religion*, pp. 132–39; The Princeton Religion Research Center, *The Unchurched American. . .10 Years Later* (Princeton, n.d.), pp. 2, 7.

97. Bezilla (ed.), *Religion in America*, pp. 44, 57, 62; "Religion Index Hits Ten-Year High," pp. 1–2.

98. Bezilla (ed.), *Religion in America*, p. 45.

99. Wade Clark Roof and William McKinney, *American Mainline Religion: Its Changing Shape and Future* (New Brunswick, N.J., 1987), pp. 44, 56.

100. Gallup and Castelli, *The People's Religion*, pp. 18, 99, 177, 183, 193; Wade Clark Roof, *A Generation of Seekers: The Spiritual Journeys of the Baby Boom Generation* (San Francisco, 1993), pp. 49, 219, 233; Kosmin and Lachman, *One Nation Under God*, pp. 10, 201, 233; Roof and McKinney, *American Mainline Religion*, pp. 54–55, 94–96.

101. Gallup and Castelli, *The People's Religion*, pp. 31–32. For a good summary of the turmoil among American Catholics since Vatican II, see Jon Nilson, "The Divided Mind of American Catholicism," in Pierre M. Hegy (ed.), *The Church in the Nineties* (Collegeville, Minn., 1993), pp. 69–85.

102. Mark Chaves and James C. Cavendish, "More Evidence on U.S. Catholic Church Attendance," *Journal for the Scientific Study of Religion* (1994): 376–81.

103. Stung by criticism of its methodology, Gallup asked people to name the church or synagogue they had attended within the last seven days. The statistical results were the same. "Do That Many People Really Attend Worship Services?" *emerging trends*, May, 1994, pp. 1, 3. The 1995 figure was 43 percent. "Religion Index Hits Ten-Year High," p. 3.

104. C. Kirk Hadaway, Penny Long Marler, and Mark Chaves, "What the Polls Don't Show: A Closer Look at U.S. Church Attendance," *American Sociological Review* (December 1993): 741–52.

105. Peter Mullen, "Are Mass Stats Off?" *National Catholic Register*, October 10, 1993, pp. 1, 6; "Researchers Dispute Church Attendance Figures," *The Living Church*, September 26, 1993, p. 6.

106. Gallup and Castelli, *The People's Religion*, p. 60. Only 16 percent see the Bible as totally humanistic, i.e., a book of fables and legends. See p. 18.

107. Miller, "Is There Any Word From the Lord?," *The Lutheran*, March, 1995, p. 8.

108. Bezilla (ed.), *Religion in America*, pp. 27, 32; "Nine Persons in 10 Believe in Heaven (But Fewer Expect to Get There," "Many Believe in Hell (Far Fewer Expect to Go There)," *emerging trends*, February 1995, pp. 2–3.

109. Kenneth L. Woodward, "The Rites of Americans," *Newsweek*, November 29, 1993, pp. 81–82. While the Gallup pollsters rarely ask specific doctrinal questions and identify the answers by denomination, what evidence they do present clashes sharply with a 1963 poll reported in Finke and Stark, *The Churching of America*, p. 229. In that poll, mainline church members believed far less than the general public! Cf. Gallup and Castelli, *The People's Religion*, pp. 62–66, 93, 102–12.

110. *Milwaukee Journal*, July 24, 1994.

111. *Wall Street Journal*, January 16, 1995.

112. Crime in America is concentrated in urban America, especially within inner-city neighborhoods. For relevant data, see John J. DiIulio Jr., "America's Ticking Crime Bomb and How to Defuse It: Ten Things to Know about Crime in America Today," *Wisconsin Interest* (Spring/Summer 1994): 1–8. Nearly a third of black American men in their twenties are serving a criminal sentence, either in prison, on probation, or on parole. Blacks, who make up 12 percent of the population, are 74 percent of the

prisoners serving time on drug charges. *Milwaukee Journal Sentinel,* October 5, 1995.

113. Gallup and Castelli, *The People's Religion,* pp. 122–24. In 1994, a *Wall Street Journal*/NBC News poll asked Americans whether the source of the nation's social and economic problems stemmed mainly from a decline in moral values or financial pressures and strains on families. Fifty-eight percent of whites chose the decline in moral values category, while only 32 percent of blacks agreed. *Wall Street Journal,* September 29, 1994.

114. *Milwaukee Journal Sentinel,* December 16, 1995.

115. See Paul R. Gross and Norman Levitt, "The Natural Sciences: Trouble Ahead? Yes," *Academic Questions* (Spring 1994): 13–29.

116. Quoted by William F. Buckley Jr. in "Let Us Pray?" *National Review,* October 10, 1994, p. 87.

117. Wuthnow, *God and Mammon in America,* p. 5.

118. Ibid., p. 155. See also pp. 171–81.

119. Editorial, "A Civilization of Love: The Pope's Call to the West," *New Oxford Review,* October 1994, p. 4.

120. C. S. Lewis, *The Weight of Glory and Other Addresses* (Grand Rapids, Mich., 1974), p. 39.

121. Paul C. Vitz, *Psychology as Religion: The Cult of Self-Worship,* 2d ed. (Grand Rapids, Mich., 1994), p. 116.

122. I John, 2:15, 5:19.

123. Steve Ebling quoted in *Milwaukee Journal,* October 2, 1994.

Chapter 3. Secular Religions

1. Crane Brinton, *The Shaping of the Modern Mind* (New York, 1959), p. 113.

2. Quoted in Louis L. Snyder, *The Age of Reason* (New York, 1955), pp. 139–40.

3. Carl Becker, *The Heavenly City of the Eighteenth-Century Philosophers* (New Haven, 1959), pp. 30–31.

4. Leo Sherley-Price (trans.), Thomas a Kempis, *The Imitation of Christ* (London, 1952), p. 88.

5. Evelyn Underhill, *The School of Charity: Meditations on the Christian Creed* (Wilton, Conn., 1991), p. 9.

6. Quoted in Snyder, *The Age of Reason,* p. 39.

7. Walter Hooper (ed.), C. S. Lewis, *God in the Dock: Essays on Theology and Ethics* (Grand Rapids, Mich., 1970), p. 58.

8. R. R. Palmer, *Twelve Who Ruled: The Year of the Terror in the French Revolution* (Princeton, 1970), pp. 323–24.

9. Quoted in Becker, *The Heavenly City of the Eighteenth Century Philosophers*, pp. 155–59.

10. Maurice Cranston (tr.), Jean-Jacques Rousseau, *The Social Contract* (New York, 1968), p. 186.

11. John Neville Figgis and Reginald Vere Laurence (eds.), Lord Acton, *Lectures on the French Revolution* (New York, 1959), p. 284.

12. Edmund Burke, *Reflections on the Revolution in France* (Chicago, 1955), p. 125.

13. Leo Gershoy, *The French Revolution and Napoleon* (New York, 1933), pp. 276–77.

14. Quoted in ibid., p. 273.

15. Bruce Fohnen, *Virtue and the Promise of Conservatism: The Legacy of Burke and Tocqueville* (Lawrence, Kans., 1993), p. 44.

16. David F. Wells, *No Place for Truth, or Whatever Happened to Evangelical Theology?* (Grand Rapids, Mich., 1993), p. 147.

17. James Hitchcock, *What Is Secular Humanism? Why Humanism Became Secular and How It Is Changing Our World* (Ann Arbor, Mich., 1982), p. 41. See David M. Potter, *People of Plenty: Economic Abundance and the American Character* (Chicago, 1958), p. 129. Tomas de Torquemada, the infamous grand inquisitor in fifteenth-century Spain, had ordered the execution of some two thousand, which is minor league mayhem compared with the actions of Robespierre and his friends.

18. Paul Hazard, *European Thought in the Eighteenth Century: From Montesquieu to Lessing* (Cleveland, 1963), pp. 160–71.

19. F. L. Lucas, *The Art of Living: Four Eighteenth-Century Minds* (New York, 1959), pp. 266, 270.

20. The exception was the almost puritanical morality preached during the maddest moments of the French Revolution. See Palmer, *Twelve Who Ruled*, p. 324.

21. Quoted in Hazard, *European Thought in the Eighteenth Century*, p. 164.

22. Malcolm Muggeridge, *Chronicles of Wasted Time, Chronicle I: The Green Stick* (New York, 1982), p. 177.

23. See Paul Johnson, *Intellectuals*, (New York, 1990), pp. 1–27. The quotation is from p. 26.

24. Hazard, *European Thought in the Eighteenth Century*, pp. 411–15.

25. Quoted in Johnson, *Intellectuals*, pp. 72–73. See pp. 52–81 for a perceptive overview of Marx's life.

26. Isaiah Berlin, *Karl Marx: His Life and Environment*, 3d ed. (New York, 1963), p. 19.

27. Ralph Lord Roy, *Communism and the Churches* (New York, 1960), p. 427.

28. Robert L. Heilbroner, *The Worldly Philosophers: The Lives, Times, and Ideas of the Great Economic Thinkers*, rev. ed. (New York, 1961), p. 115.

29. Allan Bloom, *Giants and Dwarfs: Essays 1960–1990* (New York, 1990), p. 211.

30. Berlin, *Karl Marx*, p. 259.

31. Herbert J. Muller, *The Uses of the Past: Profiles of Former Societies* (New York, 1957), p. 283.

32. Richard Crossman (ed.), *The God That Failed* (New York, 1963), p. 6.

33. Gershoy, *The French Revolution and Napoleon*, pp. 283–84.

34. J. M. Thompson, *Robespierre and the French Revolution* (New York, 1962), p. 90.

35. Jean Bethke Elshtain, "Judging Rightly," *First Things* (November 1994): 49.

36. Crossman (ed.), *The God That Failed*, p. 6.

37. Guenter Lewy, *The Cause That Failed: Communism in American Political Life* (New York, 1990), p. 303.

38. Ibid., pp. 98, 114.

39. Ibid., pp. 71–72. On this general theme, see Theodore Draper, *American Communist and Soviet Russia: The Formative Period* (New York, 1963), pp. 197–201, 268.

40. Lewy, *The Cause That Failed*, p. 303.

41. Hazard, *European Thought in the Eighteenth Century*, p. 255.

42. Quoted in Lester G. Crocker, *Diderot: The Embattled Philosopher*, rev. ed. (New York, 1966), p. 29.

43. Quoted in Lewy, *The Cause That Failed*, p. 27.

44. Harold Shukman (ed. and trans.), Dmitri Volkagonov, *Lenin: A New Biography* (New York, 1994).

45. Paul C. Vitz, *Psychology as Religion: The Cult of Self-Worship,* 2d ed. (Grand Rapids, Mich., 1994), p. 55. On science as religion, see James Turner, *Without God, Without Creed: The Origins of Unbelief in America* (Baltimore, 1986), pp. 171–251, 268. On the relationship between science and morality, see ibid., pp. 241–44.

46. Milton Mayer, "To Know and to Do," in Arthur A. Cohen (ed.), *Humanistic Education and Western Civilization: Essays for Robert M. Hutchins* (New York, 1964), pp. 209, 215, 221. Cf. Edward O. Wilson, "Science and Ideology," *Academic Questions* (Summer 1995): 73–75. Wilson assures us (p. 74) that "Understanding based on the new [scientific] information now reaches into virtually every sphere of human activity and every moral dilemma. . . . The future, if we are to have one, is increasingly to be in the hands of the scientifically literate, those who at least know what it is all about."

47. Ray Ginger, *Six Days or Forever?: Tennessee v. John Thomas Scopes* (Chicago, 1969), pp. 233, 238–39.

48. Vitz, *Psychology as Religion*, pp. x, 57. On psychology as a science, see especially pp. 40–42, 55, 141–45. See also William Kirk Kilpatrick, *Psychological Seduction* (Nashville, 1983), which calls (p. 14) psychology and Christianity "competing faiths" and compares their answers to life's problems. It has often been said that Freud saw himself as a messiah and founder of a new religion, but the point has never been better made than in Richard Webster, *Why Freud Was Wrong: Sin, Science, and Psychoanalysis* (New York, 1995).

49. John C. Greene, *Darwin and the Modern World View* (New York, 1963), p. 86.

50. Julian Huxley in the introduction to Charles Darwin, *The Origin of Species. . .* (New York, 1958), p. xv.

51. Becker, *The Heavenly City of the Eighteenth-Century Philosophers*, p. 14.

52. Paul Davies, "Physics and the Mind of God: The Templeton Prize Address," *First Things* (August/September 1995): 35. This address presents us with a classic example of the scientist whose yearning for God is blocked by the discipline that rules his mind and soul.

53. Book review by Molly Finn in ibid., January 1995, p. 50.

54. Quoted in Brinton, *The Shaping of the Modern Mind*, p. 149.

55. Daphne Patai and Noretta Koertge, *Professing Feminism: Cautionary Tales from the Strange World of Women's Studies* (New York, 1994), p. 96. The

theme of feminism as a religion is found throughout this book. See especially pp. 186–90.

56. Thomas Paine, *The Age of Reason*, (New York, 1991), pp. 115, 123, 156, 158.

57. Kenneth Scott Latourette, *A History of Christianity, Volume II, A.D. 1500–A.D. 1975* (New York, 1975), pp. 1075–77.

58. For a good summary, see ibid., pp. 1081–1105. The 1943 reference is to Pope Pius XII's encyclical *Divino afflante Spiritu.*

59. A. D. Gilbert, *Religion and Society in Industrial England: Church, Chapel and Social Change, 1740–1914* (New York, 1976), pp. 8–29. The quotation is from p. 27.

60. See John R. H. Moorman, *The Anglican Spiritual Tradition* (Springfield, Ill., 1983), pp. 128–93.

61. Charles Gore (ed.), *Lux Mundi: A Series of Studies in the Religion of the Incarnation* (London, 1904), p. 263.

62. Owen Chadwick, *The Victorian Church, Part II*, 2d ed. (London, 1972), pp. 75–150.

63. Ibid., pp. 24–28, 35.

64. Albert Marrin, *The Last Crusade: The Church of England in the First World War* (Durham, N.C., 1974), p. 7.

65. Latourette, *A History of Christianity*, pp. 1119–39.

66. Ibid., pp. 1139–57.

67. Ahlstrom, *A Religious History of the American People*, p. 358.

68. George M. Marsden, *Fundamentalism and American Culture: The Shaping of Twentieth-Century Evangelicalism: 1870–1925* (New York, 1980), p. 17.

69. Ahlstrom, *A Religious History of the American People*, p. 783.

70. Charles Howard Hopkins, *The Rise of the Social Gospel in American Protestantism, 1865–1915* (New Haven, 1967), p. 318.

71. Ibid., p. 325.

72. On the activity of mainline denominations in the Social Gospel movement, see Henry F. May, *Protestant Churches and Industrial America* (New York, 1967), pp. 182–93. The degree of participation had to with the socioeconomic level of a denomination's membership and an assortment of theological doctrines.

73. Ibid., pp. 316–17.

74. See David L. Holmes, *A Brief History of the Episcopal Church* (Valley Forge, Penna., 1993), pp. 126–28.

75. Hopkins, *The Rise of the Social Gospel*, p. 244.

76. Ibid., p. 317.

77. See Cynthia Eagle Russett, *Darwin in America: The Intellectual Response, 1865–1912* (San Francisco, 1976), pp. 19, 29–42, 147. The quotation is from p. 19.

78. Glenn Miller, "Protestants, Paideia, and Pioneers: Protestantism's First Great Cause," in Parker J. Palmer, Barbara G. Wheeler, and James W. Fowler (eds.), *Caring for the Commonweal: Education for Religious and Public Life* (Macon, Ga., 1990), p. 202.

79. Quoted in Marsden, "The Soul of the American University," in Marsden and Longfield (eds.), *The Secularization of the Academy*, p. 17.

80. Ibid., p. 19.

81. Finke and Stark, *The Churching of America*, p. 172.

82. Ibid. See pp. 154–58, 167–68, 172, 183. See also May, *Protestant Churches and Industrial America*, pp. 194–96.

83. Walter Rauschenbusch, *Christianity and the Social Crisis* (New York, 1924), p. 70.

84. Ibid., pp. 169–70.

85. Edmund A. Opitz, *Religion: Foundation of the Free Society* (Irvington-on-Hudson, N.Y., 1994), p. 27.

86. Quoted in Marsden, *Fundamentalism and American Culture*, p. 37.

87. Quoted in Richard Hofstadter, *Anti-Intellectualism in American Life* (New York, 1963), pp. 108–9.

88. Quoted in Marsden, *Fundamentalism and American Culture*, p. 38.

89. May, *Protestant Churches and Industrial America*, p. 190.

90. See Marsden, *Fundamentalism and American Culture*, pp. 104, 109–18.

91. Ibid., p. 119.

Chapter 4. Up to the Precipice

1. David L. Holmes, *A Brief History of the Episcopal Church* (Valley Forge, Penna., 1993), p. 143.

2. Sydney E. Ahlstrom, *A Religious History of the American People* (New

Haven, Conn., 1972), p. 884. The war greatly enhanced the prestige of the Federal Council, as it became the liaison between the churches and the federal government. Among other things, council officials gained a monopoly over the naming of Protestant military chaplains. Robert A. Schneider, "Voice of Many Waters: Church Federation in the Twentieth Century," in William R. Hutchison (ed.), *Between the Times: The Travail of the Protestant Establishment in America, 1900–1960* (Cambridge, 1989), pp. 108–9.

3. See Holmes, *A Brief History of the Episcopal Church*, pp. 146–47.

4. Eldon G. Ernst, *Moment of Truth for Protestant America: Interchurch Campaigns Following World War I* (Missoula, Mont., 1974), p. 171.

5. James Strachey (ed.), Sigmund Freud, *The Future of an Illusion* (New York, 1961), p. 49.

6. William E. Leuchtenburg, *The Perils of Prosperity, 1914–32* (Chicago, 1958), p. 189.

7. See Ahlstrom, *A Religious History of the American People*, pp. 904–8.

8. Schneider, "Voice of Many Waters," in Hutchison (ed.), *Between the Times*, pp. 113, 116; Paul A. Carter, *The Decline and Revival of the Social Gospel: Social and Political Liberalism in American Protestant Churches, 1920–1940* (Ithaca, N.Y., 1954), p. 126.

9. Roger Finke and Rodney Stark, *The Churching of America, 1776–1990: Winners and Losers in Our Religious Economy* (New Brunswick, N.J., 1992), pp. 165–66, 208, 232. Lutherans (excluding the Missouri Synod) grew 45.7 percent, while United Lutherans grew 43.9 percent. Both churches came late to liberalism.

10. Edwin S. Gaustad, "The Pulpit and the Pews," in Hutchison (ed.), *Between the Times*, pp. 31–32.

11. Robert T. Handy, *A Christian America: Protestant Hopes and Historical Realities* 2d ed. (New York, 1984), p. 174.

12. Walter Lippmann, *A Preface to Morals* (New York, 1929), p. 21.

13. Frederick Lewis Allen, *Only Yesterday* (New York, 1959), p. 142.

14. Dorothy C. Bass, "Church-Related Colleges: Transmitters of Denominational Cultures?" in Jackson Carroll and Wade Clark Roof (eds.), *Beyond Establishment: Protestant Identity in a Post-Protestant Age* (Louisville, Ky., 1993), pp. 161–62.

15. R. Laurence Moore, "Secularization: Religion and the Social Sciences," in Hutchison, *Between the Times*, pp. 234–40.

16. Marsden, "The Soul of the American University: A Historical Overview," in George M. Marsden and Bradley J. Longfield (eds.), *The Secularization of the Academy* (New York, 1992), p. 22.

17. Frederick Lewis Allen, *Only Yesterday* (New York, 1959), p. 167. See Lawrence W. Levine, *Defender of the Faith William Jennings Bryan: The Last Decade, 1915–1925* (New York, 1968), pp. 267–68. On the other hand, in 1926 only one out of every eight Americans between the ages of eighteen and twenty-one was enrolled in any sort of institution of higher learning. John D. Hicks, *Republican Ascendancy, 1921–1933* (New York, 1963), p. 187.

18. E.g., see Levine, *Defender of the Faith*, p. 262.

19. Quoted in Richard Hofstadter, *Anti-Intellectualism in American Life* (New York, 1963), p. 122.

20. Richard Hofstadter, *The Age of Reform, From Bryan to F.D.R.* (New York, 1955), p. 294.

21. William E. Leuchtenburg, *The Perils of Prosperity, 1914–32* (Chicago, 1958), p. 153.

22. See James Davison Hunter, *Culture Wars: The Struggle to Define America* (New York, 1991), pp. 140–42.

23. See Kenneth T. Jackson, *The Ku Klux Klan in the City, 1915–1930* (New York, 1970), pp. 18, 20, 49, 63, 241, 247.

24. See George M. Marsden, *Fundamentalism and American Culture: The Shaping of Twentieth-Century Evangelicalism: 1870–1925* (New York, 1980), pp. 212–21.

25. J. Gresham Machen, *Christianity and Liberalism* (Grand Rapids, Mich., 1923), pp. 7, 53.

26. Ibid., pp. 103–4.

27. Ibid., p. 6. The high level of Machen's scholarship is also revealed in his 1930 book, *The Virgin Birth of Christ*, designed to counter liberal disbelief in the topic. See J. Gresham Machen, *The Virgin Birth of Christ* (Grand Rapids, Mich., 1965).

28. "Fundamentalism and Modernism: Two Religions," *The Christian Century*, January 3, 1924, p. 6. *The Christian Century* was initially published in 1884 under the auspices of the Disciples of Christ. Under Disciples min-

ister Charles Clayton Morrison, editor from 1908 to 1947, the publication became stridently liberal and nondenominational, and has been called "the most influential Protestant magazine of its time." See Dennis N. Voskuil, "Reaching Out: Mainline Protestantism and the Media," in Hutchison (ed.), *Between the Times*, pp. 76–77.

29. Shailer Mathews, *The Faith of Modernism* (New York, 1924), pp. 51–52 and passim. Mathews made a distinction between modernism and liberalism, attributing a more orthodox faith to the former. See his modernist credo on pp. 180–81.

30. See Mark A. Noll (ed.), *The Princeton Theology, 1812–1921: Scripture, Science, and Theological Method from Archibald Alexander to Benjamin Breckinridge Warfield* (Grand Rapids, Mich., 1983), pp. 18–47. The quotation is on p. 35.

31. Levine, *Defender of the Faith*, p. 116.

32. Ibid., pp. 218–66, 277–92, 365. The quotation is on p. 248.

33. LeRoy Ashby, *William Jennings Bryan, Champion of Democracy* (Boston, 1987), pp. 196–97.

34. Daniel G. Reid et al., *Dictionary of Christianity in America* (Downers Grove, Ill., 1990), pp. 464, 828, 1285; Martin E. Marty, *Modern American Religion, Volume 2: The Noise of Conflict, 1919–1941* (Chicago, 1991), pp. 167, 187, 193–98. The quotation is on p. 187.

35. Ray Ginger, *Six Days or Forever?: Tennessee v. John Thomas Scopes* (Chicago, 1969), pp. 154, 162.

36. Quoted in Levine, *Defender of the Faith*, p. 333.

37. Ibid., p. 339.

38. Ginger, *Six Days or Forever?* p. 129; Ashby, *William Jennings Bryan*, p. 201.

39. See Ginger, *Six Days or Forever?*, pp. 167–80. The quotations are from pp. 170–71, 173.

40. Quoted in Ashby, *William Jennings Bryan*, p. 201.

41. Ginger, *Six Days or Forever?*, pp. 191–93, 211–17; Ahlstrom, *A Religious History of the American People*, p. 915. On the disparity in formal education between fundamentalists and mainliners, see, for example, Finke and Stark, *The Churching of America*, p. 166; Wade Clark Roof and William McKinney, *American Mainline Religion: Its Changing Shape and Future* (New Brunswick, N.J., 1987), pp. 112–13.

42. One branch had pulled out of the Federal Council of Churches in 1917, and no Lutherans participated directly in the Council thereafter.

Lutherans would be founding members of the National Council of Churches, however. Schneider, "Voice of Many Waters," in Hutchison (ed.), *Between the Times*, p. 114.

43. See Marsden, *Fundamentalism and American Culture*, pp. 191–95.

44. Finke and Stark, *The Churching of America*, pp. 218–23; Voskuil, "Reaching Out: Mainline Protestantism and the Media," in Hutchison (ed.), *Between the Times*, pp. 81–86.

45. Ahlstrom, *A Religious History of the American People*, p. 920.

46. Marty, *Modern American Religion, Volume 2*, p. 256.

47. Robert Wuthnow, *The Restructuring of American Religion: Society and Faith Since World War II* (Princeton, 1988), p. 25.

48. Holmes, *A Brief History of the Episcopal Church*, p. 150.

49. Wuthnow, *The Restructuring of American Religion*, p. 26.

50. Carter, *The Decline and Revival of the Social Gospel*, pp. 222–24.

51. George Gallup Jr. and Jim Castelli, *The People's Religion: American Faith in the 90's* (New York, 1989), p. 5.

52. Robert M. Miller, *American Protestantism and Social Issues, 1919–1939* (Chapel Hill, 1958), pp. 119–23.

53. Richard Wightman Fox, *Reinhold Niebuhr: A Biography* (New York, 1985), p. 125.

54. Miller, *American Protestantism and Social Issues*, p. 66.

55. Ibid., p. 73.

56. Carter, *The Decline and Revival of the Social Gospel*, p. 175.

57. Miller, *American Protestantism and Social Issues*, pp. 75–84.

58. Ibid., pp. 128–29, 139, 156–57, 176.

59. Ibid., p. 78.

60. Ibid., p. 83.

61. Ralph Lord Roy, *Communism and the Churches* (New York, 1960), pp. 418–25. On the 1930s, see pp. 66–122.

62. Miller, *American Protestantism and Social Issues*, pp. 66–67, 79, 109–18, 124–25.

63. Ibid., pp. 84–89, 91; Marty, *Modern American Religion Volume 2*, pp. 384–85; Carter, *The Decline and Revival of the Social Gospel*, pp. 163–79.

64. Marty, *Modern American Religion Volume 2*, p. 384.

65. Water Marshall Horton quoted in William R. Hutchison (ed.), *American Protestant Thought: The Liberal Era* (New York, 1968), pp. 193, 195.

66. H. Richard Niebuhr, *The Kingdom of God in America* (New York, 1959), p. 193.

67. Bernard M. G. Reardon (ed.), *Liberal Protestantism* (Stanford, 1968), p. 63.

68. Ahlstrom, *A Religious History of the American People*, p. 948.

69. Gallup and Castelli, *The People's Religion*, p. 61.

70. Carter, *The Decline and Revival of the Social Gospel*, pp. 134–39, 174, 202–8.

71. Ibid., pp. 211–17.

72. William McGuire King, "The Reform Establishment and the Ambiguities of Influence," in Hutchison (ed.), *Between the Times*, pp. 123–28.

73. Carter, *The Decline and Revival of the Social Gospel*, pp. 218–19. See Robert Moats Miller, *Bishop G. Bromley Oxnam, Paladin of Liberal Protestantism* (Nashville, 1990), pp. 261–68, 276, 280–89.

74. Ahlstrom, *A Religious History of the American People*, p. 953. Of course, those figures include monetary inflation and the need for new construction in the rapidly expanding suburbs.

75. Wuthnow, *The Restructing of American Religion*, p. 37.

76. Gallup and Castelli, *The People's Religion*, pp. 8–9, 30–31.

77. Quoted in Joel A. Carpenter, "Revive Us Again: Alienation, Hope, and the Resurgence of Fundamentalism, 1930–1950," in M. L. Bradbury and James B. Gilbert (eds.), *Transforming Faith: The Sacred and Secular in Modern American History* (Westport, Conn., 1989), p. 115.

78. Wuthnow, *The Restructuring of American Religion*, pp. 174–75.

79. Ibid., p. 182.

80. See George Marsden, *Reforming Fundamentalism* (Grand Rapids, Mich., 1987). This approach began to shatter in the late 1960s as renewed warfare between fundamentalists and reformers broke out. Modern-minded conservatives eventually dominated Fuller, now the nation's largest interdenominational seminary.

81. Ibid., pp. 28–29, 36.

82. Allison Stokes, "Denominational Ministry on University Campuses," in Carroll and Roof (eds.), *Beyond Establishment*, p. 176.

83. See Dorothy C. Bass, "Revolutions, Quiet and Otherwise: Protestants and Higher Education during the 1960s," in Parker J. Palmer, Barbara G. Wheeler, and James W. Fowler (eds.), *Caring for the Commonweal: Education for Religious and Public Life* (Macon, Ga., 1990), p. 208.

84. Gallup and Castelli, *The People's Religion*, pp. 36–39.

85. Chad Walsh, "Impact on America," in Jocelyn Gibb (ed.), *Light on C. S. Lewis* (New York, 1965), pp. 109–15.

86. Gallup and Castelli, *The People's Religion*, p. 9.

87. Roof and McKinney, *American Mainline Religion*, p. 164.

88. Finke and Stark, *The Churching of America*, p. 248.

89. For valuable insights on religion in the 1950s, see Alan Ehrenhalt, *The Lost City: Discovering the Forgotten Virtues of Community in the Chicago of the 1950s* (New York, 1995), especially pp. 18, 37–39, 63–64, 76, 78, 97–98, 112–35, 173–89, 222–28.

90. Gallup and Castelli, *The People's Religion*, pp. 8, 18.

91. "Trumpets in the morning," *Time*, April 11, 1960, p. 55.

92. "The Ecumenical Century," ibid., December 8, 1961, p. 77.

93. Hoge, Johnson, Luidens, *Vanishing Boundaries*, pp. 193–98. The quotation is on p. 194.

94. Paul C. Vitz, *Psychology as Religion: The Cult of Self-Worship* 2d ed. (Grand Rapids, Mich., 1994), pp. 102–3.

95. King, "The Reform Establishment and the Ambiguities of Influence," in Hutchison (ed.), *Between the Times*, pp. 129–31, 135–37.

96. Miller, *Bishop G. Bromley Oxnam*, pp. 314–17, 491–96, 517.

97. See ibid., pp. 523–29. On Matthews and Eisenhower, see Thomas C. Reeves, *The Life and Times of Joe McCarthy: A Biography* (New York, 1982), pp. 499–502. To woo conservatives, the National Council of Churches in 1961 elected a multimillionaire businessman its first lay president. Irwin Miller was a member of the Disciples of Christ and a Republican. "For the Defense," *Time*, July 14, 1961, p. 38.

98. Finke and Stark, *The Churching of America*, pp. 218, 223.

99. Gallup and Castelli, *The People's Religion*, p. 10.

100. "Ecumenical Vibrations," *Time*, June 2, 1961, p. 63; Kelley, *Why Conservative Churches Are Growing*, p. 175; Finke and Stark, *The Churching of America*, p. 230. The Rev. Ramsey Pollard of Memphis, the outgoing president of the Southern Baptist Convention, made the statement quoted.

101. Quite naturally, I recommend Thomas C. Reeves, *A Question of Character: a Life of John F. Kennedy* (New York, 1991), for the full story.

102. Hunter, *Culture Wars*, p. 254.

103. Terry Eastland (ed.), *Religious Liberty in the Supreme Court: The Cases*

That Define the Debate Over Church and State (Washington, D.C., 1993), pp. 59–104.

104. Ibid., 119–36.

105. Ibid., pp. 141, 143–44.

106. Ibid., pp. 152, 154, 165.

107. Ibid., p. 141.

108. Ibid., p. 138.

109. Ibid., p. 167.

110. "On Second Thought. . .," *Time*, August 24, 1962, p. 40.

111. Eastland (ed.), *Religious Liberty in the Supreme Court*, pp. 101, 141, 168.

112. Marsden, "The Soul of the American University: A Historical Overview," in Marsden and Longfield (eds.), *The Secularization of the Academy*, pp. 22–24.

113. Dean R. Hoge, *Commitment on Campus: Changes in Religion and Values Over Five Decades* (Philadelphia, 1974), pp. 69, 106, 127–28.

114. Robert Wood Lynn, "'The Survival of Recognizably Protestant Colleges: Reflections on Old-Line Protestantism, 1950–1990," in Marsden and Longfield (eds.), *The Secularization of the Academy*, pp. 170–79. The quotations are from p. 174.

115. Philip Gleason, "American Catholic Higher Education, 1940–1990: The Ideological Context," in ibid., pp. 234–47.

116. "Trumpets in the Morning," *Time*, April 11, 1960, p. 55.

117. "Myth in the Gospel?" *Time*, February 24, 1961, p. 48; "Episcopalians," ibid., September 17, 1965, p. 106; May 20, 1966, p. 95; October 21, 1966, p. 69; November 4, 1966, p. 53. *Time* observed correctly: "In sophisticated U.S. Protestant seminaries, such ideas are neither new nor when properly eludicated, all that unnerving." Pike, said several Episcopal colleagues, was not considered serious or deep enough a theologian to be considered a heretic. See "Theology," ibid., November 11, 1966, 56–58, 63–64. The quotation is on p. 56.

118. See the review by T. E. Utley in David L. Edwards, *The Honest to God Debate: Some Reactions to the Book 'Honest to God'* (Philadelphia, 1963), pp. 95–98, which raises the question: "Where, one must ask, will the ravages of liberal theology end?" See also Eric James, *A Life of Bishop John A. T. Robinson:*

Scholar, Pastor, Prophet (Grand Rapids, Mich., 1987), pp. 110–34, especially Robinson's statement on pp. 122–23.

119. Hoge, *Commitment on Campus*, pp. 147–48.

120. Lynn, "'The Survival of Recognizably Protestant Colleges': Reflections on Old-Line Protestantism, 1950–1990," in Marsden and Longfield (eds.), *The Secularization of the Academy*, p. 184.

121. "Roman Catholics," *Time*, April 5, 1963, p. 52.

Chapter 5. Stuck in the Sixties

1. Dean M. Kelley, *Why Conservative Churches Are Growing: A Study in Sociology of Religion* (Macon, Ga., 1986), pp. 1–10.

2. Wade Clark Roof, *A Generation of Seekers: The Spiritual Journeys of the Baby Boom Generation* (San Francisco, 1993), pp. 56–58, 169–70.

3. Wade Clark Roof and William McKinney, *American Mainline Religion: Its Changing Shape and Future* (New Brunswick, N.J., 1987), pp. 11, 13; Sydney E. Ahlstrom, *A Religious History of the American People* (New Haven, Conn., 1972), p. 1079.

4. Ibid., p. 1086; "A Church Divided," *Time*, May 24, 1976, p. 49. Between 1964 and 1994, the number of priests in the United States fell 14 percent to about 50,000. During that same period, the number of the nation's Catholics rose by almost 40 percent, to 62 million. *Wall Street Journal*, December 19, 1995.

5. George Gallup Jr. and Jim Castelli, *The People's Religion: American Faith in the 90's* (New York, 1989), pp. 11–13. The 9 percent drop was almost entirely attributable to the decline in attendance by post–Vatican II Catholics. The figure dropped from 71 percent in 1963 to 55 percent in 1973.

6. Kelley, *Why Conservative Churches Are Growing*, pp. 21–25. By the 1970s, *Time* and *Newsweek* had sharply reduced their coverage of mainline churches and religion in general, but paid increasing attention to conservative churches. See Dennis N. Vokseuil, "Reaching Out: Protestantism and the Media," in William R. Hutchison (ed.), *Between the Times: The Travail of the Protestant Establishment in America, 1900–1960* (Cambridge, 1989), pp. 77–80.

7. Gallup and Castelli, *The People's Religion*, p. 11.

8. Kelley, *Why Conservative Churches Are Growing*, p. 51.

9. Roof and McKinney, *American Mainline Religion*, p. 20.

10. *New York Times*, April 30, 1964.

11. Margaret Frakes, "United Church of Christ General Synod: Ministries Approved," *Christian Century*, July 21, 1965, pp. 919–20; *New York Times*, July 24, 1965; August 18, 1986.

12. Ibid., May 21, 1967; February 26, 1970; December 12, 1973; February 24, 1977; August 28, 1983.

13. Ibid., July 2, 1965.

14. Ibid., June 21, 1966.

15. Ibid., April 7, 1967; Everett C. Parker, "United Church of Christ General Synod," *Christian Century*, August 9, 1967, p. 1026.

16. *New York Times*, October 26, 1976.

17. Christa R. Klein, *Politics and Policy: The Genesis and Theology of Social Statements in the Lutheran Church of America* (Minneapolis, 1989), pp. 267–70.

18. *New York Times*, June 15, 1967. The schism, caused by a desire for fundamentalism as well as the rejection of liberal social issues, created the Presbyterian Church in America, now the second-largest Presbyterian denomination in the nation.

19. Ibid., May 23, 1965; April 26, May 25, 1966; March 12, 1967.

20. Ibid., May 21, 1965; June 1, 1968; May 18, 1969.

21. David E. Sumner, *The Episcopal Church's History: 1945–1985* (Wilton, Conn., 1987), p. 37.

22. Holmes, *A Brief History of the Episcopal Church*, pp. 164–65. In 1960, membership stood at more than one thousand, 24 percent of the members being in the South. At its peak, ESCRU had chapters in twenty-six cities. Sumner, *The Episcopal Church's History*, p. 38.

23. Robert E. Hood, *Social Teachings in the Episcopal Church* (Harrisburg, Penna., 1990), pp. 119–20.

24. "Episcopalians," *Time*, February 26, 1965, p. 71.

25. Hood, *Social Teachings in the Episcopal Church*, p. 121.

26. *New York Times*, September 18, 1967; Holmes, *A Brief History of the Episcopal Church*, p. 165; Sumner, *The Episcopal Church's History*, pp. 47–48. The criteria for grants stated, however, "No funds received can be used in connection with any individual or group which advocates violence."

27. For a good survey of related events, see *New York Times*, August 29, 1966.

28. "Churches," *Time*, June 10, 1966, p. 84; *New York Times*, March 7, 1971.

29. Ibid., September 13, 1967.

30. Ibid., December 8, 1972; January 17, 1973.

31. Ibid., May 22, 1969; "A Black Manifesto," *Time*, May 16, 1969, p. 94.

32. Alan Geyer, "Joy Box With No Joy: The N.C.C. at Detroit," *Christian Century*, December 17, 1969, p. 1603; *New York Times*, May 18, 1969.

33. "Churches," *Time*, June 6, 1969, p. 90; *New York Times*, June 13, 1969.

34. Ibid., July 1, 1969.

35. Ibid., May 22, 1969.

36. Ibid., June 17, 1971. Davis was found not guilty in 1972.

37. "Churches," *Time*, June 6, 1969, p. 88.

38. "Theology," ibid., July 4, 1969, p. 58.

39. "Episcopalians," ibid., September 12, 1969, p. 48; Sumner, *The Episcopal Church's History*, pp. 52–53.

40. See "Episcopalians at the Barricades," *Time*, November 2, 1970, p. 74; "Tidings," ibid., November 13, 1972, p. 104. See also John Booty, "Stephen Bayne's Perspective in the Church and the Civil Rights Movement," *Anglican and Episcopal History*, September 1995, pp. 362–68. For a view of Hines as saint and hero, see Kenneth W. Kesselus, "'Awake, thou Spirit of the watchmen,' John E. Hines's Challenge to the Episcopal Church," ibid., pp. 301–25.

41. "Reparations up to Date," *Time*, May 3, 1971, p. 51.

42. "Tidings," ibid., November 13, 1972, p. 104. See Sumner, *The Episcopal Church's History*, pp. 54–59.

43. Cf. David L. Holmes, "Presiding Bishop John E. Hines and the General Convention Special Program," *Anglican and Episcopal History*, December 1992, pp. 411–13.

44. *New York Times*, September 28, 1966.

45. Sumner, *The Episcopal Church's History*, pp. 60–61.

46. Kyle Haselden, "N.C.C. Agenda," *Christian Century*, June 16, 1965, p. 767.

47. Klein, *Politics and Policy*, p. 283.

48. *New York Times*, May 23 and June 15, 1967.

49. Parker, "United Church of Christ General Synod," *Christian Century*, August 9, 1967, p. 1027.

50. *New York Times*, February 22, 1968.

51. Geyer, "Joy Box With No Joy," *Christian Century*, December 17, 1969, pp. 1603–4; "Crunch at the Council," *Time*, December 12, 1969, p. 70.

52. Ahlstrom, *A Religious History of the American People*, p. 1081.

53. *New York Times*, May 24, 1970.

54. Ibid., October 21, 1970; Sumner, *The Episcopal Church's History*, p. 61.

55. *New York Times*, May 16, 1970; May 16, 1971. In 1972, however, the Baptists could not agree on a Vietnam resolution and remained silent. Ibid., May 15, 1972.

56. Ibid., January 5, 1972.

57. Ibid., January 17, 1972.

58. Ibid., March 28, 1972.

59. Marjorie Hyer, "NCC: Good News and Bad," *Christian Century*, July 5, 1972, p. 737.

60. *New York Times*, December 8, 1972.

61. Ibid., October 31, 1973.

62. Ibid., May 28, 1973.

63. See I Corinthians 11:3–16; 14:33–37; Ephesians 5:22–24; I Timothy 2:8–15; Titus 2:3–5; I Peter 3:1–6.

64. I Corinthians 14:37. But in I Timothy 2:8–15 Paul's teachings on women appear to be a personal desire.

65. See "The Pope on Women's Ordination" and "Abp Carey's Response" in *The Evangelical Catholic* (March/April 1995): 3–5. For good examples of the theology behind the ordination of women, see Mary Daly, *Beyond God The Father* (Boston, 1973); Rosemary Radford Reuther, *Sexism and God-Talk* (London, 1983) and *To Change The World: Christology and Cultural Criticism* (New York, 1989), pp. 45–56; Daphne Hampson, *Theology and Feminism* (Cambridge, Mass., 1990). On the traditionalist side, see William Oddie, *What Will Happen to God?: Feminism and the Reconstruction of Christian Belief* (London, 1984), and Thomas Hopko (ed.), *Women and the Priesthood* (Crestwood, N.Y.), 1983.

66. I have personally observed all these tactics and can vouch for their effectiveness. In England, women seeking ordination chained themselves to church doors.

67. See "The Women's Rebellion," *Time*, August 12, 1974, p. 60; "Sue Thy Bishop," ibid., August 18, 1975, p. 36; "Censured by the Club," ibid., October 6, 1975, p. 79; "Divided Over Women," ibid., October 4, 1976, p. 74.

68. Only the Roman Catholic magisterium kept that largest Christian church from female priests. In America, 63 percent of Catholics polled in 1993 favored the ordination of women. Of those under 30 polled, 76 percent favored women priests. A CBS–*New York Times* poll reported in *Milwaukee Journal*, June 15, 1994. See also *New York Times*, June 19, 1992, and Richard N. Ostling, "Cut From the Wrong Cloth," *Time*, June 22, 1992, pp. 64–65 for similar poll results.

69. "The Lesbian Priest," ibid., January 24, 1977, p. 58.

70. "Crunch at the Council," ibid., December 12, 1969, p. 70.

71. *New York Times*, May 19, 1971. Episcopalians elected their first woman bishop in 1988, and the Evangelical Lutheran Church in America took the same step in 1992.

72. Ibid., May 14, 1971.

73. Ibid., March 28, 1978.

74. See "Ecumenical War Over Abortion," *Time*, January 29, 1979, pp. 62–63.

75. *New York Times*, May 31, 1973.

76. Ibid., December 31, 1973.

77. K. L. Billingsley, "PC Goes to Church," *Heterodoxy*, May-June, 1993, pp. 13, 15.

78. Richard N. Ostling, "Unmanning the Holy Bible," *Time*, December 8, 1980, p. 128.

79. *New York Times*, March 30, 1981.

80. Richard N. Ostling, "O God Our [Mother and] Father," *Time*, October 24, 1983, pp. 56–57.

81. The unisex language in the 1979 book was restrained, however, and no changes were made in addressing God or Jesus Christ. See, for example, the translation of the 43rd Psalm and the Rite II version of the Nicene Creed.

82. *The Hymnal 1982* (New York, 1985), no. 107.

83. "Vexing Christa," *Time,* May 7, 1984, p. 94. During this period most Episcopalians favored the 1928 Book of Common Prayer and had not cried out for changes in their hymns. The innovations were imposed by church leaders with the approval of the General Convention. Letters to *The Living Church* strongly suggested that many clergy and laity found Christa offensive.

84. Florence King, *Lump It Or Leave It* (New York, 1990), p. 125.

85. Randolph, "Revival or Decline?," *The Evangelical Catholic* (March/April 1995): 10; "A Celebration of the Holy Eucharist in Thanksgiving for the Ministries of Women in All Orders of this Church," a special liturgy used by the 71st General Convention of the Episcopal Church, see pp. 7–9. Those on the list included the women illegally ordained in 1974 and 1975.

86. See Roger L. Shinn, *Confessing Our Faith: An Interpretation of the Statement of Faith of the United Church of Christ* (Cleveland, 1990).

87. *Milwaukee Journal,* May 16, 1992.

88. Richard J. Niebanck, "Presbyterian Recovering," *First Things* (November 1994): 13.

89. On homosexual activity, see I Corinthians 6:9–10, Romans 1:26–27, I Timothy 1:10, and Jude 7. In Matthew 5:17–20, 27–32, 48, Jesus' Old Testament view of sexual immorality is far from uncertain. (See Genesis 19:4–11; Leviticus 18:22; 20:10–13.) Marriage is commended in Matthew 19:4–6, Ephesians 5:22–23, and I Peter 3:1–7. Fornication and adultery are also condemned in the New Testament. See Ephesians 5:5; Colossians 3:5, and I Thessalonians 4:3–7. Early Church writers were unanimously agreed that sexual activity was to be limited to that between husband and wife.

90. This figure comes from Robert C. Colodny, the medical director of the Behavior Medicine Institute in New Canaan, Connecticut, who summarized half a dozen studies between 1988 and 1993. The Alan Guttmacher Institute released a study in 1993 finding that only 1 percent of men identified themselves as homosexual. *Milwaukee Journal,* April 18, 1993.

91. *New York Times,* May 2, 1972.

92. James M. Wall, "The Unreal World of an NCC Meeting," *Christian Century,* March 19, 1975, p. 275.

93. *New York Times,* January 25, 1977.

94. Ibid.

95. Ibid., July 4, 1977.

96. Ibid., June 29, 1983.

97. Jean Caffey Lyles, "Not to Decide. . .," *Christian Century*, November 30, 1983, pp. 1099–1100.

98. The United Methodist Church and the United Church of Christ entered formal dissents to the NCC's decision to deny observer status. "NCC Rejects Ties With Gay Church," ibid., December 2, 1992, p. 1097.

99. "Women's Unit Makes Grants," *The Presbyterian Layman* (March/April 1992): 26.

100. "Seminary Sued," *In Trust* (Autumn 1993): 23. Several Episcopal seminaries, including Nashotah House, Trinity, and Virginia, specifically prohibit homosexual activity.

101. "Presbyterians Delay Action on Gay Ban," ibid. The Presbyterians will ordain homosexuals who remain celibate.

102. See Jerry Z. Muller, "Coming Out Ahead: The Homosexual Moment in the Academy," *First Things* (August/September 1993): 17–24. For more on this, see Paul Hollander, *Anti-Americanism: Critiques at Home and Abroad, 1965–1990* (New York, 1992), pp. 111–15.

103. Page 23 of the May-August 1993 catalogue.

104. "Theology," *Time*, August 5, 1966, p. 69.

105. Bill Coats, "Marcus Borg, The Bible and the End of Political Theology," *Plumbline: A Journal of Ministry in Higher Education* (March 1995): 5.

106. "Is Heresy Dead?" *Time*, May 23, 1969, p. 55. See also "Episcopalians," ibid., August 25, 1967.

107. *New York Times*, May 21, 1970.

108. "Theology," *Time*, November 11, 1966, p. 57.

109. "Episcopalians," ibid., September 8, 1967, p. 82.

110. "Fading Big Five," ibid., March 8, 1976, p. 64.

111. "Episcopalians," ibid., March 22, 1968, p. 63.

112. "Troubadours for God," ibid., May 24, 1971, pp. 46, 48.

113. "The New Rebel Cry: Jesus Is Coming!" ibid., June 21, 1971, p. 61.

114. *New York Times*, September 18, 1972.

115. Marjorie Hyer, "The UCC's Relevancy Kick," *Christian Century*, July 18, 1973, p. 750.

116. "Baptism by Theater," *Time*, January 3, 1972, p. 49.

117. "Rites," ibid., July 4, 1969, p. 57.

118. Jeffrey Rubin, "The Prodigal Priest," *The Latin Mass: Chronicle of a Catholic Reform*, special ed., 1993, pp. 12–17.

119. "Christianity," *Time*, March 29, 1968, pp. 92, 94.

120. *New York Times*, February 16, 1967.

121. "The New Rebel Cry: Jesus Is Coming!" *Time*, June 21, 1971, pp. 56, 59–60.

122. Ibid., p. 61.

123. Ibid., pp. 59–61.

124. Ibid., p. 59.

125. Ibid., p. 62.

126. Ibid., p. 59.

127. Ibid., p. 63.

128. "The Pentecostal Tide," ibid., June 18, 1973, p. 91.

129. Roger Finke and Rodney Stark, *The Churching of America, 1776–1990: Winners and Losers in Our Religious Economy* (New Brunswick, N.J., 1992), pp. 239–44.

130. Christopher Lasch, *The Culture of Narcissism: American Life in an Age of Diminishing Expectations* (New York, 1991), p. 53. This point is discussed in more detail on pp. 64–65.

131. *New York Times*, November 11, 1979.

132. Ibid.

133. *Wall Street Journal*, June 13, 1995.

134. Coats, "Marcus Borg, The Bible and the End of Political Theology," *Plumbline: A Journal of Ministry in Higher Education*, March, 1995, p. 6.

135. Quoted in Tom Bethel, "Armey's Divisions," *The American Spectator*, February 1995, p. 18.

136. "Tidings," *Time*, November 13, 1972, p. 104.

137. "Episcopalian Backlash," ibid., October 15, 1973, p. 129.

138. Richard N. Ostling, "Opting for the Browning Version," ibid., September 23, 1985, p. 67.

139. Ibid.

140. See Dale D. Coleman et al., *A Catalog of Concerns: The Episcopal Church in the U.S. under Edmond Lee Browning* (Mobile, Ala., 1995), especially pp. 5–6, 10–14.

141. On the similar stance of the World Council of Churches, see Edward Norman, *Christianity and the World Order* (New York 1979), pp.

15–28, and passim; Richard John Neuhaus, *The World Council of Churches and Radical Chic* (Washington, D.C., 1977), passim, a pamphlet published by the Ethics and Public Policy Center.

142. "NCC Tackles the Reaganauts," *Christian Century*, June 3–10, 1981, p. 632.

143. *New York Times*, November 7, 1981, p. 7.

144. Jean Caffey Lyles, "Reporter's Notebook: The NCC in Cleveland," *Christian Century*, November 25, 1981, pp. 1222–23. Still, the author thought the NCC (p. 1223) "one churchly area in the U.S. where one can be sure that voices will be raised on behalf of the needy and broken in a bleak era of Reaganomic budget-cutting."

145. *New York Times*, March 25, 1982.

146. Richard N. Ostling, "Warring Over Where Donations Go," *Time*, March 28, 1983, pp. 58–59.

147. Kenneth L. Woodward with David Gates, "Ideology Under the Alms," *Newsweek*, February 7, 1983, p. 62. For more on the liberal churches and American foreign policy, see Hollander, *Anti-Americanism*, pp. 115–44.

148. Linda-Marie Delloff, "In Spirituality and in Service: The NCCC," *Christian Century*, May 29, 1985, p. 547.

149. *New York Times*, June 16, 1990.

150. Ibid., July 24, 1991.

151. Ibid., September 7, 1991.

152. Ibid., August 30, 1992.

153. "Vernon Jordan Meets With NCC Delegation," *Christian Century*, January 20, 1993, p. 48.

154. James M. Wall, "A Visit to the White House," ibid., April 7, 1993, pp. 355–56. Religious organizations on both the left and the right tend to equate their successes with political access and influence. See James Davison Hunter, *Before the Shooting Begins: Searching for Democracy in America's Culture War* (New York, 1994), pp. 182–86.

155. *Milwaukee Journal Sentinel*, December 10, 1995.

Chapter 6. Renewing the Mainline

1. Harvey Cox, *The Secular City* (New York, 1965), p. 1.

2. See, for example, Barry A. Kosmin and Seymour P. Lachman, *One*

Nation Under God: Religion in Contemporary American Society (New York, 1993), pp. 70–76.

3. Roger Finke and Rodney Stark, *The Churching of America, 1776–1990: Winners and Losers in Our Religious Economy* (New Brunswick, N.J., 1992), pp. 204–16. See also Wade Clark Roof and William McKinney, *American Mainline Religion: Its Changing Shape and Future* (New Brunswick, N.J., 1987), pp. 134–38. The Methodists, Baptists, and Disciples of Christ were frontier churches in the nineteenth century. See ibid., pp. 127–28.

4. George M. Marsden, *Fundamentalism and American Culture: The Shaping of Twentieth-Century Evangelicalism: 1870–1925* (New York, 1980), pp. 188, 202.

5. Benton Johnson, Dean R. Hoge, Donald A. Luidens, "Mainline Churches: The Real Reason for Decline," *First Things* (March 1993): 13.

6. Robert Wuthnow, *The Restructuring of American Religion: Society and Faith Since World War II* (Princeton, 1988), p. 181.

7. Wade Clark Roof, *A Generation of Seekers: The Spiritual Journeys of the Baby Boom Generation* (San Francisco, 1993), p. 52. See pp. 165–68.

8. Finke and Stark, *The Churching of America*, p. 45.

9. Wuthnow, *The Restructuring of American Religion*, pp. 161–64, 168–72. On the relationship between higher education and dropping out of all churches, see Roof and McKinney, *American Mainline Religion*, p. 176.

10. George Gallup Jr. and Jim Castelli, *The People's Religion: American Faith in the 90's* (New York, 1989), pp. 86–88, 258. See Gallup, *Religion in America, 1996,* p. 6.

11. Johnson, Hoge, Luidens, "Mainline Churches: The Real Reason for Decline" *First Things* (March 1993): 14.

12. Education appeared to have little influence on baby boomers who dropped out of church entirely. "In fact, those with a high school education or less dropped out more so than did college graduates, but postgraduates abandoned the churches and synagogues more so than any of the others." Roof, *A Generation of Seekers*, p. 55. See Edward Norman, *Christianity and the World Order* (New York 1979), p. 6.

13. Johnson, Hoge, Luidens, "Mainline Churches: The Real Reason for Decline," *First Things* (March 1993): 14–15.

14. Roof, *A Generation of Seekers*, pp. 96, 185-186.

15. Gallup and Castelli, *The People's Religion*, pp. 144, 230–33. Among those who said they had attended church within the past seven days, how-

ever, church involvement in political activity was favored 50 percent to 45 percent. Gallup also found that 39 percent of the churched and 44 percent of the unchurched thought that churches were insufficiently concerned with "social justice." Ibid., p. 139.

16. Ibid., pp. 110–11.

17. Ibid., pp. 257–58.

18. Ibid., p. 139.

19. Robert Bezilla (ed.), *Religion in America: 1992–1993* (Princeton, 1993), p. 45.

20. "Summary: Two Surveys of the Unchurched," Research Services, Presbyterian Church (USA), provided for me by Pat Hagan of the church's national office.

21. Daniel V. A. Olson, "Fellowship Ties and the Transmission of Religious Identity," in Jackson Carroll and Wade Clark Roof (eds.), *Beyond Establishment: Protestant Identity in a Post-Protestant Age* (Louisville, Ky., 1993), p. 46.

22. Gallup and Castelli, *The People's Religion*, p. 252.

23. Roof, *A Generation of Seekers*, pp. 186–87.

24. Johnson, Hoge, Luidens, "Mainline Churches: The Real Reason for Decline," *First Things* (March 1993): 17–18.

25. Gallup and Castelli, *The People's Religion*, pp. 141–43, 146.

26. Roof, *A Generation of Seekers*, p. 177. Roof and McKinney noted that mainline churches fail to attract the highly committed and lose their most faithful participants. Roof and McKinney, *American Mainline Religion*, pp. 178–79.

27. William H. Willimon, *What's Right With the Church* (San Francisco, 1989), p. 57.

28. Finke and Stark, *The Churching of America*, pp. 42–43, 237, 261 and passim.

29. Wolfhart Pannenberg, "Christianity and the West: Ambiguous Past, Uncertain Future," *First Things* (December 1994): 23.

30. Alasdair MacIntyre, *The Religious Significance of Atheism* (New York, 1966), p. 24.

31. The study of Presbyterian baby boomers came to the same conclusion. "Our findings show that belief is the single best predictor of church participation, but it is *orthodox* Christian belief . . . that impels people to be involved in church." Hoge, Johnson, Luidens, *Vanishing Boundaries*, p. 185.

32. George Eldon Ladd, *I Believe in the Resurrection of Jesus* (Grand Rapids, Mich., 1975), p. 140.

33. William Neil, *Message of the Bible: A Commentary on the Old and New Testaments* (London, 1978), pp. 16–19.

34. See Ladd, *I Believe in the Resurrection of Jesus*, pp. 80–82, 91–96, 105–29.

35. I. Howard Marshall, *I Believe in the Historical Jesus* (Grand Rapids, Mich., 1977), p. 23.

36. J. B. Phillips, *Ring of Truth: A Translator's Testimony* (New York, 1967), pp. 20–22.

37. For a brief summary of the fruits of this approach, see Rudolf Bultmann, *Jesus and the Word* (London, 1934).

38. Roger Lincoln Shinn, *Confessing Our Faith: An Interpretation of the Statement of Faith of the United Church of Christ* (New York, 1990), pp. xi, 7, 17–21, 25. The quotation is on p. 7.

39. See Thomas C. Oden, "Toward a Theologically Informed Renewal of American Protestantism: Propositions for Debate Attested by Classical Arguments," in Richard John Neuhaus (ed.), *The Believable Futures of American Protestantism* (Grand Rapids, Mich.: 1988), pp. 79–87. Oden, a Drew University theologian, shares my overall view of the mainline seminaries and calls for "a postcritical mode of Scripture study."

40. Interview with Trinity Director of Communications David Mills, July 21, 1995.

41. J. V. Langmead Casserley, *No Faith of My Own* (Lanham, Md., 1984), p. 111.

42. See Stephen Smith, "God's Body or His Creation?," *Mission and Ministry* (Fall 1990): 12–15.

43. *Seattle Times*, October 4, 1992.

44. *The [London] Sunday Times*, July 12, 1992. The Goldenberg quotation was from the back cover of Hampson's *Theology and Feminism*. The "Christian myth," Hampson writes on page 171, "is neither tenable nor ethical." She was a visiting scholar at Harvard Divinity School in 1988–89.

45. Kathy Kersten, "A New Heaven & a New Earth," *First Things* (March 1994): 10–12.

46. *Milwaukee Journal*, March 5, 1994.

47. Kersten, "A New Heaven & a New Earth," *First Things* (March 1994): 12.

48. *Milwaukee Journal,* January 29, 1994. In 1993, two thousand women gathered in Albuquerque, New Mexico, for a Catholic "Women-Church Conference" that offered more than thirty varieties of Sunday morning services, including Goddess Worship, an Indian pipe ceremony, Sufi dancing, a Holocaust remembrance, a Quaker meeting, and a "feminist Eucharist." Ibid., April 17, 1993. For much more in this vein, see Donna Steichen, *Ungodly Rage: The Hidden Face of Catholic Feminism* (San Francisco, 1991).

49. Quoted in Alan D. Gilbert, *The Making of Post-Christian Britain: A History of the Secularization of Modern Society* (London, 1980), p. 139.

50. Willimon, *What's Right With the Church,* p. 74.

51. Gale D. Webbe, *The Night and Nothing* (New York, 1964), pp. 16–17.

52. Malcolm Muggeridge, *The End of Christendom* (Grand Rapids, Mich., 1980), pp. 55–56.

53. Matthew 7:13–14. Cf. Luke 13:23–24.

54. *Pacific Lutheran Scene* (Winter 1996): 9.

55. Arthur Michael Ramsey, *The Gospel and the Catholic Church,* 2d ed. (London, 1956), p. 135.

56. Richard John Neuhaus, "The Christian University: Eleven Theses," *First Things* (January 1996): 21.

57. Review in *The Living Church,* December 31, 1995, p. 13.

58. Gertrude Himmelfarb, "The Christian University: A Call to Counterrevolution," *First Things* (January 1966): 17–18.

59. "Symposium: The Conservative Future," *National Review,* December 11, 1995, p. 96.

60. Psalm 25:9.

61. Matthew 18:1–4. See also Matthew 23:11–12; Mark 9:35–37, 10:15; Luke 9:47–48, 10:21.

62. Ephesians 4:1–2, 5:1. See also Philippians 2:3–11, 14–15.

63. I knew Bishop Pike in 1966 when we were both (for different reasons) at the Center for the Study of Democratic Institutions in Santa Barbara, California. His full and tragic story may be found in William Stringfellow and Anthony Towne, *The Death and Life of Bishop Pike* (New York, 1976).

64. Webbe, *The Night and Nothing,* pp. 31–32.

65. "Quote of the Week," *The Living Church,* January 1, 1995, p. 2.

66. Kelley, *Why Conservative Churches Are Growing,* pp. 84, 99–101.

67. Ibid., p. 132.

68. Ibid., pp. 154–55, 163, 168–69.

69. Ibid., p. 165. The liberal Stephen L. Carter, in a highly acclaimed book, assures us that "Nothing about the nature of religion requires either exclusivity or universality." Such thoughts, he claims, are solely in the minds of individual believers! Stephen L. Carter, *The Culture of Disbelief: How American Law and Politics Trivialize Religious Devotion* (New York, 1993), p. 91.

70. Kelley, *Why Conservative Churches Are Growing*, pp. 85–86. Conservatives are now set apart from mainliners and others by their attitudes on sex and the moral and public policy issues related to sex. See Gallup and Castelli, *The People's Religion*, pp. 257–58.

71. *Milwaukee Journal*, June 15, 1994.

72. Gallup and Castelli, *The People's Religion*, p. 253.

73. The Rev. Ronald F. Marshall in a letter published in *First Things* (August/September 1995): 4.

74. Finke and Stark, *The Churching of America*, p. 238.

75. Gallup and Castelli, *The People's Religion*, p. 253.

76. Elmbrook Church is Wisconsin's largest church, serving five thousand adults and two thousand children each weekend. It recently constructed a $12 million sanctuary. *Milwaukee Journal*, February 28, 1994.

77. *Wall Street Journal*, September 15, 1995.

78. Gallup and Castelli, *The People's Religion*, pp. 148–64. Of course, the mainline is not completely silent. The Episcopal Church, for example, has the Episcopal Radio–TV Foundation, Inc.

79. See S. Robert Lichter, Stanley Rothman, and Linda S. Lichter, *The Media Elite* (Bethesda, Md., 1986), pp. 20–22. Compare John Dart and Jimmy Allen, *Bridging the Gap: Religion and the News Media* (Nashville, Tenn., c. 1994), a publication of the Freedom Forum First Amendment Center at Vanderbilt University. This study concludes that charges of an antireligious bias in the broader media are false and that most media journalists are sympathetic to religion. "It appears there is more ignorance about religion than bias in the average newsroom. . . . The problem lies, rather, in a secular press reporting on a highly secularized society in which faith and beliefs are muted, privatized and extremely diverse." Still, the study concluded that "The nation's newspapers and broadcasters largely refuse to take religion seriously." See pp. 5–6.

80. L. Brent Bozell III and Brent H. Baker (eds.), *And That's the Way It IsN'T): A Reference Guide to Media Bias* (Alexandria, Va., 1990). See Ted J.

Smith III, "The Media Elite Revisited," *National Review*, June 21, 1993, p. 35. On the negative way Roman Catholics are treated in the media, see S. Robert Lichter, Daniel Amundson, Patrick Riley, and Russell Shaw (eds.), *Anti-Catholicism in the Media* (Huntington, Ind., 1993), pp. 12–137.

81. *Milwaukee Journal*, November 28, 1994.

82. Ibid., June 4, 1994.

83. *Milwaukee Journal*, March 12, 1994.

84. Michael Medved, *Hollywood Vs. America: Popular Culture and the War on Traditional Values* (New York, 1992), pp. 71–72.

85. *Milwaukee Journal Sentinel*, December 23, 1995.

86. See Wuthnow, *The Restructuring of American Religion*, pp. 225–26.

87. Ernest-Ulrich Franzen, "Promises to Keep," *Wisconsin*, the magazine of the *Milwaukee Journal Sentinel*, July 9, 1995, pp. 7–9.

88. *Wall Street Journal*, October 12, 1994.

89. For a good survey of this movement, see "The Power of a Promise Keeper," *Good News* (September/October 1995): 12–17.

90. *Milwaukee Journal Sentinel*, February 15, 1996.

91. Ibid.

92. "UM Board of Discipleship Refuses to Endorse Promise Keepers," *Good News* (September/October 1995): 16.

93. Gallup and Castelli, *The People's Religion*, pp. 146–47, 254–57.

94. Hoge, Johnson, Luidens, *Vanishing Boundaries*, p. 204.

95. "Religious Participation Among Entering Freshmen Is Slipping," *emerging trends* (January 1996): 3.

96. William Damon, *Great Expectations: Overcoming the Culture of Indulgence in America's Homes and Schools* (New York, 1995), pp. 234–41. The quotation is on page 241.

97. *Wall Street Journal*, May 12, 1994. Roman Catholic schools have not prospered since Vatican II. Enrollment fell from about 5.6 million in 1962 to 2.6 million in 1994. Ibid.

98. Ibid.

99. *Milwaukee Journal Sentinel*, December 16, 1995.

100. On contributions, see John L. Ronsvalle and Sylvia Ronsvalle, *The State of Church Giving Through 1993* (Champaign, Ill., 1995), p. 119. The embezzler was Ellen Cooke, the Episcopal Church's treasurer—a priest's wife who was paid more than $120,000 a year. See William Murchison,

"No Joy in Mudville: The National Church Reluctantly Confronts the Consequences of the Great Collection Plate Robbery," *Foundations* (July/August 1995): 4–6.

101. This is from the promotional flyer "Biblical Witness Fellowship: An Introduction to the Biblical Witness Fellowship," p. 6.

102. In a Gallup Youth Survey conducted in 1994–95, 50 percent of teenagers attended church or synagogue in the last week. This was up from 45 percent in 1992. Protestants led Catholics 60 percent to 56 percent, and people with white-collar backgrounds led those with blue-collar backgrounds 52 percent to 48 percent. "Teen Attendance," *emerging trends*, October, 1995, p. 2.

103. Gallup and Castelli, *The People's Religion*, p. 255. Gallup showed the churched far more involved in social and charitable activities than the unchurched. Indeed, 55 percent of the unchurched are "not active at all." Ibid., p. 140.

104. Media Research Center Report No. 4, "Faith in a Box," p. 22.

105. James Davison Hunter, *Before the Shooting Begins: Searching for Democracy in America's Culture War* (New York, 1994), pp. 182, 185.

106. Richard John Neuhaus, *The Naked Public Square: Religion and Democracy in America*, 2d ed. (Grand Rapids, Mich., 1986), p. 20.

107. Gallup and Castelli, *The People's Religion*, p. 252. See also pp. 254–55.

108. *New York Times*, November 17, 1993.

109. See Hoge, Johnson, Luidens, *Vanishing Boundaries*, p. 188, which makes the important point that strictness alone does not guarantee growth. The numerous Anglican sects that began to split from the Episcopal Church in 1976 are a case in point. The reasons for their failure to flourish are complex, but clerical frailties are clearly a major factor.

110. Harry Stout, *The New England Soul: Preaching and Religious Culture in Colonial New England* (New York, 1986), p. 4.

111. Matthew 7:9–10.

112. The blandness and fatuity of many contemporary sermons is discussed in Marsha G. Witten, *All Is Forgiven: The Secular Message in American Protestantism* (Princeton, 1993). The study showed much accommodation with secularism. For example, p. 132: "The God created in this speech validates human beings' incessant interest in their private inner workings. God legitimates people's fascination with the depths of their emotional experiences. This is a God whose transcendent qualities have, for the most part,

disappeared; a God who, in his immanence and understanding, smiles benevolently on the age of psychology."

113. Gallup and Castelli, *The People's Religion,* p. 253. On public attitudes about clergy, see *Religion in America, 1996,* pp. 58–61.

114. Hoge, Johnson, Luidens, *Vanishing Boundaries,* p. 207.

115. Ibid., pp. 208–10.

116. Ibid., pp. 209–10.

117. This is forecast by the sociologists Robert Wuthnow and Marsha G. Witten. See Witten, *All Is Forgiven,* p. 139.

118. Interview with James V. Heidinger II, the president and publisher of *Good News,* December 18, 1995. See his *United Methodist Renewal: What Will It Take?* (Wilmore, Ky., 1988).

119. Promotional flyer, "What Is the Confessing Movement Within the United Methodist Church?" published by the Confessing Movement, no place or date.

120. "We Confess," January, 1995, p. 1. This is the newsletter of the Confessing Movement.

121. Confessing Movement press release, April 29, 1995, issued by the Frazer Memorial United Methodist Church, Atlanta.

122. "We Confess," November, 1995, p. 1.

123. Interview with David Carlson, December 13, 1995.

124. A. Donald Davies (ed.), *Speeches, Sermons, Pictures, and Official Documents from the Episcopal Synod of America, Founded at Fort Worth, Texas, June 3, 1989* (Wilton, Conn., 1990), p. 15.

125. See ibid., p. 114.

126. "What a Little Hope Will Do!!" *The Witness: A Journal of the Biblical Witness Fellowship* (August 1995): 16.

127. Interview with David Runnion-Bareford, December 13, 1995. See his "Reformation and the Red Sox," ibid., August 1995, p. 2.

128. Interview with John Eby, December 19, 1995.

129. Interview with Robert Mills, December 27, 1995.

130. Samuel Edwards, "A Serious Case of Mixed Feelings," *The Evangelical Catholic* (July/October 1995): 11–17.

131. Interview with James V. Heidinger II, December 18, 1995.

132. Digby Anderson, "No Abiding City," *National Review,* December 11, 1995, p. 57.

133. "COCU: The Irony," *The Witness: A Journal of the Biblical Witness Fellowship* (August 1995): 6; "Issues Before Us," *Good News* (November/December 1995): 32.

134. Interview with Donald Manworren, January 2, 1996.

135. *Milwaukee Journal*, March 19, 1994. United Church of Christ theologian Donald Bloesch said in 1996: "The theological trend in the UCC is toward a new gnosticism. It could be called postmodern theology with its strong emphasis on relativism." "Reflections on the Theological Drift of the UCC," *The Witness* (Winter 1996):16. See Williams, *America's Religions*, pp. 318–19, 335, 428. New Age thought is particularly popular in California. See Kosmin and Lachman, *One Nation Under God*, pp. 78, 152–56, 204–5, 300–301.

136. Ibid., p. 155.

137. *Milwaukee Journal*, February 8, 1992.

138. James Q. Wilson, *On Character: Essays by James Q. Wilson* (Washington, D.C., 1991), p. 89.

139. Muggeridge, *The End of Christendom*, p. 19.

140. Dennis McCann in *Milwaukee Journal Sentinel*, July 17, 1995.

141. Cited by Senator Bob Dole and Congressman J. C. Watts Jr. in *Wall Street Journal*, July 27, 1995.

142. Wilson, *On Character*, pp. 50, 73, 173–74, 188.

143. *Wall Street Journal*, July 14, 1995.

144. Charles C. Grafton, *A Journey Godward* (Milwaukee, 1910), p. 86. Newman was vicar of St. Mary's, Oxford, and his sermons contributed greatly to the Oxford Movement in the 1830s. The quotation was from Ezekiel 37:3.

145. C. S. Lewis, *Mere Christianity* (New York, 1960), p. 15.

146. David Mills, "A Hope of Collapsing Churches," *Touchstone* (Summer 1995): 17.

147. Ibid., p. 20.

INDEX

263

Barth, Karl, 118, 119, 151
Barton, Bruce, 43–44, 105
Barzun, Jacques, 57
Baur, Ferdinand Christian, 85, 86
Beavis and Butt-head, 48
Becker, Carl, 70, 83
Beecher, Henry Ward, 92
Ben Hur: A Tale of the Christ (Wallace), 42
Bennett, John, 118
Bennett, William J., 6, 7, 54, 66
Berlin, Isaiah, 75
Bernstein, Richard, 47
Bettenhausen, Elizabeth, 147
Bible reading
  at home, 63, 64, 116
  in schools, 46, 129
Bible sales, 54
Biblical criticism, 85–89, 91, 96, 107, 110, 158, 178, 183
Biblical illiteracy, 63–64
Biblical Witness Fellowship, 25, 195
Birth control, 62
Black Manifesto reparations demands, 138–140
Blake, Eugene Carson, 135, 141
Bliss, William Dwight Porter, 94
Bloom, Allan, 58, 76
Boerhaave, Hermann, 70
Bolshevik Revolution, 22
Bonhoeffer, Dietrich, 117
Book of Common Prayer (1979), 148
Book of Virtues, The (Bennett), 54
Boone, Pat, 156
Borg, Marcus, 158
Bork, Robert H., 39–40
Boswell, John, 20
Bow, Clara, 107
Bowne, Borden Parker, 92
Boyd, Malcolm, 155
Bozell, L. Brent, III, 48
Braaten, Carl E., 57
Bradford, M. E., 39
Bradley, Gerard V., 47
Brauch, Manfred T., 16
Breckinridge, Benjamin, 100–101

Brennan, William J., Jr., 128
Brewer, David, 43
Briggs, Charles A., 100
Brinton, Crane, 70
Brooks, Phillips, 92
Brouwer, Arie R., 162
Brown, John Pairman, 155
Brown, William Adams, 92
Browning, Edmond Lee, 27, 159–160, 164
Brunner, Emil, 118, 151
Bryan, William Jennings, 111–115
Buchanan, Pat, 55
Buckle, Henry, 87, 113
Buckley, William F., Jr., 130
Buffon, Georges-Louis, 70
Bultmann, Rudolf, 177, 178
Bunday, Jack, 33–34
Bundy, Edgar C., 125
Burke, Edmund, 72
Bush, George, 22, 55, 163
Byham, Kim, 20

Calvin, John, 59, 78
Calvinism, 29, 38, 91
Campbell, Joan Brown, 30, 163, 164
Cannon, Katie, 18
Capitalism, 69, 87, 91, 93
Capital punishment, 57, 161
Capone, Al, 107
Carlson, David, 16, 35, 203
Carlyle, Thomas, 87
Carr, Edward Ellis, 94
Carter, Jimmy, 2, 157, 201
Carter, Paul A., 121
Casper (movie), 6
Casserley, J. V. Langmead, 178–179
Castelli, Jim, 50
Catechism of the Catholic Church, 59
Catholic Charities USA, 196
Cavendish, James C., 62
Chadwick, Owen, 89
Chandler, Russell, 207
Character issue, 8–9
Charismatic movement, 157
Charles Hodge Society, 19

Vietnam War and, 140, 142
women's rights and, 148
Episcopal Divinity School, 17, 18
Episcopalians United, 25
Episcopal Society for Cultural and
Racial Unity, 137
Episcopal Synod of America (ESA), 25,
203–204
Episcopal Women's Caucus, 20
Equal Rights Amendment (ERA), 147
Ernesti, Johann August, 85
Ernst, Eldon G., 104
Eternal Word Television Network, 189
Eucharist, 28
European Recovery Plan, 125
Evangelical and Catholic Mission, 25
Evangelical and Reformed Church, 10
Evangelical churches, 32–33, 35, 157,
158
Evangelical Foreign Missionary Associa-
tion, 122
Evangelical Lutheran Church, 1, 35, 148
Bible reading and, 64
civil rights movement and, 136, 138
finances of, 12
human sexuality and, 21, 25–26, 203
membership in, 11
Vietnam War and, 141
women's rights and, 180
Evangelical Presbyterian Church, 34
Everson v. Board of Education (1947), 127
Evolution, 83, 89, 91, 95–96, 99, 100,
102, 107, 111–114
Exit polls, 3
Extramarital affairs, 60

Faith, 50–54, 56, 61, 63–67, 123,
168–169, 171, 178, 185, 186
Faith and Values Network, 188–189
Faith of Modernism, The (Mathews), 109
Faith of Women, 27
Falwell, Jerry, 161
Family, breakdown of, 7–8, 50
Farley, Edward, 49–50
Federal Communications Commission
(FCC), 126

Federal Council of Churches, 43, 94,
95, 103, 105, 114, 116, 118, 120,
121, 125
Fellowship of Socialist Christians, 117
Feminism, 17–19, 26, 158, 179–180,
183–184
Fertility rates, 31
Feuerbach, Anselm, 87
Fife, John H., 14
Financial issues, 12–13, 115, 195
Finke, Roger, 32, 41, 52, 98, 127, 158,
167, 174, 187
Finn, Molly, 83–84
Fiorenza, Elizabeth Schussler, 179
First Amendment to the Constitution,
37, 39, 40, 127, 128
First Vatican Council, 88
Fitzgerald, F. Scott, 107
Fletcher, Joseph, 151
Foege, William, 182
Forman, James, 138–140
Fosdick, Harry Emerson, 106, 151
Fourteenth Amendment to the Consti-
tution, 127
Fox, Matthew, 26
Francis of Assisi, St., 61
French Revolution, 72–73, 77
Freud, Sigmund, 104–105, 183
Frohnen, Bruce, 73
Fuller, Charles E., 115
Fuller Theological Seminary, 122
Fundamentalism, 3, 32, 102
clash between liberalism and,
107–115
"Fundamentals, The" (pamphlets),
101–102

Galileo, 70
Gallup, George, Jr., 50, 51, 53, 56, 61,
63, 124, 169, 187, 188, 197, 200
Gang membership, 8
Gaustad, Edwin S., 106
Gaylor, Annie Laurie, 192
George, Robert P., 58
Gershoy, Leo, 73, 77
G.I. Bill, 129

Index